The Behavioral Portfolio

The
Behavioral
Portfolio

**MANAGING PORTFOLIOS
AND INVESTOR BEHAVIOR
IN A COMPLEX ECONOMY**

PHILLIP TOEWS

HARRIMAN HOUSE LTD
3 Viceroy Court
Bedford Road
Petersfield
Hampshire
GU32 3LJ
GREAT BRITAIN
Tel: +44 (0)1730 233870

Email: enquiries@harriman-house.com
Website: harriman.house

First published in 2025.
Copyright © Phillip Toews

The right of Phillip Toews to be identified as the Author has been asserted in accordance with the Copyright, Design and Patents Act 1988.

Hardback ISBN: 978-0-85719-744-3
eBook ISBN: 978-0-85719-745-0

British Library Cataloguing in Publication Data
A CIP catalogue record for this book can be obtained from the British Library.

All rights reserved; no part of this publication may be reproduced, stored in a retrieval system, or transmitted in any form or by any means, electronic, mechanical, photocopying, recording, or otherwise without the prior written permission of the Publisher. This book may not be lent, resold, hired out or otherwise disposed of by way of trade in any form of binding or cover other than that in which it is published without the prior written consent of the Publisher.

Whilst every effort has been made to ensure that information in this book is accurate, no liability can be accepted for any loss incurred in any way whatsoever by any person relying solely on the information contained herein.

No responsibility for loss occasioned to any person or corporate body acting or refraining to act as a result of reading material in this book can be accepted by the Publisher, by the Author, or by the employers of the Author.

The Publisher does not have any control over or any responsibility for any Author's or third-party websites referred to in or on this book.

*To Yuu, Akira and Sara.
You brighten every day.*

CONTENTS

Chapter Outline — ix

Introduction — 1

Part 1: Fish Swimming Out of Water — 9

    Chapter 1: The Case of Prudence Sinclair and Cornelius le Blanc—The Investor Retention Rollercoaster — 11

    Chapter 2: The Historical Accident of Conventional Portfolios—How Stocks and Bonds Create Risks for Investors — 29

    Chapter 3: The Existential Risks of the 60/40 Portfolio and the Challenges of a High-Debt World — 57

    Chapter 4: Retirement Planning Redo: Overvalued Markets, Fees, and the Behavioral Gap Create Retirement Planning Challenges — 77

Part 2: The Behavioral Portfolio — 95

    Chapter 5: Reframing Risk to Comprehensively Address Risks to Investors — 99

    Chapter 6: Building Behavioral Portfolios — 111

    Chapter 7: Behavioral Portfolios for Young(er) Savers — 145

Part 3: Transforming Your Practice with Behavioral Coaching — 157

Introduction: A thought experiment about investing — 159

Chapter 8: Communicating the Unique Value-Add of the Behavioral Portfolio to Investors — 165

Chapter 9: What Investors Tell Us They Know about Investing, and What Can Help Build Confidence in Their Portfolios — 167

Chapter 10: A Process for Avoiding Emotional/Reactive Decision Making — 177

Chapter 11: Automating Good Behavior by Setting "Defaults" in Your Practice — 225

Chapter 12: Implementing an Investor Behavioral Component in your Practice: A Step-by-Step Plan — 233

Acknowledgments — 255

Endnotes — 256

CHAPTER OUTLINE

Introduction: Transcend behavioral biases and transform your practice

This chapter provides the overarching framework that I'll be presenting. Portfolios are poorly built to meet investors' economic and physiological needs, and current advisor to client communications are ineffective at curbing investor biases and easing anxiety during market crises. I discuss my story as an asset manager who watched poor decision making and discuss how we came to build our new portfolio and communications construct.

Part 1: Fish Swimming Out of Water

Part 1 highlights the multitude of challenges confronted by advisors. I begin with an illustration of an investor living through the Great Financial Crisis, highlighting the slow path to investor dissatisfaction and getting to the root of poor investor decision making. Then, in one of the most important contributions of this book, I dive deep into the history of stocks, bonds, and balanced portfolios to show how flawed assumptions and ignored market history can jeopardize investors' livelihoods and advisors' practices. Finally, I reveal how often-missed real-world factors fundamentally change the probability of success for investors shown by retirement planning programs for the worse.

Chapter 1: The Case of Prudence Sinclair and Cornelius le Blanc—The Investor Retention Rollercoaster

Chapter 1 tells the story of Prudence and Cornelius. Cornelius is a highly educated and insightful advisor and Prudence is an astute physician client. I walk through the boom-and-bust cycles of the last 15 years to help illustrate the shifting landscape of investor risk appetites and the process of rationalization that can lead to awful decision making. Advisors reading this chapter will likely relate to this story and will understand our base case about ineffective investor communications.

Chapter 2: The Historical Accident of Conventional Portfolios—How Stocks and Bonds Create Risks for Investors

Bonds were devised to help fund governments and later corporations. Stocks were built as a means for companies to raise capital and share ownership. The conventional portfolio at its foundation is made up of combining these two assets. In other words, conventional portfolios were not explicitly designed with the intention of helping investors fund living needs, but rather are our best efforts to combine these two assets. Chapter 2 discusses market challenges associated with stock ownership as well as the major and often undiscussed risks in bond portfolios.

Chapter 3: The Existential Risks of the 60/40 Portfolio and the Challenges of a High-Debt World

Chapter 3 helps advisors visualize some of the worst historical periods for the 60/40 portfolio to draw the conclusion that these markets potentially imperil investors who are unfortunate enough to live through them and are unnavigable from the perspective of an advisor's practice. In this chapter we illustrate that advisors are ignoring historical events that happened long ago (such as the Great Depression and the bond bear market between 1945 and 1981) when doing retirement planning.

Chapter 4: Retirement Planning Redo: Overvalued Markets, Fees, and the Behavioral Gap Create Retirement Planning Challenges

Planning for investor's retirement has come a long way over the past decades with the advent of Monte Carlo analysis and income adjustment software. In this chapter I highlight obvious but missing components that materially change the chances of success for investors. I then use some of the most advanced tools currently used by financial planners to illustrate the sometimes-low chances of living through retirement and the vulnerabilities investors face based on the timing of their retirements. Finally, I explain that our current paradigm of high valuations and record global debt creates immediate risks for investors.

Part 2: The Behavioral Portfolio

The first part of this book identifies a multitude of problems with advisory communications and conventional portfolios. This section offers our solutions to those problems. Behavioral portfolios and guidance focus on how to build portfolios that attempt to meet the economic and psychological needs of investors through virtually any market. Conventional portfolios can be obliterated by extended stock market drops or hyperinflation and require that advisors ignore important historical precedents when building them. Behavioral portfolios do the opposite, they are built with an all-seasons approach that assumes that the very worst possible markets may occur. They simultaneously are built to attempt to prosper under optimistic scenarios when markets move favorably.

Chapter 5: Reframing Risk to Comprehensively Address Risks to Investors

Chapter 5 reframes how advisors think about and evaluate portfolio risks. It positions advisors as chief risk officers whose most important role is helping investors prepare for and navigate market crises. It highlights the reality that diversification may fail principally because core asset classes can correlate and move lower together during severe market crisis and suggests a new means to evaluate portfolio risk.

Chapter 6: Building Behavioral Portfolios

Chapter 6 outlines criteria for portfolios and then quantifies this in the form of a modified portfolio distribution chart that can act as a guide for investors. It presents several examples of how a behavioral portfolio can be built, as well as our guidance for its essential components. Finally, it shows that building portfolios according to these parameters can significantly improve the probability of success for retired investors.

Chapter 7: Behavioral Portfolios for Young(er) Savers

Many of the criteria for building optimal portfolios for pre-retirees and retirees are reversed for young savers. Retirees are impaired by high volatility. Young savers can benefit from high volatility during their initial years of saving. This chapter, which could be a book on its own, provides how thinking from an investor-focused perspective changes common perspectives on building portfolios for young savers.

Part 3: Transforming Your Practice with Behavioral Coaching

In investor surveys conducted by Toews' Behavioral Investing Institute, we discovered that most investors don't understand the severity of past market crises, how their portfolios are prepared to address those crises, and what the plan is when crises occur. This section guides advisors to educate investors about past markets, explain to them how their portfolios are built to address those markets, and explain in advance what plans will be taken as crises play out. The objective is to help investors potentially make counter-intuitive decisions and to help overcome the behavioral performance gap disadvantage realized by many investors. Instead of succumbing to the narrative of Cornelius and Prudence, advisors will be poised to proactively address behavioral market challenges.

Chapter 8: Communicating the Unique Value-Add of the Behavioral Portfolio to Investors

I'll explain why and how advancing yourself as a behavioral coach can be a vital part of the management and marketing of your practice, what your clients will like about it, and how to communicate this to your investors.

Chapter 9: What Investors Tell Us They Know about Investing, and What Can Help Build Confidence in Their Portfolios

In Chapter 9 I discuss the results of three separate investor and advisor surveys conducted by the Toews Behavioral Investing Institute in conjunction with the Institute of Wealth Management. We queried investors about their knowledge of past market crises, how much losses they felt that they could tolerate, and how it would affect their peace of mind if they had concrete plans for addressing market crises. We also surveyed investment advisors to get their input on the same questions and will reveal some of the disparities between what investors believe and advisors understand about their investors.

Chapter 10: A Process for Avoiding Emotional/Reactive Decision Making

In Chapter 10 I reveal our process for curbing investor biases. An analogy we have used is that of a driver without any rules of the road (no stop signs, no lines on highways, no speed limits, etc.). Drivers under these conditions would rightfully be anxious. Here, we introduce rules and set expectations. I introduce our "Investment Owner's Manual" that outlines the six biggest market challenges for investors along with a process for building confidence for each.

Chapter 11: Automating Good Behavior by Setting "Defaults" in Your Practice

Advisors can have hundreds (or thousands) of clients. Making predetermined portfolio changes for so many investors as markets vacillate is challenging, if not impossible. In this chapter, I discuss ways to automate decision making to help guide investors to implement sometimes counterintuitive portfolio decisions.

Chapter 12: Implementing an Investor Behavioral Component in Your Practice: A Step-by-Step-Plan

In this chapter I'll discuss the execution of all that advisors have learned in this book. I'll step through the processes that advisors can use to transform their practices, including how to position themselves as behavioral coaches, analyze and modify portfolios, discuss changes with investors, and provide ongoing guidance to investors.

INTRODUCTION
Transcend Behavioral Biases and Transform Your Practice

ONE OF THE most clearly understood roles of financial advisors is guiding investors away from emotional investing and towards evidence-based portfolio management. When internet stocks were valued at infinity times earnings, it was our job to steer them away from a portfolio with significant allocations to dogfood.com. During the worst days of the Great Financial Crisis in 2007 and 2008, our chief responsibilities were to avoid a sale at the bottom, to avert the stampede of the herd, and to help investors stick to their plans.

So how are we doing at accomplishing this fundamental responsibility?

According to the evidence that tracks fund flows: not well. Although some studies show that advisors have encouraged investors to invest in more diversified portfolios, other studies suggest that advisors not only fail to increase returns, but actually fare worse than retail investors managing their own portfolios.[1] Near the heights of a bull market that began at the end of the Great Financial Crisis, and again during the post-pandemic rally, investors were herding into technology stocks, special purpose acquisition companies (SPACs) that have no or little earnings, not to mention crypto currencies—despite the memory of crushing losses during the financial crisis. Flows, including advisors' managed assets, also show that investors continue to exit stocks and after significant market declines.

Overarching problems with our current advisory paradigm

A key objective of this book is to share new strategies that are being used by advisors to manage investor behavior. However, there are overarching problems that limit our ability as advisors to guide investors to successful outcomes.

First, the portfolios that we offer our clients leave investors vulnerable to severe economic events and emotional stress.

We as advisors, and our industry collectively, are vulnerable to recency bias. Recency bias isn't just relying on last year's results to predict this year's returns; it's much bigger than that. Advisors are thinking of the world through the prism of what has happened within their working lifetimes, rather than through the broader range of historical possibilities. Generational market trends hinder our ability to understand and correctly guide investors.

As a result of our vulnerability to biases, we're not preparing our investors for worst-case scenarios. By selectively limiting our screen of historical outcomes to those of the last 30 years, we're setting our investors up for potential disruption far beyond what can be managed using behavioral coaching.

Portfolio construction for many advisors focuses on minimizing portfolio variability rather than on preserving investors' likelihood of reaching their goals, and there are flawed assumptions that we make in conventional investment planning that compromise the validity of our recommendations and threaten the long-term security of our clients.

Diversification, for example, is our industry's primary risk management tool. Yet, as this book will show, the benefits of diversification among conventional financial assets breaks down during extreme negative markets (those times when we need it most). We saw a hint of this during the Great Financial Crisis. But the implications are potentially worse than recent experience suggests.

Considering true worst-case scenarios creates an imperative that financial advisors fundamentally change their business approach; otherwise, as we illustrate in this book, should those worst-case scenarios manifest, both clients' portfolios and advisors' businesses are fundamentally at risk.

Second, the way that we educate investors about their portfolios isn't effective at helping them curb biases.

Despite the abundance of literature on behavioral finance, susceptibility to biases remains a major issue. Our clients continue to follow the crowd, leaving them vulnerable to market disruption and under performance. In fact, as this book shows, the very nature of the client–advisor relationship can exacerbate rather than temper biases.

These problems negatively impact portfolios in real terms. When considering fees, overvalued markets, and underperformance due to investor behavior, the probabilities of supporting retirements can become unacceptably low and cause investors to experience stress and anxiety.

Our solutions

Performance chasing and other investor biases are a huge problem that affect millions of people. Decades have passed since behavioral psychologists concluded that innate tendencies lead most people to make bad long-term investment decisions. Yet the advisory community has yet to tackle this wrenching challenge in any comprehensively effective ways.

In order to succeed in realistically and effectively managing behavior, advisors need to:

1. Position themselves as chief risk officers instead of financial cheerleaders. There is no "likelihood" of down markets or recessions—there is a certainty. And there is a possibility of economic crash, depression, or massive inflation. Financial advisors need a deliberate, concrete, strategic approach to these risks.
2. Build portfolios that are designed to prevail or even prosper as the result of market turmoil.
3. Radically transform how they prepare investors for market disruptions in order to help curb investor biases and position investors to take advantage of the crowd's poor decision-making ability.

I will show you how to understand, measure, and track your investors' risk capacity, risk perception, and behavioral tendencies. I will also redefine risk as the probability of investor success or failure (not market volatility). I will also guide you to build holistic portfolios to fit within the psychological limits of investors and to withstand market drops, stagnation, and crises.

Transform your practice communications and add value to your investors

This book provides specific guidance to proactively address investor behavior that may negatively impact the ability to invest against the crowd, such as:

- How to plan in advance for market disruptions.
- How to coach your investors over time to embrace the counter intuitive nature of investing.
- How to ask for pre-commitments—essentially, having your investors commit to taking certain predetermined actions when market challenges occur.

A key insight of this book is that advisors must understand and embrace counterintuitive thinking and position portfolios to potentially act in opposition to the crowd. Of course, this means training investors to understand that you will allocate parts of their portfolio to asset classes that everyone else is selling.

But it gets much more interesting ...

The "herding crowd" of investors can and often does include more than just retail investors that are buying nonsensical investments due to posts by on Reddit. At the extreme end of bull market cycles, it can also include the biggest banks and asset managers who ultimately concede to a trend in order to provide access to their investors, as we have seen with crypto and SPACs.

I expand the notion of counterintuitive investing to include a pervasive investment paradox. The laws of supply and demand suggest that the more people that believe in any principle of investing, the less true it becomes. For example, the efficient market hypothesis suggests that advisors should always invest in market portfolios regardless of valuations. The reason is that either market prices correctly reflect all information, or because it is not possible to take advantage of mispricing opportunities. The problem with this hypothesis seems clear. If valuations should *never* be considered, then pricing becomes entirely driven by demand for purchases of securities without regard to fundamentals like earnings or growth projections.

While this might seem overly theoretical and hard to relate to your day-to-day practice, I assure you it is related. We saw the effects of the efficient-market mindset during the internet bubble, when advisors and their investors generally continued investing in growth stocks as a part of allocations even as prices went to stratospheric levels. Similar thinking has allowed average stock valuations to drift meaningfully higher over the past 20 years than during most of the 20th century. It has also blinded us to the long-range risks of real losses in bond portfolios due to interest rates or inflation. This is all happening with a backdrop of record global debt levels that threaten both the core asset classes of stocks and bonds.

If everyone believes that the markets are efficient and continues buying when assets are overpriced, positioning portfolios counterintuitively to take advantage of this fits with the role of helping to protect investors. But it also potentially creates opportunities to take advantage of market disruptions.

Ultimately, the principles detailed in this book unveil the compelling value you can provide your clients at a time when most traditional advisor services (asset allocation, rebalancing, tax management) are being automated. By putting these principles into practice, you will put your investors on a glide path for steadier returns and improved chances for success—which also translates into greater peace of mind for your clients.

My story

It all began with a question: "What would happen if our clients and our practice went through a prolonged bear market?"

This was the question that the owner of a financial planning firm and I asked ourselves over 30 years ago, back in 1989. The answer was obvious. The late eighties were the era of the 200-page financial plan. We had run cash flow analyses for all of our retired and retiring investors. And despite being in an affluent area referred to as the Main Line outside of Philadelphia, that cash flow analysis virtually always revealed that our investors were just barely going to be able to make it through retirement and needed to have a sizable allocation to stocks.

The answer to our question?

A prolonged bear market that lasted five years or more would devastate our clients, and potentially destroy our practice. Even though the markets hadn't experienced a bear market of that duration in decades, history showed that it likely would occur once again.

What has transpired since then is a 30-year journey that began with an exploration of solutions to help our investors avoid severe market losses, and ultimately led me to help build a full suite of tools and processes to manage investor behavior. The book walks you through the steps and missteps as I experimented with solutions and refined processes. In this book I intend to spare you the 30-year learning curve, which has proven to have a consistently sharp upward slope rather than leveling off after the initial years. My enduring passion is finding ways to improve investor outcomes and peace of mind regardless of what calm or chaos markets deliver.

Along the steep learning curve, our team recognized the performance-chasing attributes of our investors, even when guided by advisors. We consistently saw advisors migrate allocations from low-performing strategies across our platform towards higher-returning models.

Often strategies collectively would deliver on their objectives, but investors would consistently underperform due to poor timing and performance chasing.

In the starkest example, advisors moved significant assets out of hedged equity strategies, designed to help avoid losses, into fully invested conventional stock models in the final quarter of 2007 and the first part 2008, just as the stock market peaked and began its financial crisis freefall.

To summarize, our investors (who were all guided by advisors and who had the tools to navigate most any market) continually made the classic mistake. They bought at the top and sold near the bottom. Something was missing. That something, we concluded, was a new construct or a framework for guiding investor actions.

In 2011 my colleague Eben Burr and I began doing research into behavioral finance tools that we might use to help change investors' behavior. Our comprehensive review of behavioral economics literature led us to a depressing conclusion. Although there were many sources of information about investor biases, and why investors did this or that wrong, many brilliantly written and fascinating, what effectively didn't exist to our satisfaction were studies or literature discussing what to *do* about these biases.

The few books written to help guide advisors failed at both helping advisors build more investor-friendly portfolios and providing a construct for changing the way advisors guided investors. As a result, over the ensuing years we began to build it ourselves.

In 2012, my team and I began presenting the first iteration of our

"Behavioral Workshops for Advisors" across the country. These workshops were designed to introduce Behavioral Economics to advisors and to help them build a process for training clients and managing investor behavior.

We identified what we believed were the six most critical situations that present behavioral challenges for investors (e.g. significant losses, long periods of low or no returns, etc.). We then created a suite of solutions for each challenge that included: 1) recommended portfolio modifications; 2) plans of action made in advance of each challenge along with investor pre-commitments to take that action; and 3) recommended advisor communications to investors. We packaged these recommendations in what we referred to as an "Investment Owner's Manual" that provided investors as a blueprint for decision making. The effect of this effort, we hoped, would be that advisors would leave with a concrete framework on how to guide investors through some of the biggest challenges that they would confront.

The workshops were well received by the advisors that attended them. And although we considered the workshops a great success, our follow-up conversations with advisors who attended revealed a lack of follow-through on our recommendations for implementing behavioral devices into their practices.

To address this problem, in 2015, we created an updated version of the material titled "Advanced Investor Behavioral Course for Advisors." In this workshop we built upon the content from the first workshops, but provided specific instructions on how advisors could build an investor behavioral component into their practices. We added an execution agenda and began actively monitoring advisors post-workshop, in order to gather quantitative data about the results of our guidance and to improve the follow-through for advisors that attended.

In 2017, we built a coaching program to provide additional assistance for advisors who wanted to build behavioral coaching into their practices. We currently offer workshops across the country and provide ongoing coaching for advisors. Finally, in 2020, we formed the Behavioral Investing Institute, an organization with dedicated staff that is devoted to providing behavioral research and guidance to the investment advisory community.

Advisors who have applied our strategies have transformed their practices for the better. They tell us that the old way of waiting to be ambushed by behavioral challenges once investors have been overwhelmed with fear or regret now seems like malpractice. Many also brand their practices and distinguish themselves from other advisors by promoting their role as a behavioral coach who guides clients to do the opposite of the crowd.

I wrote *The Behavioral Portfolio* to share the successes that we've had in changing investor behavior and to open a debate in our industry about excessive investor risk and portfolio construction.

This book is a comprehensive presentation of what we've learned. It includes specific guidance, tools, and the process to follow to become a behavioral coach. If you methodically adopt this approach within your practice, you are on the path to add value to your clients and provide them with greater peace of mind, and you may improve their outcomes. You will also streamline your practice for greater stability and growth.

The book is divided into three sections. First, we frame financial advisors' biggest underlying challenge with the story of investor Prudence and advisor Cornelius as they navigate and make decisions during the Great Financial Crisis and the subsequent recovery. You'll see how their interactions and decisions—which seem eminently sensible and mirror the interactions and decisions of thousands of real-world investors and advisors every day—result in a failed relationship and the potential collapse of Prudence's livelihood. Then, in one of the most important contributions of this book, I dive deep into the history of stocks, bonds, and balanced portfolios to show how flawed assumptions and ignored market history can ultimately jeopardize investors' livelihoods and advisors' practices. Finally, I reveal how often-missed real-world factors fundamentally change the probability of success for investors shown by retirement planning programs for the worse.

This is followed by a section introducing and discussing Behavioral Portfolios. I define these as all-season portfolios that attempt to address the possibilities of significant bear markets in stocks as well as high or hyper inflation and rising interest rates. These portfolios are also constructed to attempt to minimize investors' anxiety and provide greater peace of mind. This section will offer a new understanding of risk and how it should be accounted for in building portfolios.

In the final section, I examine how to restructure your practice and investor communications to mitigate psychological challenges and bolster your investors' long-term success. I will provide concrete, effective ways to completely avoid the "Prudence and Cornelius" scenario.

So let us begin with the misadventures of Prudence and Cornelius as they bumble through investing during the Great Financial Crisis.

PART 1
FISH SWIMMING OUT OF WATER

CHAPTER 1
The Case of Prudence Sinclair and Cornelius le Blanc—The Investor Retention Rollercoaster

Let's begin with the hypothetical story of two accomplished professionals: Prudence Sinclair, a soon-to-retire radiologist who works at New York's Cornell Hospital, and her advisor, Cornelius le Blanc, a prominent certified financial planner whose practice is in the iconic Flatiron building in New York City.

Since the start of her career as a practicing physician, Prudence had an impressive income and was a judicious saver. Unlike many of her peers, she began saving in her 20s, and continued doing so throughout her career. Despite her constant savings, she was unwilling to accept risk with her investment portfolio and held everything in low-paying bank accounts and municipal bonds.

In 2006 she met Cornelius at a fundraiser and, on the recommendation of a colleague, decided to visit him for a consultation. With a portfolio worth just under $2.5 million, and only a few years before retirement, providing her an absolute minimum (per Prudence) of $200,000 per year would be, according to Cornelius, "improbable"—he used this term instead of the more accurate "impossible".

Cornelius and Prudence agreed on two imperatives: strive to save at least 15% more of her annual income for her remaining five years as a practicing physician and accept risk in her portfolio to produce real (above inflation) growth. To do that, she would need to leave bank CDs entirely and invest in a portfolio with at least 60% in stocks, 10% in alternative assets, and 30% in bonds, mostly made up of passive, low-cost index investments.

So, in September of 2006, Prudence made her first investments in the stock market. After decades of timidity about investment risk, and emboldened by Cornelius' academic manner and credentials, Prudence embraced this change with confidence. As Figure 1.1 shows, this allocation occurred after a three-year rally, meaning that it took place when prices were relatively elevated (buying high).

Figure 1.1: Prudence establishes a balanced investment portfolio in 2006 (and buys high)

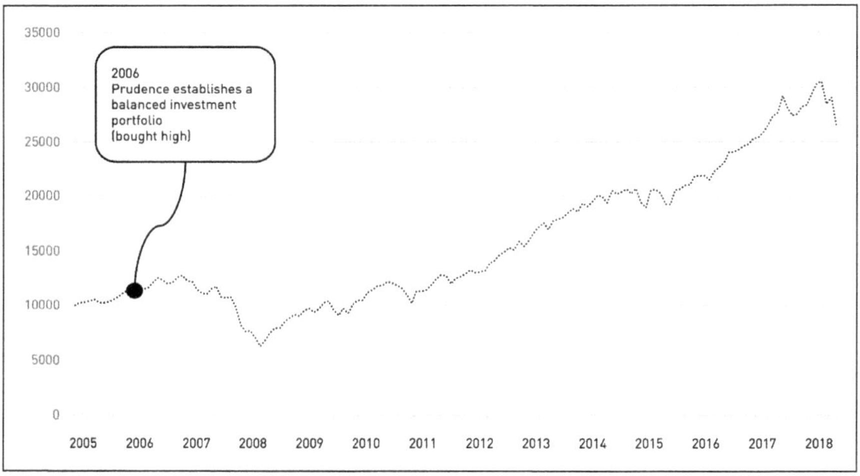

Prudence felt validated by the first quarterly statement sent by Cornelius' firm. The portfolio had risen 4.3% in only three months, more than she would have earned in an entire year in her fixed accounts. During 2007, her first full year with Cornelius as her advisor, the 7% gain in her investments produced further affirmation of her decision to accept Cornelius' recommendations. When she met Cornelius at his office in December to go over her portfolio, Prudence hugged him.

During this meeting, Cornelius carefully spelled out to Prudence how her investments addressed market risk by being invested in a diversified portfolio. If one investment moves lower, he explained, another may move higher, and the result is a dampening effect on negative market moves. Cornelius cautioned Prudence that not all years would be as decision-affirming as the last, and to prepare for periods of stagnation or even portfolio losses ahead.

2008—Cornelius' caution realized

As 2008 began, signs of market fatigue were emerging. In response to plummeting house sales, the Federal Reserve lowered the federal funds rate to 3.5% from 4.25% on January 22, and then to 3.0% only a week later. In February, median home sales fell 8.2% compared to a year earlier. Perceiving market vulnerability to a falling housing market, Fed Chief Ben Bernanke undertook several measures to bolster banks and the economy, including further reducing the federal funds rate, providing liquidity to banks and holders of subprime mortgages. On March 17, facing a liquidity crisis in the secondary market for subprime markets, the Fed held its first emergency weekend meeting in 30 years to help stem a bankruptcy by Bear Stearns, a bank that held over 10 trillion dollars in securities, whose failure would have jeopardized the global banking system.

Over that quarter, Prudence was amused as she read of house flippers and the irresponsible lenders that supported their folly. The first time she even considered that all of the news relating to the housing market might have an effect on her portfolio was in mid-April, when her statement revealed that her portfolio had losses. She hadn't lost any of her original principal. But virtually all of the gains she'd earned in the first 15 months were gone. During a brief call with Cornelius, he reminded her of his cautionary note at their last meeting. His calm tone and reminder about the way the portfolio controlled risk reassured her, so she did her best to forget about it and focus on her social and professional endeavors.

Over the next few months, Prudence's portfolio recovered some of its losses. However, by June, Prudence's portfolio and the financial markets again turned lower. In July, the Fed undertook additional measures to stem an evolving banking crisis that included the failure of Indy Mac Bank, the second largest bank failure in the history of the US at that time. On July 23, Hank Paulson appeared on news shows to make the case for bailouts of Freddie Mac and Fannie Mae. By September, markets had gone into freefall, as Lehman Brothers declared bankruptcy and the Fed purchased AIG for $85 billion. On September 18, Ben Bernanke and Hank Paulson requested a

$700 billion bailout from Congress. By the end of September, the S&P had lost nearly 20% since the beginning of the year.

Prompted by headlines and the mounting losses in her portfolio, Prudence took a more active role in monitoring her investments. She began checking her portfolio value daily through online access to her accounts at Charles Schwab. She also tuned into investment news in a way she never had as a CD and bond investor. Markets fell in October and Prudence saw her portfolio losses deepen over the next month, to 25% for the year.

On October 6, she read that on the *Today* show that morning, Jim Cramer had said, "Whatever money you may need for the next five years, please take it out of the stock market right now. I do not believe that you should risk those assets in the stock market right now."

She had never really paid attention to people like Jim Cramer, but she sensed that this kind of statement was an indication that despite Cornelius' assurances, all was not well in the financial markets. Prudence also sensed another danger signal: headlines over the past few months suggesting that even money market instruments were going through periods when they were not readily tradable. The implication, according to reputable news sources, was that there was the potential that the banking system would break, and deposits would be temporarily inaccessible.

By mid-November, Prudence was stunned to see that her initial $2.5 million portfolio—her life savings over a 40-year career!—was now worth slightly less than $1.6 million, representing a drop of 36%. As losses intensified, Prudence couldn't stop herself from obsessively comparing the current state of her investments with what her portfolio would have been worth had she just left things as they were and continued saving.

When she first began working with Cornelius, they had discussed a range of experiences that she might have, based on how the market had behaved over the past 50 years. But what was happening now felt far outside of that range. Everyday news was dominated by layoffs, foreclosures, and economic dysfunction. The wheels were off the financial system, and Prudence feared for her future livelihood.

Eventually, Prudence couldn't bear to check her portfolio value online, and even stopped opening her statements.

A discovery of Prudence's real risk tolerance

Over the following months the markets continued to gyrate, either in decidedly negative ways or through brief market rallies. But with the backdrop of bank failures and auto bailouts, Prudence's mood and perspective on her situation remained dark, even on days when stocks showed gains.

The markets finally bottomed out in March of 2009 and turned decisively higher. In June, Cornelius and Prudence met for the first time since the crisis began. Her portfolio value was still depressed, and Cornelius began by explaining how he would help her assess the situation.

As in the past, Cornelius was interested in adding perspective by looking at past market routs and their ultimate outcomes. He couldn't deny that what had transpired challenged some of his own beliefs about the stability of the financial system and the viciousness of market moves. Nonetheless, he asserted (with less confidence than he might have wished) that market history suggested a brisk rebound lay ahead.

Whereas in previous meetings, Cornelius' stately presence and honest manner had reassured her, this time Prudence was plainly anxious. Yes, markets had turned higher, but ongoing home foreclosures and company bankruptcies made the risk palpable. Prudence asked Cornelius outright if he thought that crisis was over. His answer was alarming. "Probably not."

Cornelius talked frankly to Prudence about a reset of her expectations, and her lifestyle. It would have been a stretch for her portfolio to provide a $200,000 income before the crisis. Now, with a 35% loss and two years fewer to save, it was clearly impossible (no longer "improbable"). Cornelius recognized that Prudence's psychological state of mind was a critical factor and knew that ultimately that would drive their decision making.

While neither would have sought to repeat the past year, there was a slight positive: it helped Cornelius and Prudence to understand her true risk tolerance. It was reasonable that Prudence's portfolio take on some market risk, but to tolerate full market losses was unacceptable. She would be unable to tolerate further declines financially or emotionally. Prudence cared much more about *not losing money* than making money. As a result (and as reflected in Figure 1.2), it was necessary to modify Prudence's portfolio and revise her risk tolerance.

Figure 1.2: In 2009, Prudence establishes a new risk tolerance and a new portfolio (and sells low)

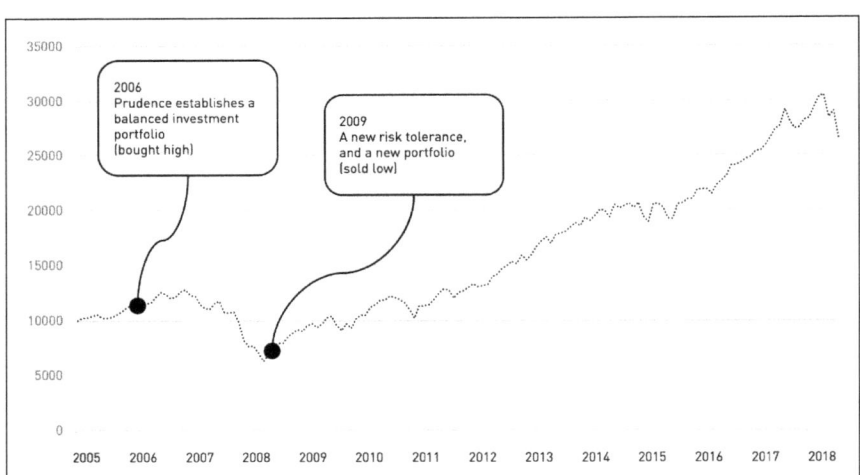

Cornelius had significant experience with more conservative approaches to growth. He increased the bond allocation up to 53% from 40%. He also changed the way he accessed equity-like exposure and migrated Prudence's stock holdings into long/short and market-neutral funds, adding a small allocation to managed futures as a diversifier. As he explained to her, each manager in the portfolio had an imbedded loss-avoidance mechanism. Long/short strategies included bets against stocks that would create gains when markets fell to help offset market losses. Market-neutral funds could be even more conservative by maintaining parity between bets for and against the markets. And while managed futures carried risks, both managers that Cornelius chose deployed explicit, algorithmically driven loss-avoidance strategies.

As the second half of 2009 began, even as depressing economic developments dominated the news cycle, Prudence felt restored to a peace of mind that she hadn't known for over a year.

CHAPTER 1

Markets inexplicably charge higher

In August of 2009, foreclosures soared to 32% higher than the previous year. In October, unemployment reached 10%, its highest level in 26 years. Inexplicably, in the face of a wall of dismal news, the stock market charged higher. By Labor Day, stocks were 10% higher (according to Prudence's Charles Schwab feed). Just before the end of the year, Prudence calculated that the S&P 500 had increased 20% since she adjusted her portfolio. Her investments were up just north of 2% since the change. She tried to take Cornelius' advice and pay attention only to her portfolio and not what the markets returned. Besides, 2% over the six months was 4% annualized, an improvement on what she might have earned in bonds.

During the following years Prudence discovered that her portfolio had a striking level of predictability. Each quarter she would open the statement that Cornelius' firm had sent to discover that it hadn't lost money, but also hadn't earned much, usually 1% or a fraction of that amount. She began to focus on the amount of her quarterly return and the amount of Cornelius' fee. About half of the time the fee was higher than or consumed virtually the whole gain on her investments for the quarter. Even when her gains eclipsed the fee, it wasn't by much.

Between June of 2009, when they modified her portfolio, and the end of 2012, she realized a total increase of 10%. During the same time Prudence calculated that the S&P 500 was up 64%. Her investment value, even after her continued contributions to her portfolio, was just over $2 million, still below her initial investment of $2.5 million six years before. But most depressing for her was that she had come to view her investments more as a source of income for Cornelius than for herself.

In December Prudence entered her meeting with Cornelius distraught. She conveyed a sense of her frustration in a call to set up the meeting with him a week earlier. As they talked in his office, Prudence became more rather than less concerned. She was 66 and her work schedule continued to prevent her from having the amount of social time that she had always craved. But it was clear to her, as Cornelius showed a cash flow projection, that her retirement would have to be delayed as much as five years, maybe more.

Prudence questioned Cornelius about each manager in her portfolio. How could they collectively gain less than one-sixth of the stock market? Cornelius stayed very much on top of each of his funds and laid out comparisons with other managers in the same asset categories. Most of the managers he had selected for Prudence's portfolio had performed in or near the top quartile of their peers. Cornelius explained that the style of management, not the managers themselves (long/short, market neutral, etc.), caused the portfolio to lag. Cornelius reminded Prudence that the focus at the time they chose the portfolio had been on making sure that losses ceased. Yes, the portfolio lagged, but that was the nature of these alternative styles of management. Some years they would languish and others they would gain.

Prudence violated her own sense of propriety when she made a comment, half-joking but with a tinge of passive-aggressiveness, about the persistent parity between Cornelius' fees and her portfolio's gains. She came to the meeting believing that something had to change. She wasn't sure what, but after the past three years she needed new options. She could return to investing in bonds, which had done much better during the past six years than her current investments, or she could leave Cornelius. In the end, she concluded, results mattered more than their shared sense of values and his affable manner.

Cornelius asked Prudence to re-evaluate her view on portfolio losses. If she could bring herself to tolerate a loss of 15% or 20%, he could recalibrate her portfolio to capture additional market gains. He reassured her that he still intended to include elements of loss avoidance with parts of the portfolio. Prudence decided to think about it and to meet again after the holidays.

Prudence stays with Cornelius and realigns her portfolio

After contemplating her options, Prudence concluded that it was too big of a project to find another advisor. She had given Cornelius a mandate to prevent losses first, which he had done. A further inducement to stay was that Cornelius, as always, already had a strategy ready. She met with Cornelius and resolved to accept a higher potential loss with her portfolio. She had no choice. Yes, bonds had earned more than her portfolio. But yields were now at only 2% and, according to Cornelius, bonds too could experience losses. Cornelius also knew her and the history of her portfolio.

By the time they met again, Prudence's angst about fee/gain portfolio parity had eased. She told Cornelius that she'd be willing to accept greater portfolio losses if it improved her chances of higher market participation. As a result (see Figure 1.3), Cornelius realigns Prudence's portfolio to take on more risk. Cornelius replaced the long/short and managed futures managers (the managed futures had performed the poorest) with several hedged equity strategies. He also added a number of broad-based Vanguard Index funds poised to fully track market gains and losses. Cornelius retained a market neutral fund, which was run by a top portfolio manager and had delivered modest but steady returns throughout the crisis and during recent years.

Figure 1.3: Prudence realigns her portfolio to take on more risk (and buys high(er))

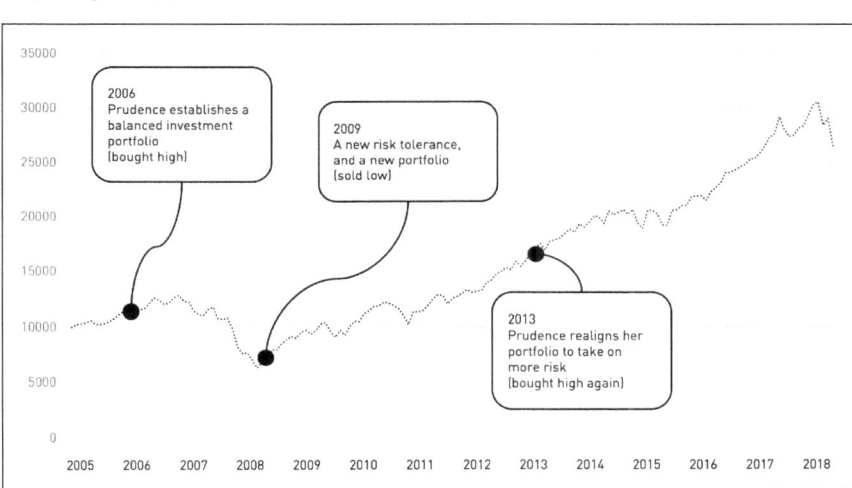

2013 turned out to be a good year. It was only the second year with really any meaningful returns, and the 14% that Prudence earned was welcome. Prudence increased the amount that she saved that year and saw her portfolio reach $2.4 million. The following two years, however, saw a return to lackluster gains. In 2014 the portfolio grew by 3%, but in 2015 Prudence lost 1%.

In early 2016, Prudence saw that her portfolio was trailing the markets once again. On the spur of the moment, she called Vanguard Funds and had a conversation with a woman in customer service. Vanguard had the best-performing funds in her portfolio over the past three years. Prudence learned about a new service that allowed her to invest in a diversified portfolio directly with Vanguard, with no cost to her beyond the small expense ratio of the funds she was invested in. She noted the name of the portfolio and decided to follow its performance alongside Cornelius' portfolio.

As Prudence correctly anticipated, the Vanguard portfolio returned three times what Cornelius' portfolio did in the first half of 2017. She called in to another person at Vanguard and learned there was an online process for entering information about her situation and opening an account. She went through part of the process, but stopped short of opening an account.

Prudence opens an online account at Vanguard

The following week, when Prudence had a few days off, she decided to complete the forms and initiate the process that would transfer funds to her new account. She twitched when she thought about telling Cornelius about her decision. Her investment results with Cornelius were horrible, and the cost savings made the decision an obvious one. But she couldn't bring herself to make the call to break the news. So she decided to wait to make the call until she had a moment when she felt more confident and articulate than she was in her current under-caffeinated state.

Cornelius receives notification of Prudence's transfer to Vanguard

When Cornelius logged onto his advisor portal at Schwab several weeks hence, he found a notice of an account liquidation. There it was. All of Prudence's accounts had transferred out the day before. Everything. Even though Cornelius had cocktails only a month ago with Prudence at a fundraiser, she had transferred everything away without an email or call. He had been ghosted at age 62 by a long-time client whom he considered a friend. As illustrated in Figure 1.4, this reallocation occurred after markets had rallied for nearly a decade, when risk was elevated and prices were again quite high.

Figure 1.4: Prudence leaves Cornelius and moves her assets to Vanguard and a full-risk portfolio (at high valuations)

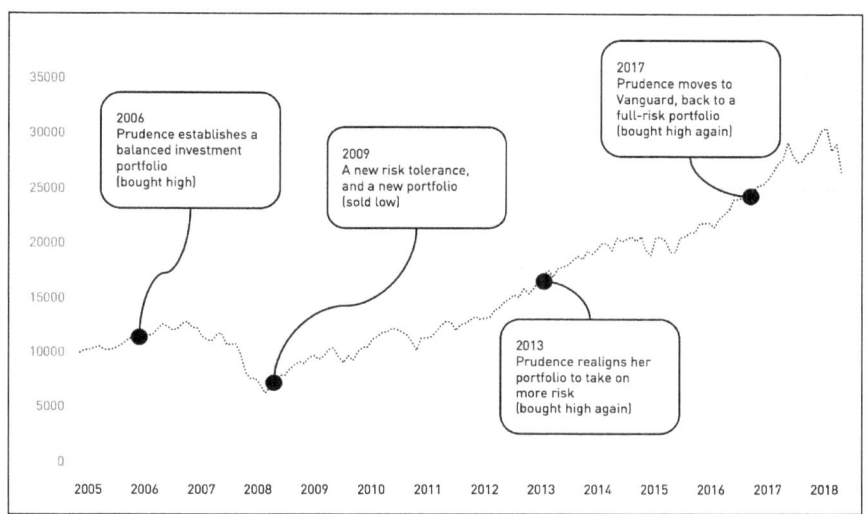

The life seeped out of him. What had she done with her funds? Was she working with another advisor? Was she tricked into investing into some high commission annuity or scheme? After 10 years, he felt a sense of ownership. Not of her assets, of course, but for her wellbeing and her vulnerability and lack of understanding of the complex world of investing.

A 10-year failed relationship

Cornelius was no average advisor. He was a practitioner whose knowledge and credentials placed him among the top echelons of his profession. He was among the very few financial advisors who had completed his CFA Charter, a designation held by asset managers that typically requires over 900 hours of study. He also was a Certified Financial Planner and had taken numerous courses in estate planning and personal taxation. He spent considerable time keeping himself abreast of new technology and asset management strategies, spending hours each evening reviewing prospectuses and journals. When it came to manager selection, his due diligence was fierce, and included portfolio manager interviews and a sophisticated ongoing performance evaluation process. In his opinion, his forte, however, was deploying this vast experience to harmonize portfolios with each investor's unique behavioral profile. By considering their financial situation and proclivity to assume risk, he would find the best portfolio fit for each investor, and then communicate in a way that helped them navigate difficult markets.

Let's review:

- Prudence is an educated and thoughtful professional who had an advisor whom she trusted and respected.
- Cornelius is an educated advisor who carefully navigates clients in portfolios that reflect their personal proclivities.
- All of the decisions made by Prudence and Cornelius were carefully contemplated and were based on her risk tolerance.
- And what were the results of their collective wisdom and careful deliberation?
- Prudence had only slightly more in her portfolio than she did 10 years prior, even though she had been adding money monthly.
- During this time, the stock market increased by over 100%, much higher than the return in Prudence's portfolio.
- Prudence exited risky assets near the bottom of the market. She repositioned her portfolio back to maximum risk levels after an eight-year bull market, when investments were again vulnerable to losses due to overvalued stocks
- Far from preventing Prudence from selling low and buying high, Cornelius provided ammunition for her to rationalize her poor investment choices.

Although the loss of Prudence was the most difficult for Cornelius, she wasn't the only client he had lost recently. Five other clients had terminated their relationships in the past year. Many had suffered similar outcomes as Prudence. All was not well with his practice. Over the ensuing weeks, he had to conclude that he had guided many clients to what both he and they would agree was a failure to meet their goals.

Are you Cornelius?

If you were an investment advisor during the financial crisis and the recovery and the story about Cornelius and Prudence sounds familiar to you, you're not alone. Many advisors felt ineffectual with their clients through the crisis and its aftermath. The decline in 2022 that included both stocks and bonds may have created similar challenges. You may have the credentials, experience, and business acumen to grow your practice and be profitable. But if it all leads toward investors who do not have peace of mind, or who fail to meet their goals, have you truly been successful?

That is the conclusion I came to after analyzing how many advisors' clients were faring, and it's the reason that I began researching investor behavioral solutions years ago. Advisors may be recommending strategies that deliver their desired returns, but investors aren't realizing those returns because they're leaving after products perform poorly, and entering after investments perform well. In the next section, I'll deconstruct the advisor/client relationship to find out why this happens so often.

Maintaining business relationships with clients may force you to execute flawed/biased decisions

Investors earn lower returns due to behavioral biases, leading them to chase performance or exit near market lows. Intuition suggests that investment advisors would help curb biases. Yet the few studies that look at investment advisor outcomes suggest that in practice, just the opposite happens. The reason for this is a combination of advisors' own vulnerability to behavioral biases and the nature of the business relationship that advisors have with their clients.

In this section, I'll help bring clarity to the question: who guides investment decisions, you or your client?

In an NBER working paper, a group of researchers concluded that advisors not only fail to de-bias their clients, but often *reinforce* biases.[2] Similarly, a study in the *Journal of Banking and Finance* showed that the performance of advisor-managed investors (net of fees) may underperform that of investors who manage their own portfolios, supporting the more nuanced assessments about advisors' failure to curb investor biases. In this 2009 study, Tullio Jappelli, Andreas Hackethal, and Michael Haliassos tracked over 32,000 randomly selected accounts at a brokerage firm that allowed investors to select if they wanted to manage accounts themselves or use an investment advisor. The study revealed that advisors tended to lower returns, raise portfolio risk, increase the probability of losses, and increase trading frequency and portfolio turnover.[3]

Understanding the advisor/client relationship

Many factors affect advisors' ability to help investors efficiently navigate markets. The first, and perhaps the most obvious, is that advisors themselves are vulnerable to recency bias. Recency bias is the tendency of stock market participants to evaluate their portfolio performance based on recent results, and to use this information to make often incorrect predictions about how the stock market will behave.

Just as occurred during the internet bubble of the 1990s, advisor-managed accounts showed a strong bias towards large cap growth strategies in the years after the global pandemic began. Why? Because large cap stocks significantly outperformed most other conventional asset classes. Just the opposite was true immediately after the Great Financial Crisis. During that period, advisor-driven asset flows were biased towards bonds and alternative strategies rather than conventional large cap stocks.

Cornelius was formidably well informed, yet he guided Prudence to follow the worst impulses of investors. As hard as it may be for advisors to admit, assets under their direction move mainly along with the crowd, not in opposition to it. You, too, are likely vulnerable to the behavioral biases that we often assign to undisciplined or inexperienced investors.

To lay blame exclusively on advisors' biases, however, would be an oversimplification of the complex, long-term nature of advisor–client relationships. The nature of the business relationship that advisors have with their investors can cripple advisors' ability to curb biases.

As an advisor, you are a fiduciary *and* a businessperson. You have an obligation to act in an investor's best interest, but you also need to ensure that your business remains profitable. Those two roles present a conflict. The extent to which investors unwittingly influence their advisors' recommendation is illustrated by the experience of an advisor friend of mine who was attempting to guide his investors through the internet bubble and its subsequent burst.

The advisor, "Dylan," is located in a small town in Pennsylvania. He became an investment advisor after college, following the path of his father.

In the latter half of the 1990s, with markets setting new highs, Dylan made the decision to begin shifting his investments to trend following strategies that were designed to capture most market gains but potentially avoid significant downturns. The common trade-off with these types of strategies is that they often trail markets during rising periods.

For those of you that weren't in the investment industry during that time, the second half of the 90s were go-go years for the stock market. Twenty percent return years were so common that investors began to expect them. Between 1995 and 1999 there were several times that the stock market fell by as much as 25%. But these declines each lasted only two or three months, and were followed by recoveries and then even more gains. As the internet bubble was expanding, investors began to view these drops as opportunities to buy more stocks. The notion that markets could continue lower was effectively erased from investors' imaginations. The trend following models that were executed were effective during 1997 and 1998 at capturing significant gains. They also helped avoid the few brief downturns along the way. Dylan and his investors were pleased.

In 1999, growth stocks went off the rails. Although they began the year already overvalued by virtually any measure, that year the NASDAQ Composite index increased another 86%. I remember that I spent much of my time that year speaking at client events, comparing the price of internet stocks to the price of tulips during the episode of Tulip mania in Holland during the 17th century, and recommending that investors deploy risk-management strategies across their portfolios.

The growth in 1999 came with high volatility, with the stock market vacilating lower, and then quickly higher. This environment was suboptimal for the trend following strategies, which went defensive a number of times that year, only to buy quickly back in at higher prices. By the end of the third quarter in 1999, Dylan's clients were trailing the markets by 15%. Due to these whipsaws, some clients showed losses compared with double digit market gains.

For Dylan and his clients, the combination of underperformance along with the pain of watching trades occur at exactly the wrong times created a toxic environment. Dylan, who belonged to the country club in his community, stopped golfing and avoided social contact with his clients whenever possible. Dylan was ashamed for having recommended the models. His investors were embarrassed for him. As a result, in a quick couple of weeks that year Dylan moved all of his investors out of the trend following models and back into conventional investments that tracked the markets without any loss-avoidance methodology.

As you might imagine, the decision to exit strategies that could become fully defensive near the end of 1999 was super bad timing, as that year marked the end of a 20-year bull market, and the beginning of one of the most momentous market declines in years.

The trend following models that Dylan abandoned exited markets at the end of March and missed the majority of declines during the internet bust years of 2000–2002. But Dylan's investors were not in those models any longer. They were invested in strategies that fell along with the stock market.

Dylan's decision to adopt tactical models near the top of the market was ultimately proven correct. However, he wasn't able to maintain this course. If he had asked his investors to stay invested in these models when they were underperforming so dramatically, they would have left his practice. In his small community, where everyone knows everyone else, this would have jeopardized his business. He made a rational decision that it was better to be wrong along with the crowd than run the risk of being wrong alone.

In Cornelius' case, he and Prudence agreed on each course of action that they took. Dylan was essentially *forced* to change his clients' investments in order to stay in business. This extreme example helps answer the question that we asked at the beginning of the chapter: who makes the investment decisions, you or your clients? My experience strongly suggests the answer is that the ultimate decision makers are our clients.

Studies confirm my experience. They show that asset flows for investment advisors and even institutional investors exhibit the same performance-chasing tendency that afflicts retail investors.[4]

The iconic investor Sir John Templeton summed up wise investing when he advised us to: "buy when others are despondently selling and to sell when others are avidly buying." Our greatest value to our investors is to do as Templeton suggests and help them resist emotional investing and to act in opposition to the crowd. If advisors are ineffective at managing investor behavior and follow the herd along with their investors, the implications for our industry are sobering. It means that when there is an asset bubble similar to internet stocks, meme stocks, or cryptocurrencies, the next time that the stock markets crash, or the next time that markets become wildly overvalued, the advisory community at large will again be ineffective at curbing the portfolio-destroying behavior that we've witnessed in the past.

Advisors can guide investors to make counterintuitive decisions. But the current method that many use to onboard, communicate, and guide investors isn't working. Investors must be taught to both understand and embrace counterintuitive decision making with a new set of tools.

Before getting into investor communications, however, I'll be spending a fair amount of effort on discussing the problems that plagued Prudence and Cornelius from the outset: the pitfalls of conventional portfolios.

CHAPTER 2
The Historical Accident of Conventional Portfolios—How Stocks and Bonds Create Risks for Investors

MODERN PORTFOLIO CONSTRUCTION is a victim of historical accident. Different financial products were created to meet specific needs. Bonds helped finance governments (and later companies), and stocks allowed investors to pool equity funding for companies. The means of purchasing stocks and bonds has improved greatly, creating an enormous number of investment products. Yet the evolution of investment product creation has focused on improving inefficiencies and methods of purchasing securities rather than on products that meet the unique needs of investors at different stages in their investing lives.

As a result of this centuries-long accidental evolution, modern portfolio theory answers the question, "How can we best buy and combine these things to reach the maximum return for a given level of risk?" rather than "How do we build portfolios that conform to the specific needs of our investors?"

Deconstructing conventional portfolios

Vast academic effort has been expended to build a rich body of theory that supports portfolio construction. That, along with the enormous number of investment products and strategies available, obscures the fact that most portfolios are made up primarily of just two core holdings that have existed for centuries: stocks and bonds.

Understanding the risks presented by conventional strategies requires a deeper look at stocks and bonds, the two basic building blocks behind over 90% of investors' portfolios. The way our industry frames these two building blocks understates their risks.

In this chapter, after looking at these two building blocks, I'll examine portfolio construction. I'll illuminate flaws in the assumptions that support modern portfolio theory and conventional portfolio construction, and illustrate its shortcomings in meeting what investors need from their portfolios.

Stocks—a victim of their own success

In this section, I'll examine stocks carefully, investigating how they can function as intended in investors' portfolios, but also how they can "malfunction" in ways that the financial industry tends to ignore.

Stocks are the engines of portfolio growth. As shown in Figure 2.1, stocks have a clear history of producing gains. Even after inflation, which has averaged 3.11% from December of 1927 through 2023, the S&P 500 has provided returns of 6.7% per year. That means that after advisor fees and other costs for owning stocks, there is ample room to produce real growth for investors.

Figure 2.1: Stock market gains historically have been a great source of growth, providing 6.7% per year more than inflation since 1915

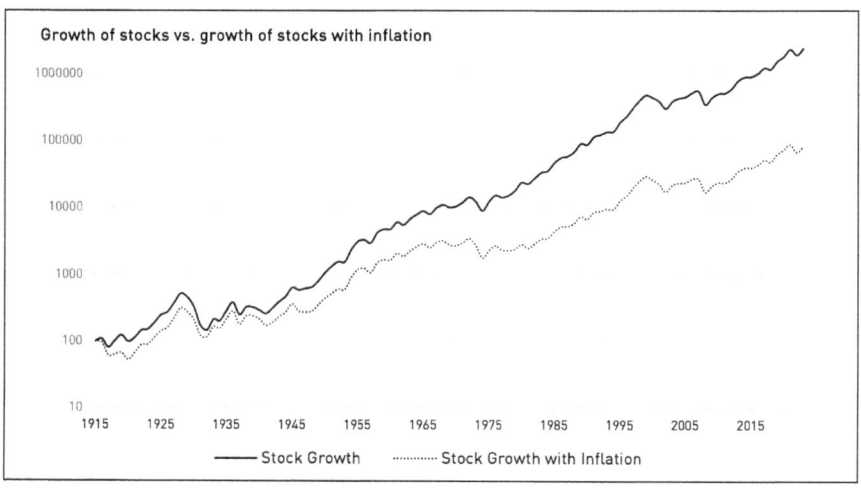

For those concerned about losses in stocks, market historians point out that, as long as investors held US stocks for 20 calendar years or more, they would never have realized a loss over the period from 1926 to present.[5] That period includes the worst decline that any advisors contemplate today, which is the 84% decline in stocks during the Great Depression.

Confidence in stocks is further bolstered by the most respected minds in the industry such Eugene Fama, who won a Nobel Prize for his work on the efficient markets hypothesis. In fact, losses in stocks are framed in many cases not as "losses," but as "volatility." Volatility suggests that downturns are momentary phenomena that are ultimately erased by recovery and further gains. Studies routinely scour stock market data to reach the same apparent conclusion: the profitability and resilience of stocks is certain, and it is folly to invest otherwise.

This one-sided perspective on stocks has allowed the entire industry to abstract stock market historical data from the instruments themselves, which are companies that earn or lose money, and can succeed, but can also fail and go bankrupt. It has also allowed the amount that we pay for the earnings of companies to drift higher, even as the markets have cycled through significant turbulence. This level of über confidence in the long-term prospects for the stock market calls into question the possibility for gains ahead. But even more significant for our investors, it significantly increases the risk not just of volatility, but significant losses.

To help investors understand how stocks are valued on exchanges, I often ask them to think first about small private companies that they may own or know of. There is a rule of thumb that the value of a mom-and-pop small business is two to three times one year's earnings before income taxes.[6] An investor buying such a company would earn a high annual return of 30% to 50% per year at this rate, but would also take on considerable risk that the business might not be able to generate those earnings in the future.

As companies grow and ultimately become public firms that issue stock on exchanges, the amount that we pay for them more than quadruples to an average of 16 times earnings (for S&P 500 companies).[7] That means that an S&P 500 company would produce earnings of 6.5% that could be distributed to investors as dividends or invested by the company into increasing future growth. That return seems low historically when considering that the average yield on a 10-year Treasury that is backed by the US government is 5.86%,[8] and stocks can fall in value significantly. Based on that earnings comparison, current earnings alone don't account for the high price we pay for publicly listed companies. The reason that we pay high prices for companies also isn't primarily based on the assets of the companies. Currently, the book value of the S&P 500 makes up just 23% of its valuation.

If an investor isn't being rewarded in the form of current earnings or current assets for taking on the added risk of owning a stock, what are they paying for?

The answer is that the majority of the value in the stocks that our investors own is based on an *expectation of earnings growth*, not just in the coming year, but over five or 10 years or longer. When we buy stocks, we aren't primarily buying bricks and mortar, brand names, or masterful management teams, we're quite literally buying *optimism*. (My nine-year-old and 12-year-old start literally every sentence with "literally" or "no offense but," so prepare yourselves!) If we own optimism, the primary risk to stock values occurs when market participants become less optimistic or even outright pessimistic. As fast and extreme as market participants can change from optimistic to pessimistic, stocks can lose value. As much as we'd love for some floor to exist under stocks value, it's that simple.

When stocks rally into the stratosphere, an optimism bubble inflates that creates an intrinsic level of risk for our investors that is not fully appreciated or understood by many investors. Based on how many managers evaluate stocks, and the fact that valuations are primarily driven by expected earnings growth, a change in expected earnings growth can dictate an outsized change even in the price of a widely respected company's stock.

For example, if analysts change a five-year earnings growth forecast from 5.0% to 2.5% annually, present value calculators might show that that justifies a loss of 30% of a company's value, even before an actual decrease in earnings is experienced. A decline in expected earnings growth from 5% to 0% annually using simple modeling calculators could dictate a nearly 50% drop in stock prices. Again, without any actual change in earnings, a vacuum of optimism can rapidly deflate the value of a company.

Adding to the potential size of stock moves is that stock earnings have historically been highly variable. They haven't just gone from positive projections to zero growth. Earnings can decline too. As shown in Figure 2.2, the biggest declines in S&P 500 earnings occurred in the early 20th century and during the Great Financial Crisis, which saw declines of 87% and 82% respectively. If a company's long-range earnings estimates ever becomes negative, it can decimate a stock's value.

Figure 2.2: The biggest declines in earnings of S&P 500 companies were massive—87% in the early 20th century and 82% during the Great Financial Crisis

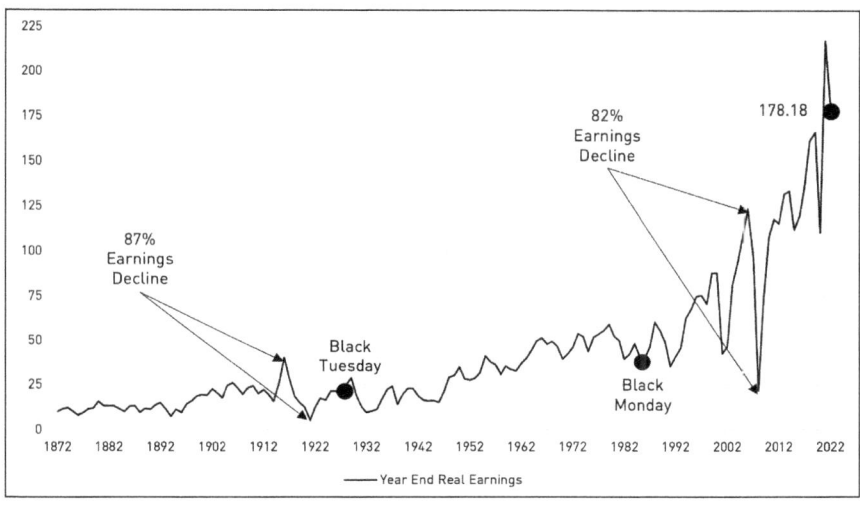

Variations in how much we pay for each earnings dollar created even greater risks

In addition to this already volatile mechanism for pricing stocks, the amount that we pay for a dollar of earnings fluctuates greatly. For example, although on average we have paid 16 for each dollar of earnings for S&P 500 stocks, the price/earnings (P/E) ratio has ranged from a high of 123.0 to a low of 5.3 (as shown in Figure 2.3). That range of valuations is enormous, with a decline from 123.0 to 5.3 representing a 95% decline. In other words, with all things being equal, and company earnings in the index completely unchanged, it would have been possible based on levels of optimism and pessimism during different markets for stocks to lose 95% of their value.

Figure 2.3: The real price/earnings ratio history of the S&P 500 shows a wide range—as low as 5.3 times earnings and as high as 123 times earnings

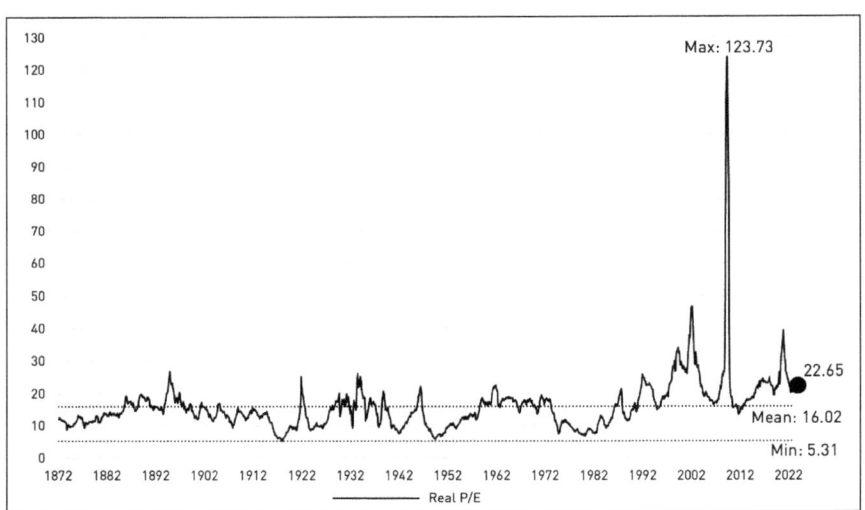

We have identified two factors that primarily determine stock values:

1. Projected earnings growth, and;
2. How much we pay for a dollar of earnings.

Unfortunately, these two factors tend to be interdependent. When the economy is in decline, this often means decreasing earnings projections. This in turn decreases optimism and potentially lowers the amount that investors are willing to pay for each dollar of earnings. When earnings projections are rising, this tends to increase the amount that investors are willing to pay for each share of earnings due to increasing levels of optimism.

This interplay between earnings growth and levels of optimism/pessimism acts like leverage on stock market gyrations. Let me illustrate with a simple example of the effect of stock declines.

If earnings decrease 33% as they did during the three-year period between 1988 and 1991, and stocks remain at constant multiple of, for example, 15 times trailing earnings, it would justify an equal decline in stock prices of 33%. If, however, as a result of market pessimism about growth prospects, market participants were only willing to pay 10 times earnings for stocks (down from 15), a 33% earnings compression would cause stocks to fall 55%.

If trailing earnings are 29, as they have been a number of times in the past decade, that same scenario, a decrease of 33% in earnings and a compression to a P/E of 10, justifies an 77% decline. A decline to the historically low P/E of 5.31 would create an 88% loss (shown in Figure 2.4).

Figure 2.4: When decreases in earnings are combined with a lower P/E paid for stocks, losses can be amplified significantly

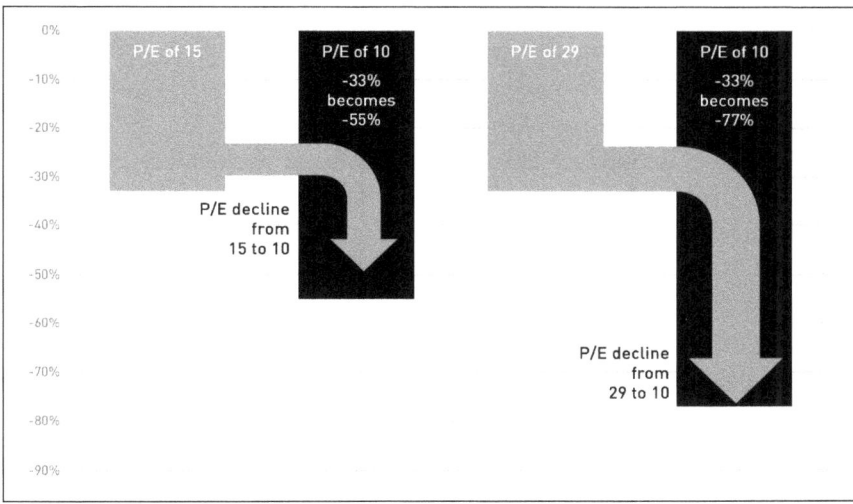

How can a 33% change in earnings cause a loss of 477% of an investor's portfolio? Many investors eschew ever buying stocks on margin, which means that an investor is buying more securities than they have committed in capital (leverage) because they understand that when prices turn against you, it is possible to lose all your money, or even more than you have invested. Yet, all stock investors experience the volatility associated with leverage because of the multiplier effect that price/earnings ratios can have on stock prices.

The changing views of how much each dollar of earnings is worth has leverage-like effects during rising as well as falling markets. During bull markets, as P/E ratios climb, risk escalates.

Despite risks, cognitive dissonance prevents advisors from reacting to inflated markets

When valuations become excessive, the response of the advisory community has been to continue to build portfolios as usual. They're aware that the situation has changed, but cognitive dissonance, the habits of how we build portfolios, along with confusion and a lack of realistic solutions to overvalued markets, prevents advisors from adapting.

This intellectual paralysis, combined with the oppressive academic data supporting the efficient markets hypothesis, has allowed US stock market valuations to drift at times to irrational levels.

Most view periods of elevated valuations as momentary overpricing lapses that come and go. Yet few realize the average price/earnings in the past decades—the amount that investors are willing to pay for each share of earnings—has moved significantly higher. The 20-year average P/E level of the S&P 500 has increased from levels averaging 13.80 since 1892 to a current average of 24.81. In other words, during the past 20 years, we were comfortable paying 80% more for the earnings of S&P 500 companies than we were historically. This is shown in Figure 2.5.

Figure 2.5: During the past decade, the 20-year average of how much investors are willing to pay for stocks has been elevated, reflecting complacency about market risks

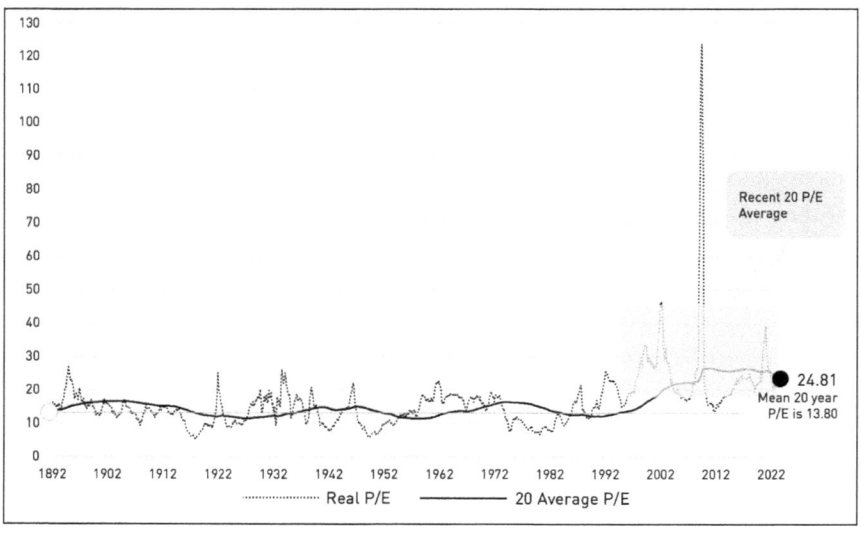

Frequent periods of high valuations make bear markets commonplace. Over the past 120 years there were losses ranging to nearly 20% during every decade. Stocks entered bear markets that averaged losses of 36% twice per decade during these years. These declines challenge an investor's ability to meet their goals, in addition to wreaking havoc on their emotional well-being. The data for the number of bear markets per decade and the DJIA decline in each of these bear markets is shown in Figure 2.6.

Figure 2.6: Every decade since 1900 has seen a bear market of nearly 20% at least once, with an average of two bear markets per decade and average losses of 36%

	Years	Number of bear markets	DJIA percentage decline				
	1900s	3	-49%	-46%	-32%		
	1910s	2	-47%	-40%			
	1920s	1	-47%				
	1930s	5	-89%	-52%	-37%	-23%	-22%
Significant	1940s	1	-24%				
declines are	1950s	1	-19%				
part of the	1960s	2	-37%	-27%			
	1970s	2	-45%	-27%			
fluctuations of	1980s	2	-36%	-24%			
the markets	1990s	2	-21%	-19%			
	2000s	2	-54%	-38%			
	2010s	1	-19%				
	2020s	2	-37%	-22%			

Average number of bear markets	Average loss
2	**-36%**

Stock market declines can and have been greater than during the Great Financial Crisis

We all have a sense of how much our investors are willing to tolerate fiscally and psychologically. For most, losses like those that we experienced in 2008 pushed investors to their limits. Due to recency bias, when I query an audience of advisors about the worst-case scenarios that they try to prepare their investors for, virtually everyone points to the Great Financial

Crisis. While that stock market decline was among the most severe that has occurred in the past 100 years, it certainly wasn't the worst in several respects.

First, the S&P 500 fell 55%—much less than the maximum loss of 84% realized between 1929 and 1932. But the size of declines is only one factor that affects investors. When the duration of declines increases, the impact on the ability of investors to maintain income and tolerate its psychological effects are more severe. During the Great Financial Crisis, stocks bottomed after only 16 months, and experienced a fierce recovery beginning in March of 2009. It took 4.5 years for the market to fully return to break even.

Figure 2.7: When illustrated as a shaded drawdown chart, it's easy to see the significance of the drawdown during the Great Depression relative to that during the Great Financial Crisis

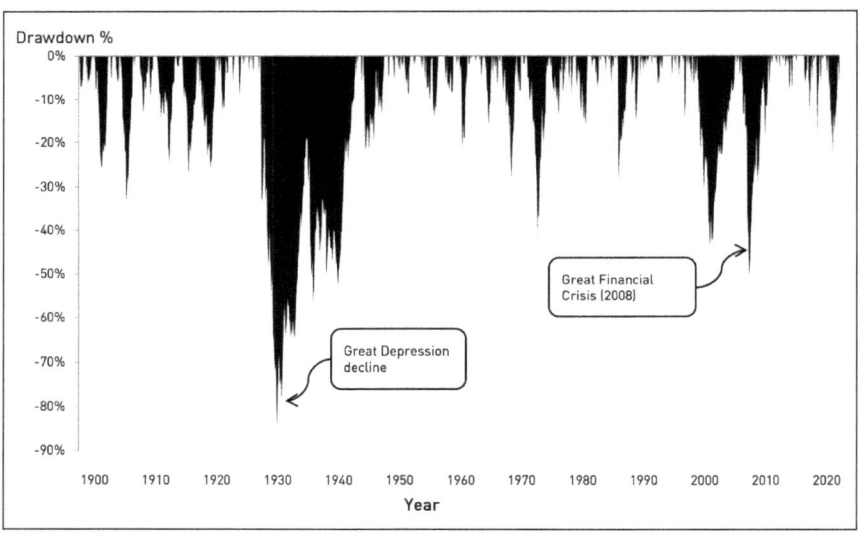

The initial decline of 84% realized during the Great Depression, by contrast, occurred over three years, between September of 1929 and June of 1932, rather than the 16 months experienced during the 2008 financial crisis. Stocks turned higher in 1932. However, the stock market didn't recover during a strong rally between June of 1932 and March of 1937. In fact, even after that rally, stocks were still lower by almost 39%, nine years after the bear market began. This was followed by another significant drop that lasted until 1942. Over the course of the bear market, the S&P 500 dropped a whopping 67% and lasted 12.7 years. Stocks didn't fully recover to their original value until 16.4 years from the decline's inception. As is shown in Figure 2.7, when combining both time under water and the amount below break-even, losses during the Great Depression were four times as severe as what we experienced during the Great Financial Crisis.

As a reader, you're no doubt having this thought: "I understand that to be true, but the Great Depression occurred because of innumerable policy blunders as well inadequate measures to prevent bank failures. Our Federal Reserve and banking safeguards will prevent us from experiencing depressions of that magnitude again."

I hope you are right. But as an investment advisor who is being relied on to guide investors, it's worth examining the validity of this statement from an historical perspective. It's also worth considering how investors view your role in defending against improbable events like the stock market debacle during the Great Depression.

The Great Depression was not a one-time event—events like this have recurred and likely will occur again

Before the "Great Depression" that we commonly refer to occurred, historians referenced a previous "Great Depression": the period between 1873 to 1896. Today, this period is referred to as the Long Depression. During the Long Depression, the United States suffered its longest period of economic contraction, at 65 months. The depression of the 1930s by comparison was 43 months of contraction, according to the National Bureau of Economic Research (NBER). Between 1873 and 1879, the worst years for the United States, 18,000 businesses, 10 states, and hundreds of banks went bankrupt.

Other depressions in the United States include the depression of 1807, 1815–1821, and the depression of 1920–1921.

Events over the past decade illustrate economic vulnerabilities that could lead to depressions. During the Great Financial Crisis, banking regulations from the 1930s were inconsequential to prevent the meltdown of credit default swaps and other financial derivatives. Those new products, which evolved faster than regulators could address the risks that they posed, caused the failure of Bear Sterns, the bankruptcy of Lehman Brothers, and led many other financial institutions to the brink. Hank Paulson, the acting Secretary of the Treasury, wrote: "I didn't want to be the treasury secretary that presided over the onset of another great depression, and I have no doubt today that, that is exactly what our country would have faced had our actions fallen short."[9] Those at the highest levels of control during this time openly acknowledge that success at avoiding a collapse was far from certain. Even with quick action by the Treasury and the Fed, stocks plummeted 55%, real estate declined by 18%, and unemployment increased to 10%. The global economy did not fall into a depression (defined as an extreme recession that lasts three or more years, or which leads to a decline in real gross domestic product (GDP), of at least 10% in a given year) during the Great Financial Crisis, but we were clearly on the brink.

The global pandemic is a second and stark example of economic vulnerabilities to exogenous shocks. During the initial months of the pandemic, US GDP plummeted 9%. In response, the Federal Reserve took dramatic steps to backstop financial assets and even began to outright purchase investments that were falling in value, and the government poured trillions of dollars into the economy paid directly to individuals and businesses. Any number of factors, such as a higher COVID fatality rate or a government less willing to bolster the economy could have led us into a depression.

Finally, as a way of expressing the impotency of current banking regulations at preventing crises, it's worth considering cryptocurrencies. One significant contributor to the economic collapse during the initial years of the Great Depression was the failure of thousands of banks. Without the Federal Deposit Insurance Corporation (FDIC) and strong bank regulations, people, businesses, and the banks themselves saw their money vanish. And obviously vanishing money is super bad for the economy.

If this sounds eerily familiar, it's because we innovative humans managed to create a new type of "currency" in the form of cryptocurrencies that are held in some cases by crypto trading firms that can operate without insurance or oversight from any regulatory body. As one might have been able to predict based on the wild speculation that has taken place in the crypto world, brokers such as Celsius, Genesis, and FTX collapsed due to leverage and rapidly declining prices in Bitcoin and other alt-currencies. All of the tight regulations of the global banking system did exactly nothing to help defend against this new currency that traded outside of banks and brokerages. From the peak in the crypto market in November of 2021, markets tumbled in 2022 to erase over $1.8 trillion.[10] When money vanishes due to these new instruments, it's no different than the vanishing money associated with banks during the Great Depression. This scenario represented risk being created outside of the system of regulation that then poses systemic economic risks.

Contemplating how losses like those during the Great Depression would affect your clients and your practice is sobering, and we will explore a visualization of a balanced portfolio during the depression in a later chapter. However, we would probably all agree that few if any clients would still be visiting you at your office and paying a quarterly fee for your advice if the stock portion of their balanced portfolio was 63% lower after 13 years. (That's 63% lower before they paid your annual fee … for 13 years). The assertion that those investors would recover their losses and go on to see substantial gains ignores the high probability that they are no longer investors at all, at least not stock market investors.

Advisors dismiss the possibility of events like the Great Depression as having such a low probability that it is just noise. After all, what's the probability that a 1-in-100-year event will affect your investors?

Higher than you think. Clients who begin saving in their 30s may have an investing time horizon of 60 years or greater, with potentially 30 of those years in an income distribution phase. Such long investing horizons subject investors to an increased chance that they will participate in extreme turbulent markets. Investors with a 30-year time horizon would have had a nearly one-in-three chance of being an investor during some part of a Great Depression that occurs once every 100 years. Arguably, when markets are priced at elevated levels, chances of extreme negative markets increase. In our chapter on risk, we look at additional macro factors that are associated with great depressions and reach … depressing conclusions.

Before I summarize our discussion of stocks, it's imperative that I bring up the starkest example of all developed country stock market stories in the past 100 years: Japan. Japan sets the record for the worst developed country stock market performance in the past century, by a lot. But it's ignored by many in the investment advisory profession when considering stock market outcomes.

Figure 2.8: Japanese stock losses have been massive, in terms of both percentage and duration

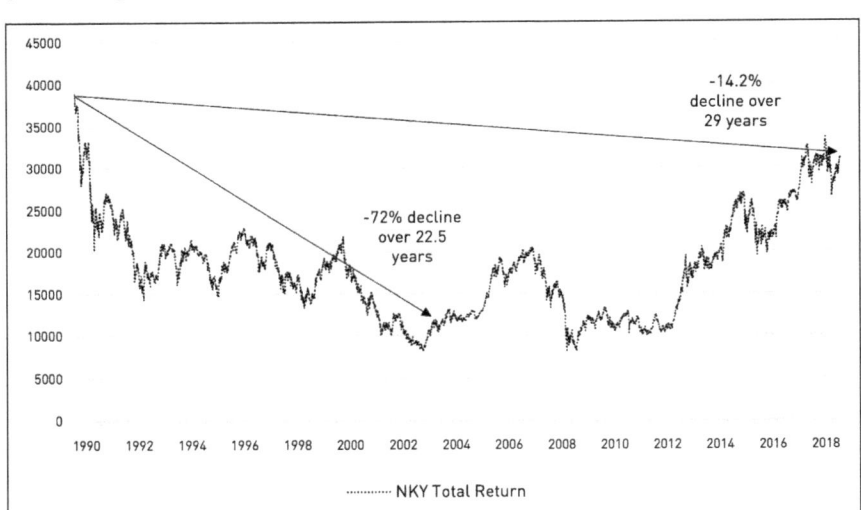

As you can see in Figure 2.8, from the peak of the Japanese stock market at the end of 1989, the Nikkei 225 total return index has lost 14% 29 years later. In 2012, 22.5 years after the peak in the index, Japanese stocks were 72% lower. The decline has been caused by low growth, unfavorable demographics, poor public policies, business and banking weaknesses, and high unemployment.

The United States is not currently in a similar situation to Japan prior to the crash of their bubble, and it is easy to lay out all the mistakes that were made by banks, corporations, and the government in Japan as being improbable in our own economy. Yet, the decision to ignore the possibility of this decline is a result of what I have labeled proximity bias. It didn't happen in a Western developed country, but such a decline in a highly functional and efficient economy like Japan shows us that these types of declines are possible and could happen in the US.

The experience in Japan is a stark challenge to the notion that if investors hold stocks for 20 years or longer, they would never have realized a loss. Japan is early among developed nations to experience unfavorable demographic trends that will affect Europe, the United States, and ultimately China. As populations shift towards more retirees and fewer people in their prime earning, productive years, there are legitimate questions about the ability of economies to grow at levels seen in the past century. Unprecedented levels of global debt is another factor that can't be ignored. Increasing debt lowers long-range growth prospects for economies, and increases both the probability and magnitude of financial crises.

Stock market rollercoaster induced nausea

Stocks have created tremendous wealth for investors and are necessary components of many or even most portfolios. Yet, they carry risks that have the power to devastate our investors and our practices. During periods of growing optimism, company earnings increase, and the amount that we pay for those earnings increases at the same time, creating a leveraged effect on stock prices. The increase in the amount that we pay for each dollar of earnings makes it appear that companies are performing better than they are.

During these market rallies supply/demand dynamics supersede stock fundamentals as the primary driver of stock prices. How far down the rabbit hole we go depends on a lot of factors. But the levels of detachment from reality appear unbounded if one looks at periods such as the internet bubble, where stocks without earnings or even earnings prospects were priced at billions of dollars. Outsized returns, especially over prolonged periods, force investors and their advisors to make greater allocations to stocks as a percent of their portfolios, which acts as a positive feedback loop to increase stock prices even further. This happens in both the retail and advisor-managed marketplace. It may be obvious but is worth pointing out that flows into stocks relative to other assets increase with perfectly poor timing: near or at peak P/E levels when the prospects for stock market gains become poorer, and the chances for losses and the size of losses peak. Because of the ineffective means of communication and behavior management, advisors have been able to do little to prevent this trend, if they even have an interest in trying.

When markets turn lower, this all plays out in reverse. Declining P/E ratios act like leverage when declining earnings growth or outright earnings declines combine with lower valuations. As negative momentum builds, supply/demand dynamics once again take over, with little correlation or concern for realistic long-term earnings prospects or stock market history. Now, instead of viewing stocks as a bargain, investors become net sellers of stocks. The greater the opportunity and the better the bargain that stock prices represent, the greater the sales become.

Framing stock market ownership for retired or retiring investors

Would you ask an investor who was retiring imminently to start or purchase a business? Probably not. Retiring investors have less time and ability to tolerate declines than younger investors. Investing a sizable portion of a retired investor's portfolio in a business exposes them to what is referred to as idiosyncratic risk, which refers to risk created from just one asset. Because it's just one business, failure could cause excessive losses.

Investing in diversified funds or portfolios lowers idiosyncratic risk and few advisors hesitate to recommend these portfolios to their investors. Yet, as we have shown, while idiosyncratic risk is largely eliminated, systemic risk may be higher on exchange-traded stocks than smaller private companies due to the substantially higher valuations that we pay for publicly traded companies.

There is a direct correlation between how volatile portfolios are and the probability that retired investors will run out of money. When markets become overvalued, the probability that the average retired investor will meet their goals potentially becomes even bleaker. The time for investing a majority of a portfolio in speculative investments is not during retirement, yet that is what we ask investors to do.

Before moving on to discuss bonds, the second core asset class, let's summarize what we just discussed about stocks, and juxtapose that alongside how we've been taught to think about them:

Volatility vs. risk

Common perspective: We're taught that stocks are sometimes "volatile," but that if investors hold them for 20 years or longer, they would have always realized a positive return.

Reality: As a result of extreme losses, stock ownership can permanently impair capital. Worst-case scenarios over the past century would have caused investors to leave the stock market and would have left many investors destitute.

Median valuations

Common perspective: When priced at median price/earnings, stocks are reasonably priced and are not susceptible to significant losses.

Reality: Because price/earnings ratios and earnings themselves fluctuate in a wide range, stocks priced at average valuations can still experience extreme losses due to earnings decreases and P/E compression.

Depression stock market risk

Common perspective: Improvements in bank and market regulations, and wiser Fed policy, render the possibility of a depression so small that it can be ignored when planning for investors.

Reality: Depressions recur. Businesses innovate and evolve, creating new systemic risks that are unaddressed by outdated regulations. Exogenous risks, like the global pandemic, can potentially decimate economies with little or no notice and can occur regardless of the health of economies.

Bonds: The "stable" anchor of portfolios that may pose the greatest risk to our portfolios

Bonds are perceived as the safe asset class. However, history shows that they can produce profoundly negative outcomes for investors that last for decades. It's been a generation since bonds have experienced a long-term negative market. As a result, advisors and their investors are both vulnerable and oblivious to their risks.

One of the most iconic investors in our industry was Jack Bogle, the late founder of the index fund giant Vanguard Funds. He was a veritable hero who benefited investors immensely by steering them away from high-expense products and into index products that have minimal costs. The company he founded manages $7.2 trillion worldwide as of 2023 and is among the largest global money management firms.

Throughout his career, Jack Bogle focused on two primary mantras: 1) invest in low-cost index funds that allow you to keep more of your money, and; 2) balance your portfolio among stocks and bonds to provide stability and diversification.

Bonds generally *do* add stability to portfolios. While stocks fluctuate according to industry- or company-specific information or economic changes, bonds are less vulnerable to price adjustments as both principal and interest are backed by their issuers.

Investors can expect a trade-off between risk and return, however. The greater stability of bonds translates into lower returns for investors. Since 1915, corporate bonds have returned 6.6% on average.[11] After inflation, which averaged 3.3% over the same period, bonds produced 3.5% real growth. That's only about half of the real return provided by stocks (6.7%). If we assume advisor- and fund-related fees of 1.65%, real growth of corporate bonds declines to 1.9%.

So why does the headline of this section assert that bonds may pose the "greatest risk?"

Bonds have fallen by as much as 17% in a single year,[12] but this doesn't come close to matching the 84% drawdown of stocks during the Great Depression. The risk posed by bonds is more complicated than straightforward principal losses. Namely, bonds have three primary sources of risk:

1. Default Risk
2. Interest Rate Risk
3. Inflation Risk

I'll now move on to discuss each of the three primary risks to bond portfolios and evaluate how they have combined to potentially devastating effect for long-term investors. I'll also look at present challenges to bonds based on current high levels of global debt.

Default (credit) risk

The first and easiest risk to understand is default risk. If a bond issuer is unable to pay the interest or principal (or both) of a bond, then an investor can realize a loss. The way to think about default risk is that everything is fine until it's not, and then it's really not. Once an issuer is unable to make a payment, challenges escalate quickly. Rating agencies lower the issuer's ratings, making it more difficult or impossible to fund operations or refinance debts. The result can be that bondholders are forced to accept a reduction or elimination of interest payments and may only collect a portion of their original principal, or none of it. In the case of the bankruptcy of a company, a bondholder can lose everything.

Fortunately for holders of diversified corporate bond funds, defaults for investment-grade bond portfolios are infrequent during normal markets. The Schwab Center for Financial Research showed that the investment-grade corporate bond default rate was 0% in 14 of the 22 years from 2001 through 2022, and the highest annual default rate was just 0.75% in 2008 during the Global Financial Crisis.[13] However, default rates have been much higher. During the railroad crisis in the 1870s there was a three-year period when defaults totaled 36%. And during the Great Depression, defaults were 13% during the worst three-year period.[14]

A note about investment-grade bond defaults: although I cited a "zero" percent default rate during 14 of the 22 years above, this misrepresents the situation somewhat. As company finances (and their ability to service bond debt) deteriorate, companies tend to be reclassified as "high yield" or "junk." If these companies later default, this is reflected as a below-investment grade company default. So, more companies that were once considered investment grade find their way to actual defaults than is reflected in the figures cited here.

All of these statistics relate to corporate bonds. Often not fully considered is the default risk on government bonds, also referred to as sovereign debt. On the surface, debt backed by governments would seem to be safer, but history suggests that sovereign debt risks can eclipse corporate bond risks in the right circumstances. In *This Time Is Different*, Carmen Reinhart and Kenneth Rogoff documented the history of sovereign debt defaults and found that since 1800 there were 250 instances of default, equaling more than one per year. In our section on risk, I'll more fully examine the risks to fixed income

Interest rate risk

The second risk to bond portfolios is interest rate risk. When interest rates rise, interest paid on new bonds is higher than the older bonds that are held in an investor's portfolio. The lower-yielding bonds become less desirable and can demand a lower price on the secondary market. Assuming that a bond is held to maturity and does not go into default, an investor will receive the full principal owed. However, because most bonds that are owned by individual investors are held in mutual funds or ETFs, the principal value of the fund typically declines as interest rates rise. A rule of thumb is that for every five years of duration, a 1% increase in interest rates translates into a principal loss of 5%. In 2022, as rates increased on short-term bonds by roughly 3%, bonds lost 15%, conforming with that rule of thumb.

Inflation risk

The third risk to bonds is inflation. If an investor holds bonds, and inflation moves to a higher level than the interest paid on those bonds, an investor realizes a loss of purchasing power, even though nominally it may appear that they realized a net gain from interest collected.

Figure 2.9: Cumulative years of high inflation add up, totaling as much as 121% or a more than doubling of prices

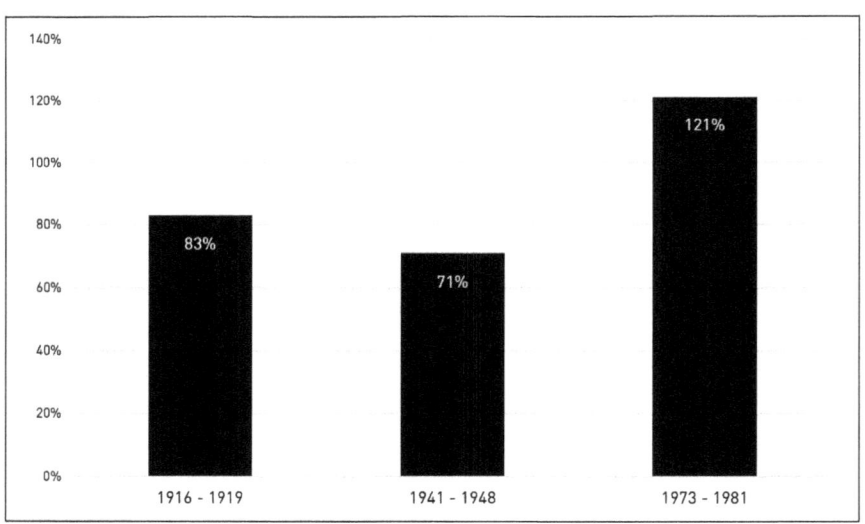

Source: www.econ.yale.edu/~shiller/data.htm

Although individual year inflation increases have only briefly once moved higher than 20% per year, cumulatively inflation has increased significantly over multiple years. As shown in Figure 2.9, between 1916 and 1919, for example, inflation in the US increased 83%. Between 1941 and 1948 inflation increased by 71%. But the worst episode of inflation occurred between 1973 and 1981, when inflation increased 121%.

Is this as bad as inflation and, as a result, bond markets can get? Not by a long shot. In the United States we've been lucky to have rarely experienced a hyperinflation market, defined as inflation of 20% per year or higher. But other countries, even developed countries, have experienced inflation that dwarfs our experience in the United States. In 1795 France saw inflation as high as 304% in one month. In 1923 Germany experienced inflation of 29,500% in one month, or 20.9% in one day.

More recently in 1990 Argentina experienced inflation of 197% in one month, and Russia's currency collapse led to a 245% inflation increase in 1992.[15] Inflation isn't always caused by traditional wage and pricing pressures. The most extreme inflation originates from countries' inability to service debt. A poignant example of this was after World War I when Germany was unable to make reparation payments and began excessively printing marks. As developed countries continue to increase public debt, the risk of currency and economic crises increases, increasing the odds of correlated losses in stock and bond portfolios. As you think about inflation in portfolios, always expand your perspective to include the global experience and realize that inflation has been much, much worse than the US all-time high inflation rate of 20% annually in 1918.

For bond owners, including typical corporate or government bonds, high inflation directly reduces purchasing power. When inflation increases cumulatively by 100%, as it has in the United States, that translates to purchasing power losses of 50% (plus interest earned on bonds, minus principal losses due to rising interest rates). But at higher levels of inflation like those seen internationally, it could mean virtually wiping out the real value of a bondholder's portfolio. Investors are affected inversely depending on how conservative their allocation is. Perversely, conservative investors (those that "can't afford to lose") that own only bonds, like Prudence before she met Cornelius, have the highest risk from inflation and interest rate increases. Figure 2.10 shows the decline in purchasing power at varying levels of inflation.

Figure 2.10: The amount of purchasing power lost when inflation increases significantly

Inflation Increase	Investor Loss (purchasing power)
10%	9.1%
20%	16.7%
50%	33.3%
100%	50%
200%	66.7%
500%	83.3%
1000%	90.9%

What does inflation risk look like for more aggressive investors, who have higher allocations to stocks?

The answer may surprise you. Due to the correlation between high interest rates and inflation, and the fact that rising interest rates tend to have a depressive effect on stocks, one might assume that inflation is correlated with poor stock performance. But that hasn't been the case on average. During the three instances of high inflation in the US, inflation averaged 9.8% per year. During those same years, the S&P 500 averaged a return of 9% per year. Stocks failed to provide above-inflation growth during that time, but they at least kept pace with inflation. Something bonds didn't do.

Why?

Inflation is a measure of consumer prices. Increasing prices can translate into greater company revenue and potentially greater profits (on a nominal basis). In other words, even though high interest rates tend to be negative for companies' growth, those companies act as a pass-through for prices, helping to immunize investors' stock portfolios against the effects of inflation. That means that stocks are likely to lessen the effects of inflation when bonds are vulnerable to severe losses.

The ability for stocks to produce gains during inflationary periods, however, applies only to normal inflationary periods. During hyperinflation, where currencies are essentially collapsing, this no longer necessarily holds true. Currency crises are potentially so disruptive that commerce collapses, destroying value in both stock and bond portfolios.

Is high or hyperinflation *really* something advisors need to consider when building portfolios? Yes. The chances that any one year realizes inflation of 10% or greater was only 1-in-10 since 1913. However, because inflation periods are clustered, with inflation bouncing above and below that 10% threshold over longer periods, the three episodes of high inflation accounted for almost one-fifth of the time between 1913 and 2023. Long investing horizons for investors of 60 years or more mean that the chance that investors would have experienced a high inflation episode are more probable than not.

As global debt increases to unprecedented levels, it increases the possibility that a currency crisis, even a global currency crisis, could happen. Pretending that high or hyperinflation can't happen exposes investors in fixed income to risks that they are likely completely unprepared for if they are invested heavily in bonds. As an advisor, failing to address potential inflation in portfolio design leaves you and your investors vulnerable to an obvious and recurring historical risk. Incorporating inflation risk contingency planning should be a critical part of portfolio design.

The three risks to bonds can combine to deliver decades of real losses

During the worst periods for bonds, rising inflation, rising interest rates, and defaults worked together to create a wealth-destroying combination. Figure 2.11 shows real (or after inflation) returns of the Dow Jones Total Return Bond Index from 1915 through 2023. There were three significant bond bear markets during the past 100+ years. From 1915 to 1921 bonds lost 44% of purchasing power. Recently, bonds lost 24% as the Federal Reserve raised rates. The whopper, however, is a bond bear market that lasted 36 years, from 1945 to 1981. During that time, bonds lost 21% of their purchasing power. As bad as this appears, this is the return of the index, not what most investors would have realized. Net of advisors' fees and assumed underlying fund costs (assumed to be 1.5% per year), an investor would have lost 58% of their purchasing power. A loss of half of one's money in bonds is astounding, but that the loss occurred over such a long period, possibly one's entire investing life, is remarkable. This loss occurred over a period when interest rates rose from lows of 2.5% to 13.9%[16]

Figure 2.11: The Dow Jones Bond Total Return Index has experienced three bear markets since 1915, with the most significant lasting for 36 years, between 1945 and 1981

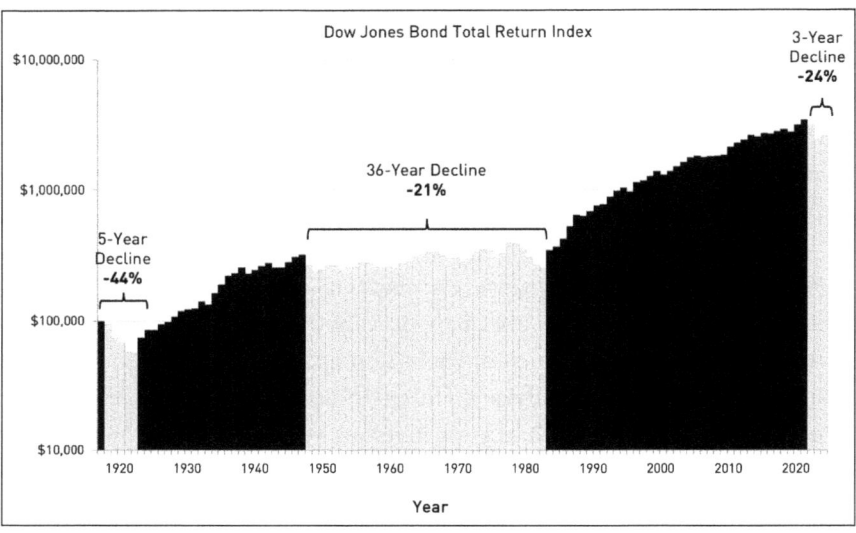

Inflation played a significant role in the real losses realized in bonds during the longest bond bear market. From 1945 until 1948, and again from 1973 to 1981, the US saw inflation range as high as 15% per year.

Until recently, advisors more or less ignored the prospect of bond losses when planning for their investors, especially when planning for conservative investors. The likely reason for this is recency bias. We hadn't had bond losses in over four decades, until 2022. As a result, and as is highlighted in Figure 2.12, investors' perspective is warped through the fishbowl of significant gains realized from 1981 through 2021.

Figure 2.12: Prior to the recent bond bear market, bonds did so well for so long that bond investors only experienced the "fishbowl" effect of bond gains since 1981

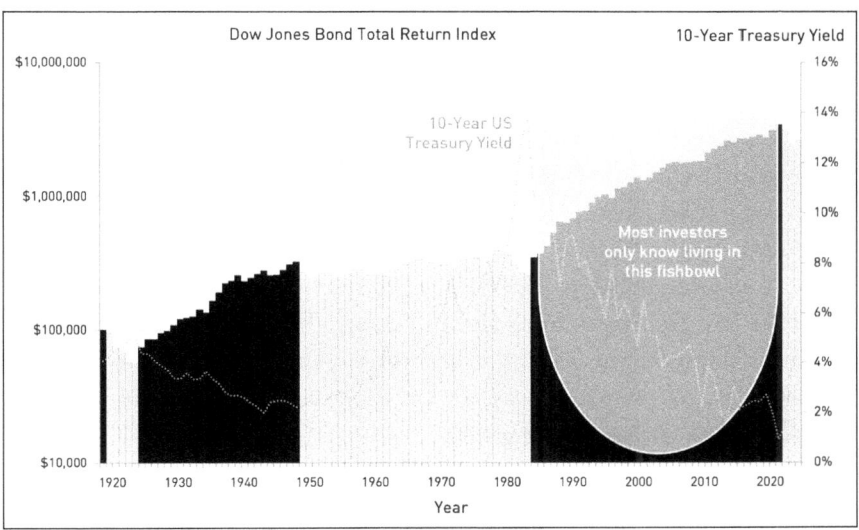

As with stocks, advisors are experiencing cognitive dissonance. It is easy to conclude that bonds are safer, and that's where a conservative investor's assets will be concentrated. Trying to solve the riddle of how to build in contingencies for bond losses is not easy.

To summarize: bonds are considered the safe asset class yet they represent the hidden risk in our investors' portfolios. Due to their vulnerability to inflation, combined with risks of increasing interest rates and defaults, bonds have experienced real losses over longer periods than stocks. While stocks are more volatile, they tend to recover after declines and have not been susceptible to losses that extend three decades or more (except in the case of Japan, of course). I'll talk more about unique investor behavioral challenges presented by bonds in the second half of the book.

Balancing portfolios among stocks and bonds is a flawed and unreliable diversification strategy

In this section, I'll show how bonds are an unreliable diversifier for stocks. Bonds can act as a buffer against stock market losses, but in some cases bonds magnify risks and correlate with stocks. I'll then illustrate how, when these factors are considered, along with realistic assumptions about managing portfolios, the probability of success for retiring or retired investors can become unacceptably low, especially when stocks and bonds are overvalued and have low expected returns ahead. Finally, I'll show how true worst-case scenarios for balanced portfolios are not navigable for advisors and their investors in any pragmatic way, an assertion that is virtually ubiquitously ignored by the advisory community.

Many times, bonds *do* add stability to stock portfolios. In normal markets, when stocks decline, a flight to safety can create demand for bond portfolios, driving up prices. The variables that affect the ability of bonds to be an effective diversifier include valuations, interest rates, inflation, and the huge but generally uncontemplated problem that corporate stocks and corporate bonds both rely on the viability of the same corporate entities.

Stocks become more vulnerable to losses when valuations are high. Similarly, bonds have more exposure to losses when interest rates are low and/or inflation is increasing. The 36-year decline of bonds that began in 1945 coincides with the generational lows in interest rates reached in the 1940s as is illustrated in Figure 2.13 by showing the 10-year treasury yield against the history of bond bear markets.

Figure 2.13: The beginning of the bear bond market in 1945 coincided with a 10-year treasury yield near 2%, which is ominously similar to the low rates in 2021

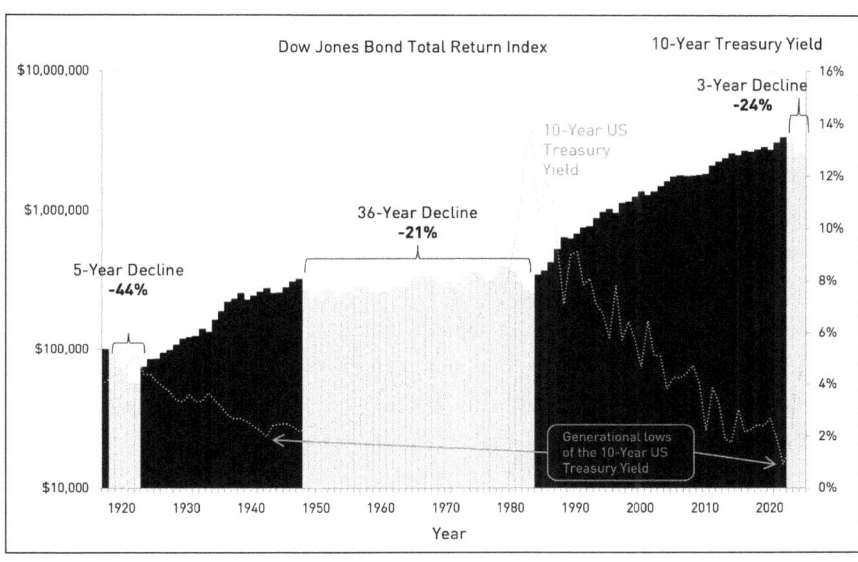

When stocks are trading at elevated valuations at the same time that interest rates are low or susceptible to increases, the probability that losses in both asset classes will occur increases. In the past century there were five times when stocks and bonds both experienced meaningful real losses, as shown in Figure 2.14. The worst experience occurred between 1916 and 1920, when both stocks and bonds experienced real losses of over 40%.

Figure 2.14: On five occasions over the past 110 years, stocks and bonds both experienced real losses simultaneously, showing that bonds are not always an effective means of diversifying against stock losses[17]

1916 to 1920	1946 to 1947	1972 to 1974	1977 to 1981	2022
Equities: **-47%**	Equities: **-25%**	Equities: **-49%**	Equities: **-8%**	Equities: **-23%**
Bonds: **-44%**	Bonds: **-26%**	Bonds: **-14%**	Bonds: **-36%**	Bonds: **-22%**

In some cases when both asset classes experienced losses, stocks were trading at elevated price/earnings ratios at the beginning of the period. However, in all cases either inflation was high, or interest rates were increasing, or both were moving higher.

As we saw during 2022, the effectiveness of the diversification that bonds provide for stocks depends largely on luck. Sometimes bonds will negatively correlate and insulate against losses, other times they'll equal losses, and still other times bond losses will increase stock market losses.

Another potential problem with the stock–bond diversification solution, however, is that corporate bonds and stocks rely on the same companies to support the valuations of both.

Why is this important? As breathtaking as the stock market decline during the Great Financial Crisis was, its short duration helped mask the vulnerability of corporate bonds. When an economy seizes up, lowered revenue and profits or outright corporate losses compromise companies' ability to service bonds. The Great Depression saw bond defaults rise as high as 13% over its worst three-year period. But a better measure of the potential recession/depression impact on bonds is during the three-year period during the "Long Depression" (1873–1879) where bond defaults reached 38% over three years.

The impact of the ability of bonds and stocks to correlate during economic downturns isn't fully realized until crises become severe and their durations are long. However, the simple fact that companies under duress will see their stock market prices decline at the same time that they lose the ability to support bond payments makes diversification meltdown more probable if economic duress becomes severe. This is when loss avoidance from diversification among asset classes is the most important.

The most cataclysmic type of market for stock/bond "diversified" portfolios hasn't occurred in the United States for over a century, but would be realized if inflation soars and interest rates rise at the same time that the economy falters and stock prices plummet.

I hope I've made clear the risks to stocks and bonds individually. However, in the next chapter I'd like to discuss in depth the foundational approach that most advisors use some variation of: the 60/40 balanced portfolio. Specifically, I'll step you through a time when a balanced portfolio would likely have brought about an end to your practice, and your clients livelihoods.

CHAPTER 3
The Existential Risks of the 60/40 Portfolio and the Challenges of a High-Debt World

The Corona Bias

From 1915 to 1918, the Great Influenza pandemic killed an estimated 25–50 million people across the globe. A century later, a new coronavirus spread throughout a global population with little to no immunity to protect themselves.

Similarly, generational asset trends are so long term in nature that advisors come to them with a "lack of immunity," effectively unaware of their potential negative effects on portfolios. As an example, I discussed earlier how bonds experienced a 36-year bear market during the rising rate period between 1945 and 1981. This was followed by 40 years of bond market prosperity. They transitioned from an investment that produced real losses in almost all markets to a stable source of growth. These generational trends may be one of the most consequential determinants of investor success.

Most advisors are familiar with recency bias, which implies that investors focus on recent returns when making current decisions. Megatrends that last for 40 years transcend recency bias, shaping the way an entire generation views specific asset classes and fundamental views on how to invest. I have labeled this the "Corona Bias," as it implies that these megatrends are completely ignored, but ultimately may come to dominate and change everything. In other words, "Corona Bias" means that while we may completely ignore historical events and find them exceedingly difficult to contemplate, doing so could potentially be devastating for our investors.

To help illustrate this point, imagine two circles, one inside the other (see Figure 3.1). Inside the smallest circle are events or market trends that have occurred recently enough to be considered relevant. Advisors think about these events when they build portfolios because either they have lived through them or they are recent enough in memory to seem relevant. Currently these would include the losses in stocks and bonds in 2022; the pandemic market decline and rally; and the Great Financial Crisis. They might also include the internet bubble for older advisors that were already in the profession in the early 2000s. As the circle becomes larger, it encapsulates events that occurred further back in time. Included here would be the great bear bond market beginning in 1945; the Great Depression-era decline in stocks; and events that occurred in other parts of the world, such as the over 30-year stock market decline in Japan.

Figure 3.1: Advisors prepare portfolios for crises that they have lived through or are more recent, but may ignore those that occurred longer ago

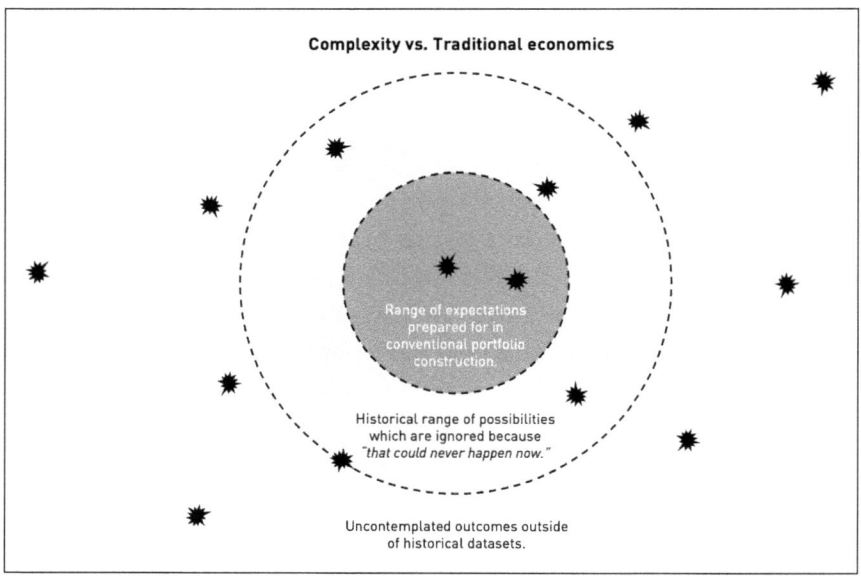

Because these events occurred so long ago, they lose relevance for advisors. As a result, portfolios are built in ways that do not prepare investors for their possible recurrence. Outside of the second circle are potential market events that have never happened before but are possible based on a broad understanding of the vulnerabilities of the markets. These contingencies are ignored by everyone.

Depression-era visualization

Hopefully, the story of Prudence and Cornelius helped you understand the challenge that we all face in trying to manage decision making as markets vacillate. Similarly, I aim to highlight events that are generally ignored by advisors and explore their potential impact on investors and their practices.

Understanding that we're working with the Corona Bias, which means that these events are almost impossible to contemplate, I will conduct a time-stamped virtual walk-through as these events played out, revealing the effects on both investors' portfolios and advisors' business. If this succeeds, at the end of the visualization, you will fully appreciate the implications of the Corona Bias and the extent of the risks it presents.

A balanced portfolio worst-case visualization

For this worst-case visualization, I chose to focus on the worst stock market experience in the past 100 years: the Great Depression. In this visualization, an investor and advisor start out with a 60/40 balanced portfolio invested in the S&P 500 and the Dow Jones Bond Total Return indices. The investor is assumed to pay all-in fees (for funds, platforms, and advisory fees) of 1.6%. In a study by Bob Veres, advisors self-reported fees that were slightly higher, at 1.65% per year. I assume an annual rebalance for the portfolio at the end of each year back to its target allocation.

The initial shocking stock market crash from 1929–1932

For many, their primary (and perhaps only) market knowledge of the Great Depression is the Black Tuesday crash of October 29, 1929, which saw stocks fall 10.2%—more than they had ever fallen on a single day in US history. That infamous stock market crash started in September and continued through November of that year. From the beginning of September in 1929 to the end of the year, the S&P 500 fell 32%.

Several factors punished the economy and the stock market in the early stage of the Great Depression. First, the FDIC and the Securities and Exchange Commission (SEC) had yet to be created. As a result, bank failures began to surge. It's hard to imagine now, but in many cases bank failures translated into the complete and sudden evaporation of the wealth of individuals and businesses. In the initial years of the Great Depression, there were over 16,000 bank failures.[18]

During those early years, bonds did well and, despite defaults, produced positive total returns. Putting this four-month stock market loss into perspective for our businesses and our investors, and taking into account the gains in bond portfolios, a 60/40 portfolio would have declined 18% (see Figure 3.2)—a large but not insurmountable loss.

Figure 3.2: Balanced portfolio losses during the first four months of the Great Depression

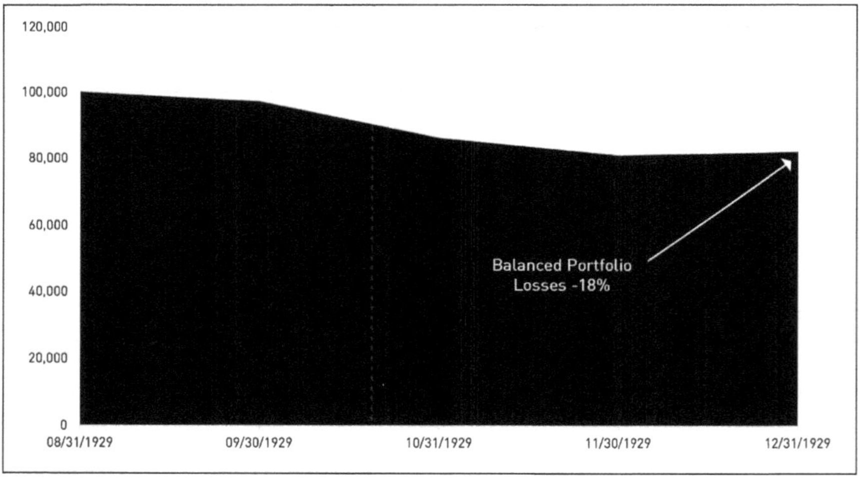

Smoot-Hawley tariffs legislation is enacted, sending stocks lower

The loss in the final quarter of 1929 was among the fiercest seen in the US markets. But instead of recovering, stocks continued their decline.

As bank failures helped catapult the economy into recession, Congress passed the Smoot-Hawley tariffs legislation in June 1930, imposing tariffs on over 20,000 imported goods. The aim was to help protect American workers and encourage the US production of goods. However, over 25 countries responded by increasing tariffs on American goods, likely lowering productivity in the US and abroad as the demand for goods globally was compressed. Unemployment surged from 3.2% at the end of 1929 to 8.7% by the end of 1930.

This all translated into further pressure on stocks. After falling 32% in the final months of 1929, stocks dropped a further 25% in 1930. Again, bonds produced gains and helped temper stock market losses. By the end of 1930, a balanced portfolio would have lost 30% (as shown in Figure 3.3).

Figure 3.3: Balanced portfolio losses during the first 16 months of the Great Depression, which look similar to those experienced during the 16-month Great Financial Crisis

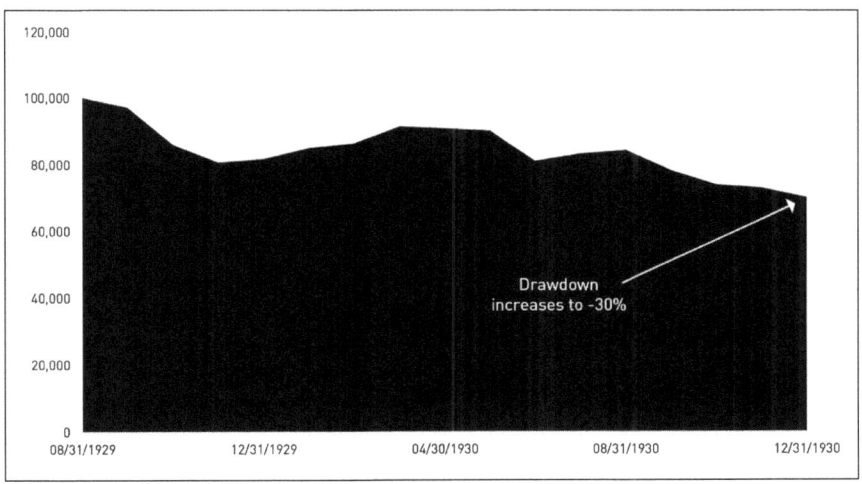

The first 16 months of the Great Depression resemble the Great Financial Crisis

To try to understand the emotional and fiscal impact of the decline up to this point, the timing and portfolio losses by the end of 1930 are similar to the losses and change in unemployment realized during the more recent Great

Financial Crisis. Between November 2007 and February 2009, the same balanced portfolio lost 28%. Both losses occurred over a 16-month period, and both were accompanied by economic events that made for a perfect storm of behavioral biases against remaining invested. GDP compression was more severe in 1930, declining 8.5% relative to declines of 0.1% and 2.5% in 2008 and 2009. For those of you who were investment advisors during this period, try to remember how awful things felt in March 2009, after once-in-a-generation losses crushed our economy, our investors, and confidence in the financial markets. For me personally, it was a depressing time. It felt like the bottom had fallen out of the economy and the financial system was on life support. For investors, it felt like a breaking point. Mercifully, during the Great Financial Crisis, the March bottom was followed by a fierce rebound. From the lows in March to the end of 2009, the S&P 500 increased 70%. Had the market continued lower in 2009, it's difficult to believe that investors would have been able to tolerate more losses. As difficult as it is for us to imagine how continued losses might have looked, the Great Depression shows us that from similar lows, that's exactly what happened.

Depression stock market losses continue

Instead of rallying in 1931—as we might have expected having lived through the Great Financial Crisis—the stock market and the economy imploded. Ask yourself: "What would be the worst possible fiscal response by the government to the imploding economy during this time?" If you answered, "Increase taxes," that would be correct. In 1931, President Herbert Hoover proposed increasing taxes in order to prevent the federal government from falling into debt as tax revenues decreased. Fortunately, although Hoover's Republican Party controlled Congress, they voted against this idea. While tax rates did not increase, the focus on keeping the government out of debt rather than supporting the economy with additional spending meant that the economy continued in freefall in 1931. The unemployment rate increased to 16% and GDP fell another 6.4%—now 14.4% lower since the beginning of the depression. As shown in Figure 3.4, stocks fell another 43%, bringing balanced portfolio losses since the start of the Great Depression to 53% in just under two and a half years.

In stark contrast to the Great Financial Crisis, when you might recall friends holding off on purchasing their next flatscreen TV, many people during the Great Depression were very poor and could barely afford the food which they needed to survive. As a backdrop to an abysmal economy, beginning in 1931, the Dust Bowl engulfed a section of the Great Plains, including parts of New Mexico, Texas, Oklahoma, Colorado, and Kansas. Black blizzards of soil that concealed the sun swept across the plains, sometimes reaching as far as the East Coast.

Due to a lack of demand, the US experienced deflation beginning in 1930, with prices dropping 15% from their peak by December 1931.

Figure 3.4: In 1931, the stock market fell another 43%, bringing balanced portfolio total losses to 53%

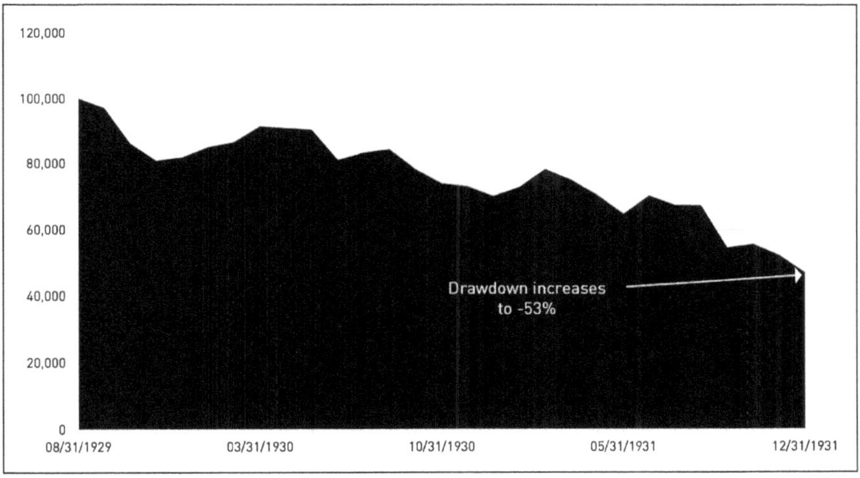

Stock market bottoms in 1932 as unemployment surges

While investors would have already experienced an almost unimaginable decline by the end of 1931, markets continued lower, with the S&P falling another 43% in the first five months of 1932 to reach its maximum loss of 84%. From the end of 1930 (by which time the market had already realized losses similar to the Great Financial Crisis, which were accompanied by many of your clients begging you to exit the markets), stocks fell an additional 68%— more than the total loss experienced during the 2008 debacle. Bonds also lost 22%, bringing total losses for a balanced portfolio to 67% (see Figure 3.5).

Figure 3.5: A balanced portfolio bottoms in May 1932 during the first of two bear markets of the Great Depression, with losses of 67%

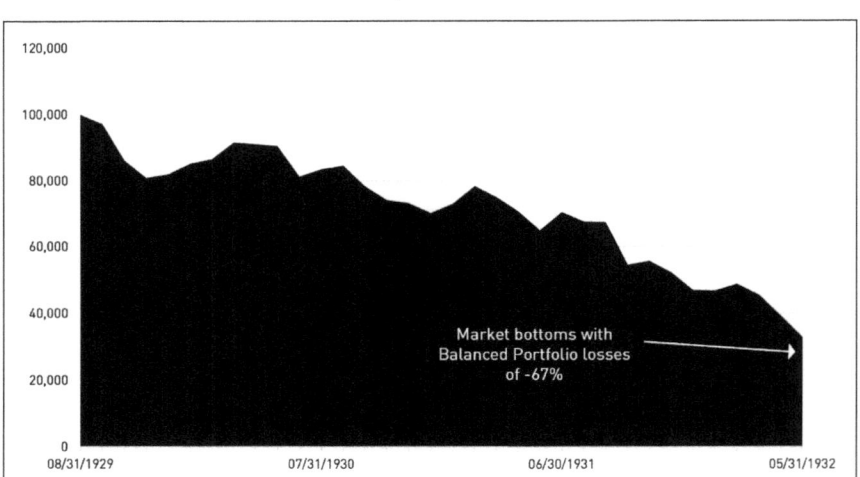

Unemployment increased to nearly 24%. People who no longer had jobs or who were paid lower wages needed to turn to their investment assets for sustenance—assuming they had assets to draw from—at a most inopportune time.

Impact of distributions

So far, I have not discussed the impact that distributions would have had on balanced portfolios. The period from 1929 to 1932 was the only significant deflationary period in the past 100 years. That would have helped retired investors, as a 4% withdrawal of $4,000 from a $100,000 portfolio would have been reduced by roughly 25% to approximately $3,000, lowering the impact of distributions from a collapsing portfolio. Yet despite the effects of deflation, stock losses brought the drawdown of a balanced portfolio during these years from 67% without withdrawals to 72% assuming withdrawals, leaving just 28% of an investor's original capital (see Figure 3.6).

Figure 3.6: Taking into account a distribution of 4% (adjusted for inflation), the drawdown of a balanced portfolio would have been (gulp!) 72% in May 1932, leaving just 28% of an initial portfolio

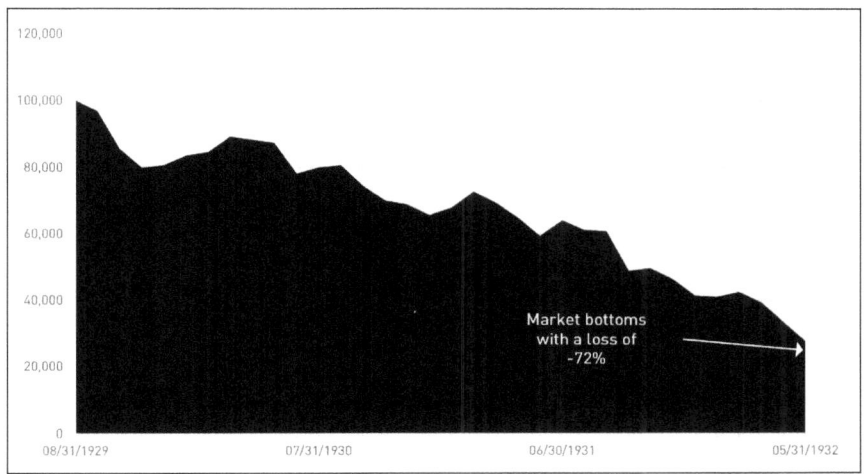

Rebalancing increased the total drawdown, creating a brutal investor landscape

I'm going to pause the historical narrative for a moment to highlight a reality that may surprise investment advisors.

The most ubiquitous and unquestioned belief within the advisor community is that rebalancing is prudent and necessary. In fact, rebalancing is used as a rhetorical anecdote to address falling markets. "If markets fall, that's great, because we'll rebalance and buy more shares, and that's a good thing," is a common statement. Or even: "The worse it gets, the better, because we'll get more shares when we rebalance." Few advisors would think twice about the seemingly benign notion of doing systematic rebalances across their portfolios. Yet when datasets are expanded to include the Great Depression or Japan's stock market decline, maximum drawdowns are increased—potentially significantly—where an asset class like stocks falls over multiple years. The longer that markets fall consecutively, the greater the impact.

The main objective of a rebalancing strategy is to prevent higher risk/return asset classes from becoming too great a portion of a portfolio. If that happens, a 60/40 stock bond portfolio can become an 80% equity (or higher) portfolio due to the outsized returns of stocks relative to bonds, causing the risk of the portfolio exceeding the original parameters set by an advisor. Over the long term, rebalancing moves assets from the more profitable asset (stocks) to a lower-return asset class (bonds), rather than allowing the higher-profit asset to continue growing at a faster pace. As a result of this rebalancing, which many advisors execute across their practices quarterly or annually, portfolio returns are likely reduced.

This is confirmed by a study by the Vanguard Group,[19] which shows that returns as well as risk, as measured by standard deviation, are reduced. So the benefit of rebalancing, if any, is to maintain consistent risk levels across investor portfolios.

During the initial years of the Great Depression, as stocks were suffering annual losses ranging as high as 44%, bonds played a role as a stabilizer and were at times profitable. During such multi-year declines, if each year assets are reallocated from bonds into stocks, this increases portfolio exposure to an asset that again experiences significant declines. This type of reallocation increases both losses and portfolio drawdowns, and presents behavioral challenges for investors as, year after year, they follow their investment advisor's advice and make the "mistake" of allocating additional assets to a falling investment. As shown in Figure 3.7, during the initial three-year decline of the Great Depression, rebalancing the portfolio annually at the beginning of each year would have caused a balanced portfolio to lose an additional 9% before bottoming in May 1932.

During these initial years of the Great Depression, advisors would have rebalanced not once, but three separate times. On each occasion, rebalances were followed by decent gains in bond portfolios and fierce losses in stocks. Throughout my 36 years in the investment field, I have never seen a challenging investor retention scenario that even comes close to this.

Figure 3.7: Although rebalancing is viewed as a way to reduce risk, an annual rebalance increased the drawdown during the initial bear market of the Great Depression by 9%

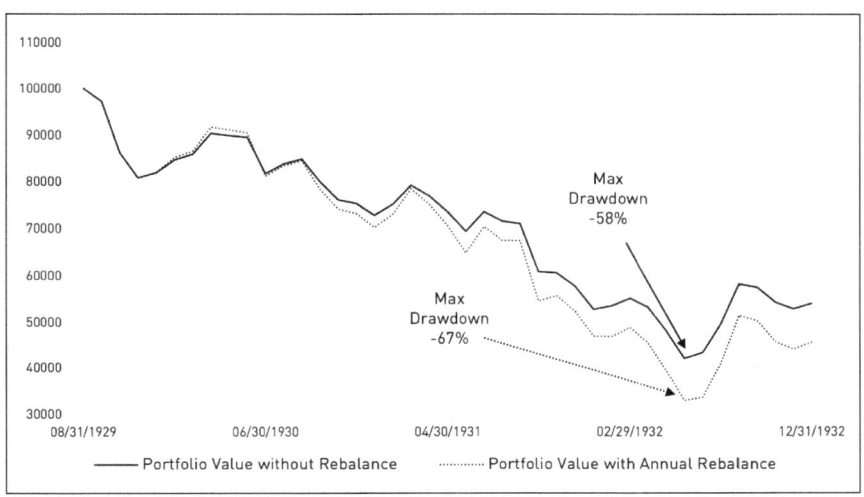

Moreover, just as portfolio diversification is effective at lowering risk during most markets but breaks down during extreme crises, rebalancing not only is ineffective at reducing risk, but increases investors' exposure to depletion of capital during the worst that markets have to offer. This is another example of how advisors and investors fail to prepare for and don't consider the possibility of the direst types of markets and are susceptible to the Corona Bias.

After the crash: stocks enter a vacillating bull market

The Fall of 1932 brought elections. Herbert Hoover's approach to fiscal austerity had arguably crushed the economy. Encampments of homeless people sprang up during this time that came to be known as "Hoovervilles"—not a great public relations boost to re-election. Franklin Roosevelt, a Democrat and cousin to former President Theodore Roosevelt, promised to fundamentally change the government's approach to government support for the economy.

Franklin Roosevelt won that election decisively, with 472 electoral votes to a mere 59 for Hoover. Roosevelt immediately began government programs to increase employment and rescue the economy. These programs, referred to as part of the "New Deal," included (among others) the National Recovery Administration, which promoted fair competition between governments; the Public Works Administration, which between 1933 and 1939 funded 34,000 projects across the country that ultimately employed over 8 million workers; and the Civilian Conservation Corps. To fund these programs, Roosevelt and Congress began running fiscal deficits.

Leading up to the elections that year, stocks finally found a bottom in May 1932, falling 84% in just under three years. The bull market that began that month played out as significant but short bursts of gains followed by longer-duration losses or languishing markets. For advisors and their investors, the down months in some cases produced bear market moves and would have added to the negativity of a depression economy. Furthermore, if investors had exited the stock market during the brutal decline between 1929 and May 1932, they either would have had to re-enter quickly after rallies began or would have missed the bulk of gains.

A balanced portfolio would have gained 56% in three months beginning in May 1932, only to fall 21% over the following six months. The market then rallied 63% over six months but fell 9% over the next one and a half years. Beginning in March 1935, stocks realized their biggest stretch higher, increasing 130% over almost two years.

Although this convincing two-year rally might have created enough positivity to potentially lure investors back into stocks, the economy was still suffering. Unemployment, while improving, was still 14.3% in 1937—down from 25% at its peak in 1933, but significantly higher than the 3.2% level in 1929 at the beginning of the Great Depression (see Figure 3.8).

The impact of the gains in balanced portfolios on investors, and the ability of the rally to resuscitate accounts back to their original principal, depended on whether investors were drawing income from their portfolios and whether they were able to stick to their strategy throughout the decline and recovery. Investors holding a constant (rebalanced) allocation to stocks and bonds throughout managed to see portfolios recover their original principal amount plus a gain of 6% by February 1937, eight years after the decline began (see Figure 3.9).

CHAPTER 3

Figure 3.8: Unemployment surged to 25% during the initial years of the Great Depression, but decreased during the five-year bull market ending in 1937

Figure 3.9: After falling 67%, stocks rallied strongly between 1932 and 1937, pushing a balanced portfolio slightly positive at +6% (not including distributions)

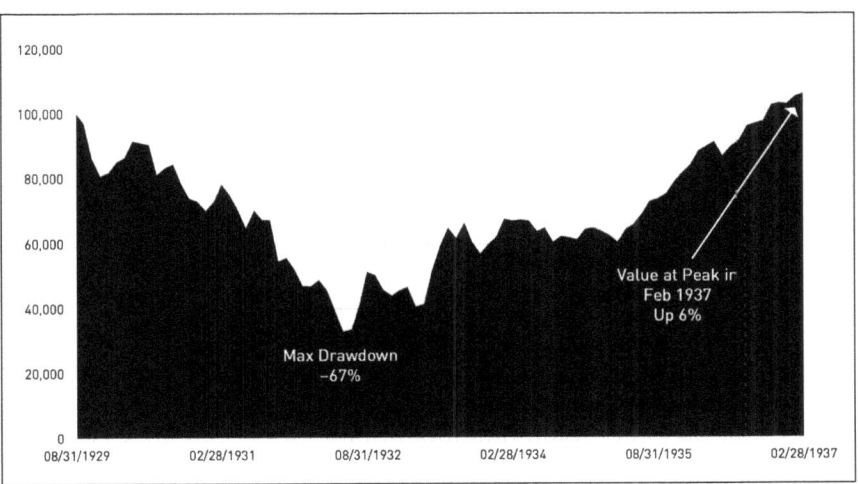

However, as is reflected in Figure 3.10, investors drawing 4% (adjusted down in this case for deflation) never came close, seeing a balanced portfolio increase back up to 63% of its original value (a 37% drawdown).

Figure 3.10: Taking into account retirement distributions, a balanced portfolio didn't come close to recovering and was still down 37% at the end of the bull market in 1937

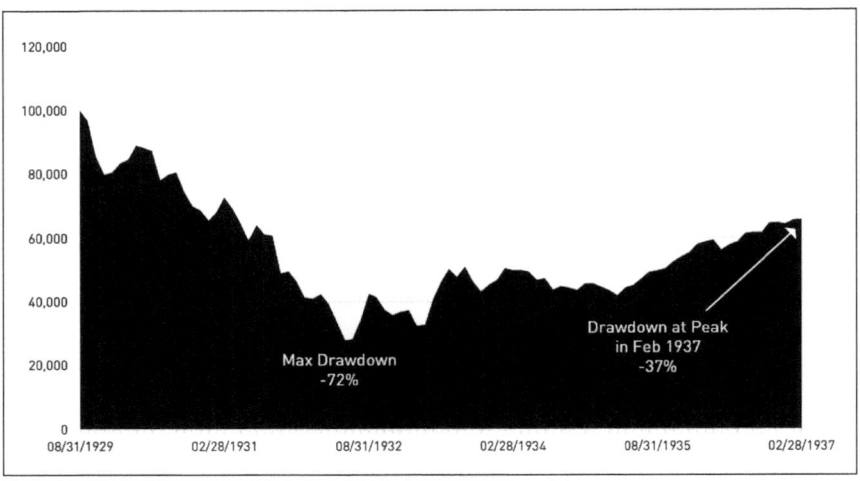

Following an eight-year dismal market, stocks enter a second, even longer bear market

In 1937, in response to growing sentiment about returning to a balanced budget, Roosevelt and Congress began cutting back on a number of New Deal programs. The move was enough to help nudge the economy and employment lower once again. Unemployment in the following years reached as high as 20%. The stock market again turned lower and entered a durable bear market that saw stocks fall 50%. Over that time, a balanced portfolio lost 38%. As a reminder, this is 10% more than the decline that a balanced portfolio experienced during the Great Financial Crisis—except instead of lasting 16 months, as it did during the Great Financial Crisis, it lasted five years.

For investors not drawing incomes, a balanced portfolio would have ended the period from September 1929 to the end of April 1942 being down 23%—a loss that would have occurred over nearly a 13-year period.

Withdrawing investors fared worse, ending April 1942 down 68% from the original value in their portfolios (see Figure 3.11). Because of the severity of the drawdown, these investors would have ended up depleting their portfolios entirely (assuming that withdrawals were not decreased), as subsequent market gains were not enough to sustain investor income.

Figure 3.11: Investors drawing income from their portfolios would have ended the second bear market with their balanced portfolio down 68% over a period of 13 years

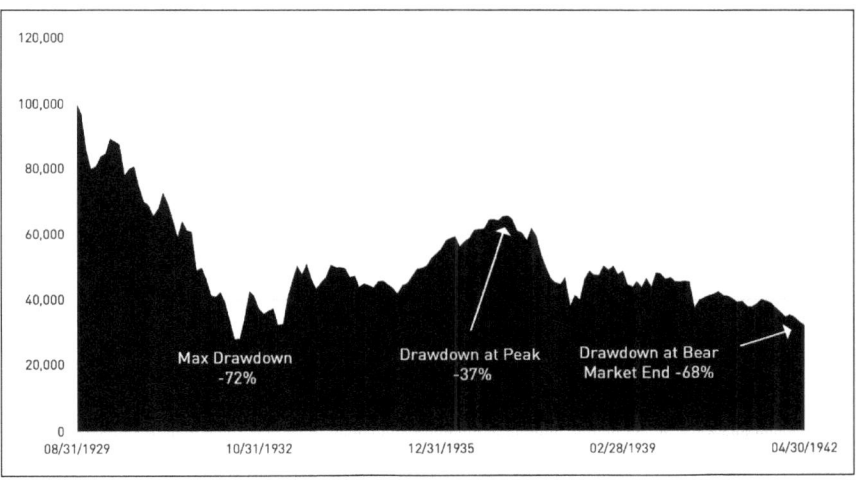

Putting the Great Depression decline in the context of your investors and your practice

When I consult advisors about stress testing portfolios, I always include a conversation about stress testing their practices through true worst-case scenarios. There's little question about the impact that a Great Depression-like decline would have on investors. But what about other real-world variables that could play a role?

One factor that would inevitably affect an advisor's practice is attrition. To illustrate this, I added some pragmatic assumptions about what impact the dramatic market moves during the Great Depression might have on an advisor's business. Once markets reach a certain level of distress, investors leave advisors or leave the markets. Losing half of one's money in a balanced portfolio clearly reaches that level. As a result, I assumed that an advisor would have had attrition of 15% of assets under management (AUM) in 1931 and 15% again in 1932. During the ensuing bull market, I assumed that an advisor added a generous 15% new investor assets each year between 1932 and 1937, with attrition of 15% per year during the final years of the bear market. I also assumed that half of investors were taking distributions of 4% annually, while the other half were not.

Including these factors in the analysis shows that an advisor level of AUM would decline to 30% of its original value by 1932 (a 70% compression); increase back to 80% of its original value by the end of 1937; and then decline all the way down to 22% of the original value by December 1942, 14 years later (see Figure 3.12).

Figure 3.12: During the Great Depression, investment advisors' practices would have been on a rollercoaster, potentially decreasing to 22% of AUM

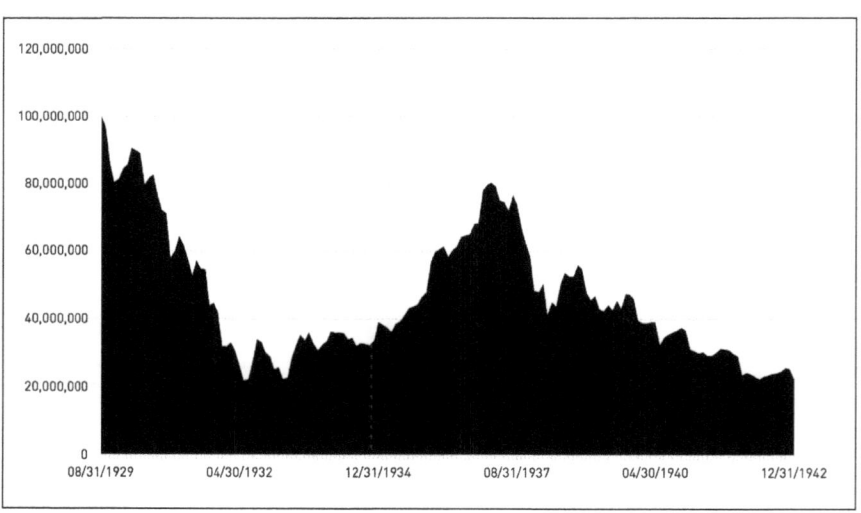

In the Spring of 2020 and 2021, my asset management firm conducted investor and advisor surveys about market crises and bubbles along with the Investments and Wealth Institute (an astute association of advisors whose AUM averages $450 million). During a presentation sharing the results of this survey, we asked the advisors attending how many thought that they could survive a Great Depression level of decline. Fifty-two percent thought that their practices would fail.

Conclusions from our Great Depression visualization

What are the biggest takeaways for advisors from a Great Depression market visualization?

First, for investors drawing 4% from portfolios, a balanced portfolio would have been depleted if spending was not adjusted to account for a decreased account value. For investors not drawing from portfolios, it would have taken more than 13 years to recover the original value.

Second, few if any investors would have been able to remain invested in a balanced portfolio that had a meaningful allocation to stocks; and in my opinion, many investors would leave an investment advisor that rebalanced into fierce declines for three years. Due to the relatively strong performance of bonds and the brutally long duration of the stock market rout, advisors and their investors' attitudes about stocks as an asset class would have fundamentally changed.

Third, advisors' businesses would have been ruined unless they switched to recommending solely fixed-income portfolios or otherwise adjusted their advice away from an AUM revenue model.

The worst trade of the century

After watching advisors manage their businesses and make allocation decisions for 36 years, I'm convinced that very few advisors would have been able to maintain significant allocations to stocks during the Great Depression. Those that did survive might have pivoted early on or during the second phase of the bear market to bond-based portfolios or other fixed-income strategies. That shift could have represented the worst possible trade at the worst possible time, especially if it occurred during the final stages of the 1937 to 1942 bear market.

Recall our discussion about the 36-year bear market in bonds. That decline began two years after the stock market bottomed at the end of the

Great Depression. At the same time, stocks entered a decades-long massive rally. If investors and advisors switched to bond-based portfolios during the Great Depression, they would have missed out on among the strongest bull markets in US stock market history. Just as selling stocks and buying bonds would have had a devastating effect on portfolios, buying into stocks at the end of the Great Depression would have been the counterintuitive best trade of the century—one that I am persuaded few would have been able to make.

One final point. I've been referring to this visualization as a "worst-case scenario." It's not. Recall my earlier observation that the Japanese stock market has been in decline now for over 30 years. What we've just looked at here is nothing compared to the consequences of investing in Japan during that time. Proximity bias—the tendency to only consider things that happen in our part of the world—helps prevent us from going there.

In summary: the huge market moves during and after the Great Depression would be a nuclear bomb on investment advisory business as it exists today.

A few antidotes to the Corona Bias

- Understand that this time is not different: Although we may be smarter, better, and more productive than any generation before us, similar advances throughout history have not protected us from significant market disruptions.
- Include the entirety of relevant historical outcomes when building portfolios, without weighting them based on proximity or recency: Remove the dates and geographies associated with market events. Instead, rank historical events based on their severity. Then stress test portfolios for their ability to endure each event.
- Plan for risk events based on their probability of occurring over an investor's investing time horizon, rather than during any one year: As discussed in our conversation about bond bear markets, astute readers will have observed when reading our Great Depression visualization that we have only experienced a depression once during the past century, and those odds are so low as to appear to be irrelevant. However, investors have long investment horizons. Young investors may have an investing horizon of 60 years.

Although a risk event may have only a one-in-100 probability of occurring in any one year, when a young investor has a 60-year time horizon or a retiring investor has a 30-year time horizon, the probability that a risk event will occur becomes much more likely.

I've discussed at great length the challenges presented by the markets and by conventional portfolios. In Chapter 4, I'll show how these portfolio dynamics—as well as some factors that are often not considered in retirement planning—directly increase the probability that investors will outlive their assets.

CHAPTER 4

Retirement Planning Redo: Overvalued Markets, Fees, and the Behavioral Gap Create Retirement Planning Challenges

As an advisor, you likely have a sense of wellbeing about the ability of your investors to provide for their retirements. This chapter may well erode that state of calm. Despite the numerous software solutions for helping plan for investors, an industry-wide "optimism bias" is preventing advisors from accurately understanding the confluence of forces that affects retirement success, and recent above-mean returns for stocks and bonds severely distort perceptions of investors' vulnerabilities.

Studies confirm that investor biases lower returns; yet that behavioral performance gap is absent when doing retirement distribution analysis. We also know that high valuations likely lower probabilities of success; yet many times that reality is excluded as well (it is included in some projection programs). Finally, an advisor's fees can be included in retirement projections; but what about all other fees, such as fund and platform fees? When including all variables, the probabilities of investor success can become dismal. Advisors reading this are likely thinking, "But that's not my experience—my investors are fine." Yep, but we've just been through a period when balanced portfolios have increased roughly average amounts (rather than the lower quintile) of return experiences. This has happened during a period of historically low interest rates and rising equity valuations—factors that may work against the probabilities of success over the coming years. In other words, we're afflicted by the Corona Bias. We are assuming that stocks will increase as they have for the past decades, and that bonds (despite recent losses) will provide real gains and portfolio stability, as they did for the 40 years prior to 2022.

So, what are the chances of investor success during retirement using conventional portfolios when taking into account all of these variables? In this section, I'll look at a number of scenarios that help answer that question. I'll begin with the most simplistic way of evaluating portfolios that many advisors used decades ago; but I'll expand the set of variables to include the effects of volatility, all-in portfolio fees, investor behavior, and even market valuations. Finally, I'll look at one of the newest ways to address market challenges to retirement, which is reducing income to address lower portfolio values and prevent an investor from running out of money. The results show that when all factors that can affect investors are considered, the probability of sustaining a desired retirement income can become unacceptably low.

In the late 1990s, when I worked with a financial planning firm on the "Main Line" outside of Philadelphia, we completed cash flow analyses for all of our new investors. We took investors' assets and income needs and calculated what return they needed to earn before beginning to construct their portfolios.

At the time, we—along with many other advisors—completed the most basic type of analysis. I'll give an example here, as is summarized in Figure 4.1. Let's look at an investor who is 65 years old, has $1 million of assets, and needs to draw 4% of that during retirement. Finally, assume that this investor has a 30-year life expectancy[20] and will spend their assets down to $0.

The return of a balanced portfolio[21] has been 10.33% since 1916, during which time inflation increased by an average of 3.3% per year.

This is the type of analysis that investors might make if they think about their ability to retire. It assumes that the average return plus inflation is what a portfolio returns *every* year. And according to this simplistic analysis (see Figure 4.2), it shows that a balanced portfolio would have no problem making retirement distributions to this investor and would grow the portfolio from $1 million to more than $8 million over 30 years. What is unrealistic about this analysis, of course, is that it assumes the returns will be exactly the average of 10.33% every year, without downturns along the way.

CHAPTER 4

Figure 4.1: A summary of the assumptions for a retired investor who needs to draw 4% from their portfolio for 30 years

Age	65
Investment assets	$1,000,000
Income drawn from investments	$40,000
Life expectancy in years	30
Assets remaining after death	0
Balanced portfolio return	**10.33%**
Assumed inflation	3.3%

Figure 4.2: The simplistic analysis when assuming that a portfolio returns the same each year shows that an investor would easily meet their retirement goal

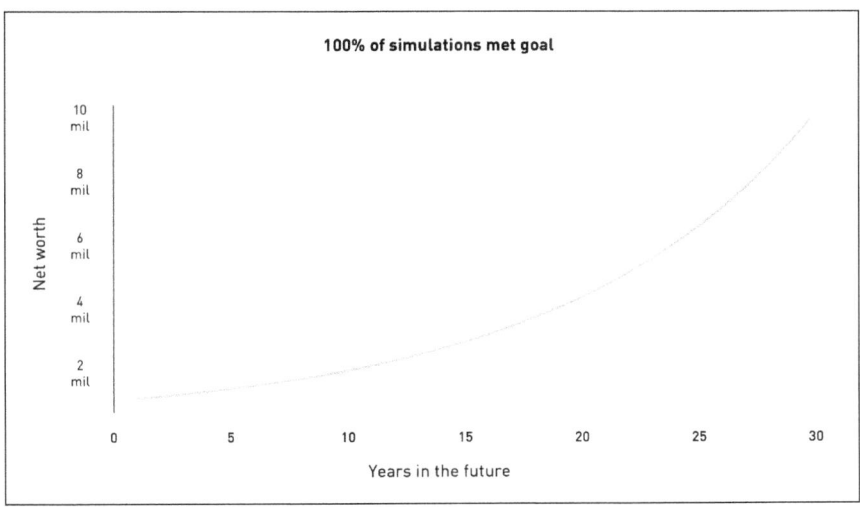

79

We all know that returns vary dramatically around this average. To address this, most goals-based software today includes a standard deviation variable that addresses variable levels of returns.

Using Monte Carlo analysis—a method of analyzing many potential return scenarios using a mean return and amount of return variability expressed by a portfolio's standard deviation—we can attempt to determine the probability of a retiree living through retirement under a wide range of potential return scenarios. When including the average standard deviations of a balanced portfolio of 13.38%, an investor's odds of having assets last throughout their 30-year life expectancy decrease slightly to 96% (see Figure 4.3). In 4% of these scenarios, investors run completely out of money before they reach their life expectancy.

Figure 4.3: When drawing 4% from this retirement portfolio and including variable returns reflected by a standard deviation of 13.38 of a balanced portfolio, an investor's odds of not outlasting their portfolio through retirement are still strong, at 96%

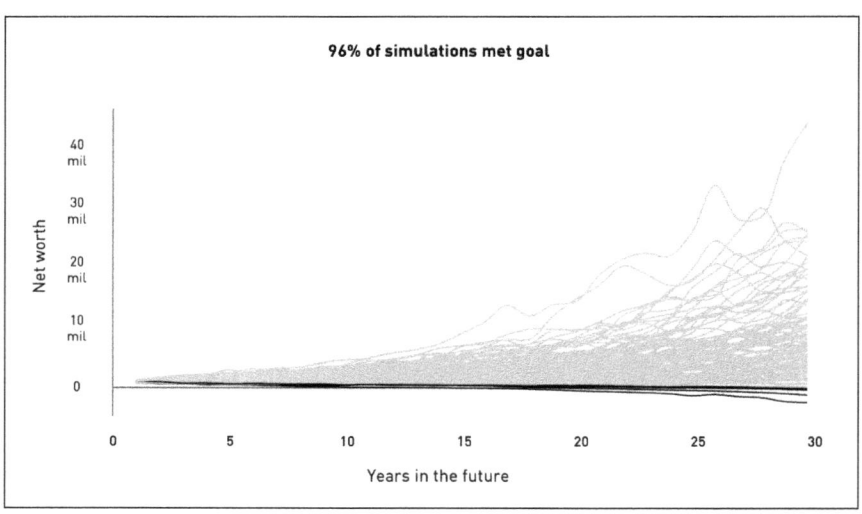

But those odds assume that investors are perfectly rational; that they rebalance portfolios back to a 60/40 stock/bond balance each year regardless of market moves; and that they pay no fees and can achieve index returns. It also assumes that markets are not overvalued at the start of an investor's retirement in order to make that assumed historical average return.

These aren't realistic assumptions. But let's consider this to be the baseline argument that supports the two things that proponents of conventional balanced portfolios like the late Jack Bogle consider sacrosanct: invest in low-cost index funds and balance portfolios between stocks and bonds.

Thinking about probabilities and retirement

Before moving on and looking at more realistic scenarios that consider investor behavior, I'd like to discuss the cavalier way that I just glossed over the 4% possibility that an investor would run out of money based on our portfolio plan, describing it as "pretty good odds."

The investment industry, like every other business, has its own way of thinking about risk. It's not uncommon for investment professionals to build portfolios that have a 70%, 80%, or 90% probability of success. This means that portfolios are built so that in only three or two or one in ten times, historically, would an investor run out of money based on their needs. Of course, the amount that investors draw from their portfolios is variable, so even in dire situations, investors can always adjust their living standards lower if their portfolios lose money, reducing the chance that they will completely run out of money. Even considering this, however, the way most advisors couch probabilities of "success" is at odds with how we view risk in other aspects of our lives.

If you are currently in your 30s, you may feel like you're immortal—and you practically are. There's a 92% probability (depending on your gender) that you'll live to be 60. But if you're also the primary income source in a family with children, it would be considered irresponsible not to have a sizable life insurance policy to protect your family during those early years. Other examples are starker. Are you always exiting the pool during a thunderstorm? Your chances of being struck by lightning during your lifetime are one in 3,000. Nervous during take-off and landing? The odds of that plane going down are one in 5.3 million.

For whatever reason, our industry views this level of probability of failure (10%, 20%) as acceptable, where in most other areas of our lives it would be viewed as a risk that needs to be insured against. Think about a one-in-10 risk that your house burns down, or a bridge fails, or a ship capsizes in a stormy ocean. For an investor, an investment portfolio is often the sole source (plus social security) of retirement sustenance. It easily qualifies as a risk significant enough that is worth insuring against, if possible. Our view is that a one-in-10 chance of running out of money is high enough odds of failure to create significant psychological and economic challenges during turbulent times. Hidden within this statistic are other return scenarios where a portfolio may be under significant distress and finish below the original principal value; and still others where a portfolio loses significant amounts of money, but eventually recovers and sustains the investor during their lifetime. In other words, in an analysis showing that an investor has a 20% probability of running out of money, this may mean that 30% of the time, losses would be so significant that it would take an investor to the breaking point and cause them to leave their plan.

As I'll show here, incorporating real-world factors such as the behavioral gap, valuations, and fees dials probabilities of "success" potentially much lower than one in ten. In the second part of the book, I'll drill further into the psychological effects of declines on investors; but it is safe to say that the possibility that investors will run out of money based on a carefully devised financial plan helps explain why they lose confidence. When news about the market is the most pessimistic, investors assume that they are living that low probability event and need to take action to protect their livelihoods.

Retirement analysis under more realistic scenarios

Do we live in a perfectly rational world? Do you and your investors deploy Spock-like emotionless decision making about their investments? Most investors don't.

Each year, Morningstar conducts research to evaluate the difference between what investors earn on their funds and the returns of the funds themselves—sometimes referred to as the "behavioral gap." This report is a convenient way to measure the effect of investor biases on the returns they earn. If, as an example, a fund performs very well, it might attract significant assets as a result. However, those new assets are invested *after* stellar results are realized. If the fund then performs poorly, this brings the average returns of investors in the fund to levels lower than the fund itself. In its 2022 *Mind the Gap* study,[22] Morningstar found that on average, investors' returns over the previous 10 years trailed funds' returns by 1.7%. This is consistent with prior 10-year periods ending December 2021 (-1.7% gap), 2020 (-1.7%), 2019 (-1.5%), and 2018 (-1.6%). Advisors who run a tight ship and feel that they have control over the allocations of their investors may be skeptical of this underperformance statistic, and you can decide for yourself if you want to include this in your own assumptions for retirement planning. However, some studies referred to earlier suggest that performance between advisor and investor-guided assets is indistinguishable. Also, I will say, as a manager that markets to thousands of advisors, some level of performance gap absolutely conforms to my experience witnessing performance chasing. Most recently, as large cap growth in 2021 trounced all other asset classes, assets poured into large cap growth stocks. A study that we completed on our own hedged equity strategies was that poor timing of entry and exits produced significant annual underperformance relative to holding our strategies through all markets, and these are marketed exclusively to investment advisors.

How many advisors take underperformance due to behavioral errors into account when completing retirement projections? In our experience, very few—making this one of the biggest forecasting errors in retirement scenario planning. The assumption is that investors will have perfect timing and will be able to hold and rebalance through all markets, when everyone understands that investor behavior will likely affect returns. Prudent analysis suggests that advisors should take the likelihood that poor timing will affect results into account in retirement plans.

If we assume that investors trail performance by the 1.7% shown in Morningstar's study and reduce the portfolio return by that amount to 8.63% (see Figure 4.4), an investor's chance of running out of money in their lifetime increases to 13% (see Figure 4.5).

Figure 4.4: Investors likely trail market benchmarks due to investor bias and poor timing. Here we have reduced the portfolio return by the 1.7% Morningstar behavioral gap

Age	65
Investment assets	$1,000,000
Income drawn from investments	$40,000
Life expectancy in years	30
Assets remaining after death	0
Balanced return less behavioral gap	**8.63%**
Assumed inflation	3.3%
Standard deviation	13.3

Figure 4.5: Taking into account the behavioral gap, the chances of an investor's portfolio lasting through retirement decline to 88%

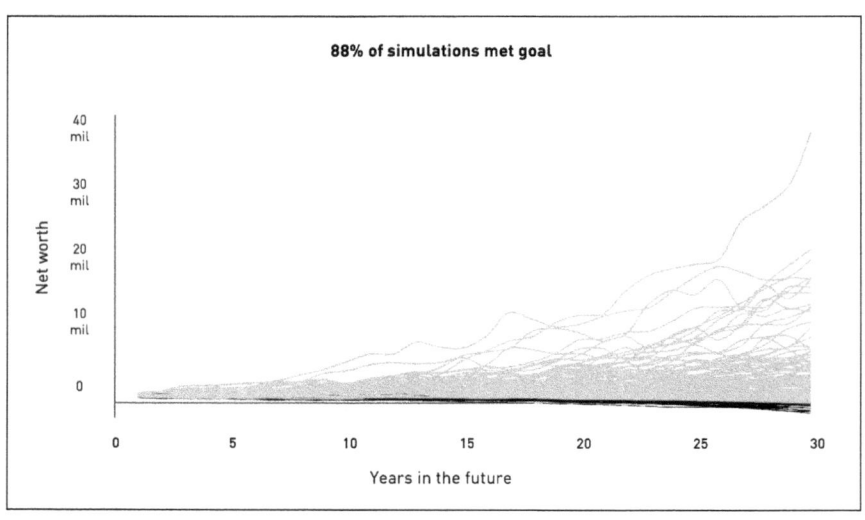

CHAPTER 4

Adding in the effect of fees

This book is designed for investment advisors. And the advisors that we work with charge a fee that averages 1% on AUM. Other costs to portfolios include the expense ratios of funds, transaction costs for buying and selling securities, and in some cases platform or back-office fees for providing administrative services. A study by Bob Vere's Inside Information showed all-in fees for financial advisors were 1.65%. In some cases, this isn't high enough; but clearly, some advisors can deliver portfolios with much lower fees.

Subtracting all-in fees and the effects of the behavioral gap would deliver returns to investors of 6.98% (see Figure 4.6).

Figure 4.6: Taking all-in portfolio costs into account in retirement assumptions reduces the return of a balanced portfolio further, to 6.98%

Age	65
Investment assets	$1,000,000
Income drawn from investments	$40,000
Life expectancy in years	30
Assets remaining after death	0
Balanced return less behavioral gap and fees	**6.98%**
Assumed inflation	3.3%
Standard deviation	13.3

If we adjust our analysis to reflect fees, the probability of success drops to 72% of scenarios (just shy of a one-in-three chance of failure, as shown in Figure 4.7).

Figure 4.7: Taking into account the behavioral gap and portfolio fees, the chances of not outliving your portfolio fall to the concerning level of 72%

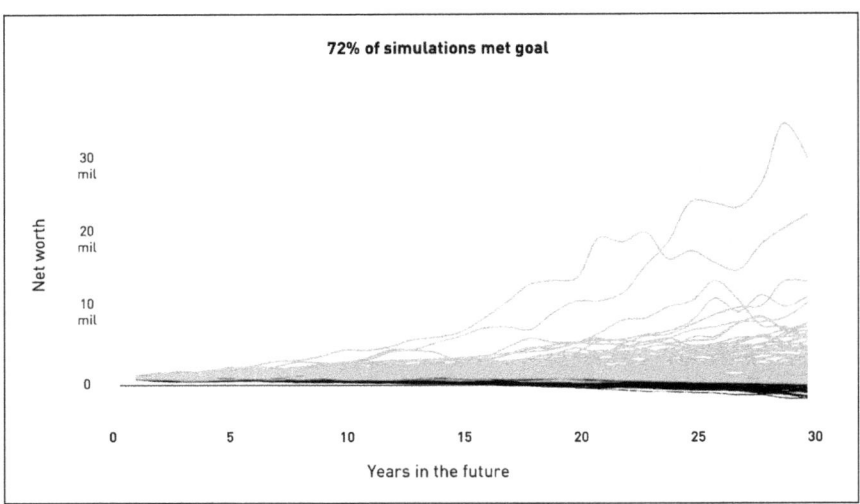

Before introducing potential overvalued markets, I would like to explicitly make the point that this is a baseline scenario for investors who hold a balanced portfolio and draw a 4% income for 30 years. Many variables could affect this result. As an example, studies show that retirees require less income as they enter the final stages of retirement. Some investors could be very good at sticking to their plan and may have little or no "behavioral gap." Advisors could be particularly good at keeping fees to a bare minimum. All of these factors would improve investors' prospects.

However, I would like you to put yourself back into your mindset during our Great Depression visualization. Then understand that if one of your clients taking distributions is on a return path where their portfolio is below their original principal at retirement by, say, 25% or 50%, most others likely will be too. Even if markets help solve the problem of losses along the way, the risks at depressed levels are high and a 28% probability of failure is clearly lower than where you want to be.

CHAPTER 4

The impact of market valuations on expected returns

There are times when markets are priced at such bargain prices that high returns appear virtually guaranteed. There are other times when markets are priced so high that gains are expected to be paltry or even negative for the coming years. Efficient markets advocates ask investors to subscribe to the same portfolio recommendations regardless of where markets are priced because the "average" returns for the strategy meet investors' objectives historically.

In the past 10 years, stocks have been priced at such high valuations and, prior to 2022, with such low interest rates that both core asset classes have had expected returns below average. Earlier we discussed that markets have priced stocks at different levels over time relative to their earnings. Over the past 140 years, stocks on the S&P 500 index have been priced at between five and 123 times companies' earnings, with a mean level of 16 (as shown in Figure 4.8). The P/E ratio of stocks at the time that an investment is made can be predictive of the returns that an investor can be expected to achieve. Over the past decade, stocks have routinely been priced above 25 times trailing earnings, which is 40% above their mean level.

Figure 4.8: As shown earlier, the amount that investors pay for stocks (based on earnings) varies wildly. This can be negative for investors that invest when valuations are high and subsequent returns are low

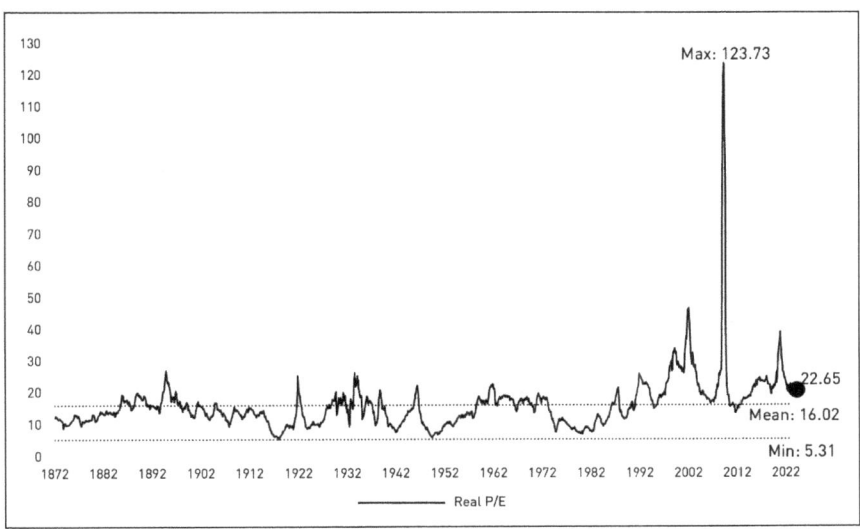

Three variables potentially affect projected portfolio real (above inflation) returns. First, as discussed above, stock valuations can be predictive of future returns. Although studies have shown that the P/E ratio of stocks in any one year is a poor predictor of long-term performance, longer-term averages of P/E ratios—such as Robert Shiller's 10-year CAPE index, which is an average of price earnings over 10 years—is highly predictive. When valuations are high, as indicated by the CAPE 10 or CAPE 20, future returns are more likely to be low; and when valuations are low, it could mean expected returns are higher than average. The concern for advisors attempting to manage risks for investors is the case where returns are potentially lower, or even much lower, than the average return of 10.33% for a balanced portfolio. A second variable that can affect returns is what bonds are yielding at the start of a period of retirement. This is a discovery I made when doing research for this book. When a person begins retirement, if yields on bonds are low, the real return delivered to portfolios from bonds would likely be minimal over a very long projected period of 30 years (see Figure 4.9). As we discussed earlier, when looking at bonds, they can realize real losses over periods as long as 30 years.

Figure 4.9: When starting yields are low, the 30-year return of bonds tends to be lower. This figure is based on a study of the Dow Jones Bond Index from 1915 through 2023 and reflects real 30-year returns of bonds based on the starting 10-year treasury yield

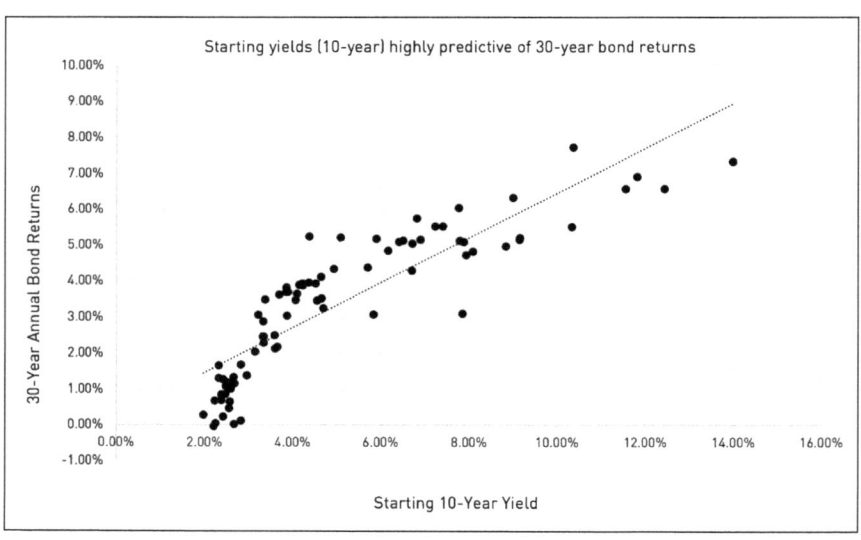

This occurs as bonds potentially lose principal as interest rates move higher, with a negative impact on returns of a balanced portfolio. Finally, inflation plays a major role in determining the real returns delivered to an investor during their retirement. Historical real losses in bond portfolios are due to both principal losses and inflation.

To determine the variation of returns of balanced portfolios, I analyzed all 30-year periods from 1927 to present to determine how wide the variance of returns could be from average returns. Although one might assume that over periods as long as 30 years, returns would be similar and any variation would be smoothed out as markets returned to normal, that is not the case. Real returns varied widely, by as much 4.7% per year. The lowest example of a 30-year return was 2.6% below average real returns and the highest was roughly 2.2% above average real returns.

When starting yields are very low and stock valuations are very high, it is predictive of a lower potential balanced portfolio return for investors than average. Of great concern is that this criterion (high valuations, very low yields) is exactly what investors faced at the end of 2021, when the ten-year bond was near historic yields of 1.52% and the CAPE index was at 38.3, suggesting that markets would underperform significantly over the following 30 years.

Considering that both stocks and bonds can at times be expected to produce sub-par returns due to high P/E ratios and low interest rates, I estimated the negative potential impact to balanced portfolios by using the bottom quintile of 30-year real returns of a balanced portfolio, which is 1.83% below average returns used in our calculations (assumptions summarized in Figure 4.10).

Considering this potential underperformance, advisor fees, and the behavioral impact of poor decision making, a balanced portfolio in an underperforming market distributing income of 4% has a 48% probability of success, or a 52% probability of running out of money before reaching a 30-year duration (see Figure 4.11).

Figure 4.10: If investors realize the lowest quintile of historical real returns of a balanced portfolio, this would mean 1.83 lower returns, further compressing returns of our assumptions to 5.15%

Age	65
Investment assets	$1,000,000
Income drawn from investments	$40,000
Life expectancy in years	30
Assets remaining after death	0
Balanced return less behavioral gap, fees, and lower return due to overvalued markets	**5.15%**
Assumed inflation	3.3%
Standard deviation	13.3

Figure 4.11: Representing a worst-case scenario of average fees, a normal behavioral gap, and the bottom quintile of balanced portfolio returns, the chances of your portfolio lasting through retirement drop to a dismal 48%

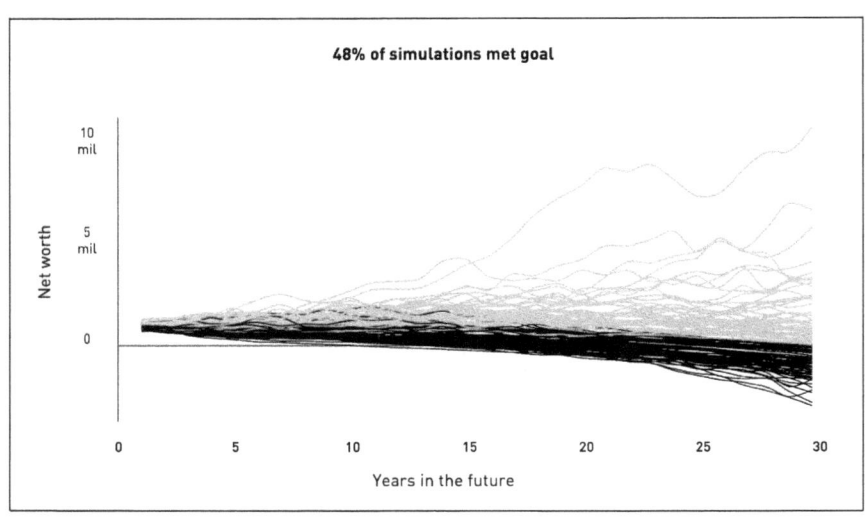

Fortunately, asset class return projections are considered in some of the most commonly used financial planning software programs. For example, Money Guide Pro includes asset class projections in its Monte Carlo analysis retirement projection analysis. The result is that at times when markets are elevated, advisors are forced to share bleak assessments of the probability of success with their investors. The development team at one such firm was forced to suggest that "a 50% or 60% probability of success is fairly respectable right now" when examining the probabilities of what would have seemed like affluent investors during recent discussions.

Putting it all together: how multiple factors affect retirement planning

The above analysis is linear and reduces return expectations for investor behavior, fees, and overvalued markets. However, each individual factor may lessen the effect of the others. For example, if an investor is out of the market due to bad timing of investment choices, their fees may be lower during that period. Also, the effects of an overvalued market may not be as significant for investors who panic and exit risk assets. So, depending on each investor's situation, our analysis suggests a range of probabilities of success for fee-paying clients from a low of 48% when markets are overvalued to a high of 72% when markets are priced at median valuations or are fairly valued. If investor behavior is optimal or if advisor fees are reduced below what is shown here, those odds improve even more.

Changing the conversation: adjusting income to address longevity risk

In the past decade, retirement specialists have proposed a number of solutions to address market challenges that retirees face. One way that advisors can potentially reduce the risk from overvalued or declining markets is by purchasing a fixed immediate annuity to pair alongside their investment portfolios. These annuities lock in a fixed rate of return and provide a guaranteed payout to retirees regardless of market gyrations. Should an investor experience significant market downturns during the initial stage of their retirement, having this fixed, guaranteed income can help them maintain a level payout. On the surface, this makes sense. What this does not address is the possibility that an investor experiences high or even hyperinflation (defined as greater than 20% per year). As we have already shown, a major determinant of the real return of portfolios is the starting yield on bonds. Especially if yields are low, locking into a below-average rate for the duration of an investor's retirement could actually guarantee lower returns rather than guarantee success. Although the maximum level of inflation in the US is just north of 20% in any one year, that is not the case globally. At a time of unprecedented global debt and stretched government budgets, high inflation is more rather than less likely. If a retiree puts money into an immediate fixed annuity, this decision is irrevocable and creates risk from inflation where it decreases risks from stock downturns.

A second alternative introduced to address longevity risk is adjusting a retiree's income to account for portfolio variations. If portfolios fall and penetrate a lower guardrail, withdrawals can be adjusted down. Alternatively, if portfolios increase beyond a certain upper guardrail, incomes can potentially be increased. This solution is groundbreaking for two reasons. First, it changes the conversation away from "chances of running out of money" and "probabilities of success" to "making adjustments" as markets evolve. In other words, it's a real-world strategy for addressing the economic impact of portfolios declining during retirement. But it also addresses the question for investors about what specific action can be taken by investors and advisors if markets decline. This can be a desirable behavioral tool that I will discuss in more depth in the part of the book devoted to behavioral communications.

Based on this basic idea, a company called Income Labs has built a way for advisors to incorporate guardrails into retirement distribution planning. It allows advisors to show investors what the impact of historical events would have had on their ability to draw income, and to illustrate for clients how making these adjustments would address the possibility that they might deplete their portfolios.

Although using guardrails to reduce withdrawals during times of market stress is clearly desirable, when incorporating the behavioral gap, fees, and overvalued markets, significant market downturns like the Great Depression can cause income to decrease to unrealistic levels.

To provide several examples, during the period from the beginning of the crash associated with the dotcom bubble era in 1999, an investor's income would sometimes have decreased and other times have increased, but would have been effective at preventing portfolio depletion. In October 2002, an investor would have been asked to reduce income from a 4% initial withdrawal by 16% (from an inflated $3,650 to $3,070).[23] The investor would have been able to increase income along with inflation after that reduction until the Great Financial Crisis, when they would have been forced to make an additional income decrease by 33% below the initial target income level. In June 2014, however, the investor would have been able to increase their income almost back to target levels.

During the Great Depression—a time when we realized not inflation, but deflation—ostensibly an investor would have been able to reduce their spending along with decreasing prices. However, even after changing income needs to adjust for deflation, an investor would have had to decrease their income by an additional 35%—all the way down as low as $1,600 (from $3,300)—at the same time as they watched their portfolio decline from $1 million to $347,000 over nearly three years. Despite the subsequent market rally and income adjustments, the portfolio would have remained far below its initial value of $1 million.

As we will discuss later in this book, modifying the portfolio to reduce drawdowns, combined with reducing income to account for portfolio losses, could function as a powerful antidote to address losses.

The entire conversation around reducing income assumes that an investor can and will do so—potentially a far from safe assumption, as many advisors will attest. However, in my opinion, every advisor who does retirement planning should include Income Labs or similar strategies in their planning discipline.

Let's summarize our critique of conventional balanced portfolios:

- Adding an allocation of bonds to stocks adds stability to portfolios and lessens drawdowns—unless it doesn't. In certain markets, especially when interest rates are low or during periods of high inflation, bonds may lose value and may increase portfolio drawdowns.
- Most retirement planning tools project using returns that assume perfect execution/behavior. But studies show that investors' poor timing for buying and selling investments lowers real-world returns by as much as 1.7% per year.

- Advisor and all other fees must be considered in order to get a realistic assessment of investors' net expected returns.
- Asset prices and the level of interest rates at the time that an investor creates their portfolio may predict future returns. Investors should not ignore this and assume *average* investment returns when doing portfolio planning.
- Real-world financial planning that considers all of these factors for retiring investors today predicts a risk of failure of between 12% and 53% based on conventional asset allocations.

In the first part of this book, I've identified everything wrong with conventional portfolios. In Part 2, I'll discuss our solutions to those problems. The focus is on how to build behavioral portfolios—that is, portfolios that attempt to meet the economic and psychological needs of investors through virtually any market.

PART 2
THE BEHAVIORAL PORTFOLIO

Conventional portfolios can be blown to pieces by extended stock market drops or hyperinflation and require that advisors ignore important historical precedents when building them. Behavioral portfolios do the opposite: they are built with an all-seasons approach that assumes the very worst possible markets may occur. They are simultaneously built to attempt to prosper under optimistic scenarios when markets move favorably.

Conventional portfolios demand that investors conform to the vagaries of the markets and overcome innate tendencies to react to negative market conditions. Behavioral portfolios acknowledge the relatively universal tendencies of investors and attempt to create the smoothest glide path to achieve their goals. Behavioral portfolios eschew benchmark centricity in favor of an explicit investor orientation.

In this part of the book, I will reframe ways to think about portfolio risk, lay out specific criteria for building behavioral portfolios, and create a qualitative framework for defining them. I will then provide an example of an all-seasons approach to investing. Finally, I will return to the question of probabilities of investment success and show how behavioral portfolios can potentially improve the probabilities that investors won't outlive their assets.

Adopting behavioral portfolios is a big deal, folks. Leaving benchmarked centricity in favor of behaviorally modified portfolios transforms the portfolio construction process. Although the acceptance of alternative investments is broadly recognized in the advisory community, a satisfactory framework and toolset for leaving the standard approach to investing has not been articulated (in my opinion). In this part of the book, I will attempt to do just that.

Recall the "Corona Bias" graph in Chapter 3, shown again in Figure 5.1 below. Inside the smallest circle are the historical events that most advisors prepare for; in the larger circle lie historical events that advisors do not prepare for due to the time that has passed since they occurred; and outside of that circle are events that have never occurred but are possible.

Behavioral portfolios are built with contingencies in place to attempt to *address all markets* (within reason). In other words, under our approach, advisors acknowledge historical precedent and adopt a more consequential role as managers of clients' existential portfolio risks.

Figure 5.1: The Corona Bias. Advisors prepare portfolios for crises that they have lived through or are more recent, but may ignore those that occurred longer ago

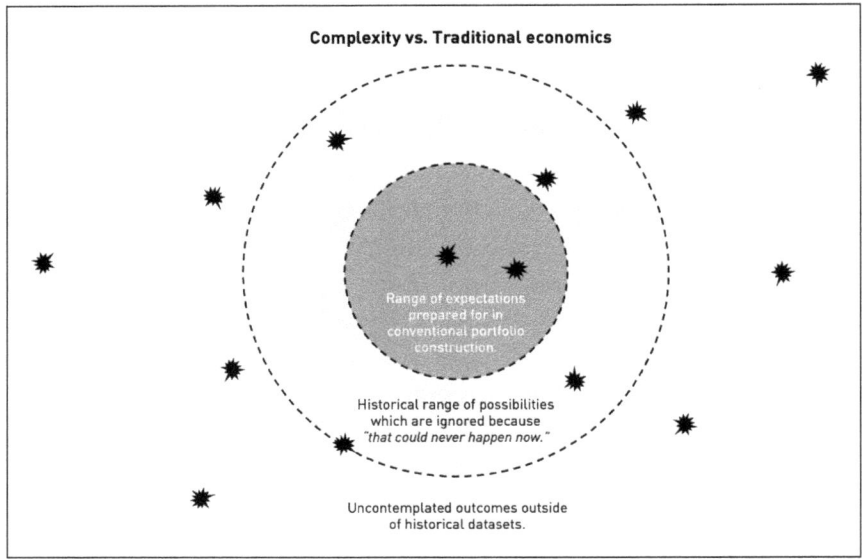

In the following chapter, I'll discuss how to change your perspective about risk, putting you on a path to become your clients' chief investment risk officer.

CHAPTER 5
Reframing Risk to Comprehensively Address Risks to Investors

Before getting into specific criteria about how to build behavioral portfolios, it is imperative that I eviscerate virtually every aspect of how the investment advisory community thinks about and measures risk. This will be fun: like taking the red pill in *The Matrix* and discovering, "Oh no—we've all been dreaming!" Let's start with my favorite topic that can put any audience to sleep: diversification.

Diversification in conventional portfolios is a mirage

Economist Harry Markowitz introduced modern portfolio theory in a 1952 essay, for which he was later awarded a Nobel Prize in economics. Modern portfolio theory states:

> given a desired level of risk, an investor can optimize the expected returns of a portfolio through diversification. This is done by investing in less correlated assets and grouping correlated assets together with those that move in opposite directions to each other, so as to reduce risk for a given return.[24]

A key tenet of modern portfolio theory is that the means of reducing risk is including assets in a portfolio that are uncorrelated. If one asset moves lower, another may not—or may not move down as much. This reduces the volatility of the portfolio.

Diversifying portfolios during elevated markets, however, is like skating beautifully on thin ice. You practice skating from the age of 18 months until 18 and then suddenly: crash—you're in icy water!

The industry really woke up to the fragility of the assumption about uncorrelated assets during the Great Financial Crisis, when correlations among assets tightened significantly. A portfolio diversified across domestic and foreign equities and domestic corporate bonds saw most assets move lower as the crisis peaked in October 2008. This is confirmed by studies that show assets correlate during crises.[25]

Intuitively, it is easy to understand the problem that many investors who deploy the capital asset pricing model and modern portfolio theory have failed to grasp. If asset prices are tied to the health of the economy and the economy falters, then during extreme markets, many or even most assets will eventually correlate and diversification will fail. It's that simple, folks. One could argue that government treasuries could (and have) negatively correlate and move higher during severe economic stress. Perhaps; but at some level of turbulence in a country's economy, especially one with high debts, even the currency that backs government treasuries is vulnerable to failure.

As bad as the Great Financial Crisis was, I encourage advisors to use their imaginations about how this scenario would have been had the government and central bankers not succeeded in bolstering the failing economy. During 2008, bonds performed admirably in the initial months leading up to the worst equity declines in October and November. They did so and continued to perform because companies' balance sheets allowed them to keep interest payments current. Had the economy stayed in a depressed state, reduced revenues and profits or outright losses by companies would have severely compromised their ability to fund interest payments, causing cascading bond defaults and significant declines in bond funds. These losses would have mounted at the same time as stocks were under pressure. Private equity and real estate are other asset classes that are directly tied to the economy, even though the adjustment in their prices can take more time as economies fail. If the method that financial advisors use to achieve risk avoidance is to invest in non-correlated assets, but virtually all assets that are deployed in portfolios become positively correlated during severe crises, that loss-avoidance strategy sucks (sorry—is flawed). Diversification in conventional portfolios reveals itself as a temporary mirage that, in severe crises, doesn't exist. I compare this strategy to tying life preservers to different parts of a sinking ship.

This is a point not to be missed: *diversification—the primary risk management tool used by the investment industry—fails when crises become severe if advisors are limited to conventional asset classes.* The Great Financial Crisis was just a warning shot of a potentially much bigger crisis to come. Astute advisors must recognize this as a reality and embrace new strategies for finding non-correlated assets to manage risk in their investors' portfolios.

Why accurately defining risk is so important to investors

"Risk management" is just a phrase to theorists and academics. But for investors—especially individual investors—the most extreme form of risk translates to: "Am I able to support myself or am I broke?" For most people, financial wellbeing ranks second in importance after their own health and that of their family.

So how should we define "risk"? The most meaningful definition for our investors is "the risk of failing to meet life's goals." "Failure" ranges from not meeting aspirational goals to lowered living standards to becoming destitute.

Risk management is critically important because it translates into an investor's physical and emotional wellbeing. In Chapter 4, we showed how the probability of running out of money during retirement can approach unacceptable levels. Running out of money is clearly the most extreme example of financial failure. But even among the successful return paths in our hypothetical examples of a conventional portfolio, there were inevitably significant drawdowns and lackluster markets. These produce uncertainty and anxiety for investors that, even when ultimately resolved by the markets, negatively impact their mental wellbeing.

If our aim is to seek stable returns and provide peace of mind to investors, we need to be comprehensive in our approach to risk management. Even widely accepted methods of reducing risk should be examined for their validity and, when lacking, should be replaced with new strategies. As you have likely perceived, this means venturing outside of conventional means of approaching risk, finding assets that might negatively correlate or have very low correlations during market crises, and even seeking new ways of managing risk that might be created in the evolving marketplace for investment products.

Conventional risk management: volatility

Volatility is deeply embedded as the conventional tool for measuring risk. It is a mathematically elegant way to express risk across individual securities and overall portfolios. As we stated earlier, modern portfolio theory is "a mathematical framework for assembling a portfolio of assets such that the expected return is maximized for a given level of risk." The way that risk is measured in modern portfolio theory, which dominates portfolio modeling, has generally been standard deviation, or absolute volatility. The higher the standard deviation, the higher the risk.

The problem with this measure of risk is that investors are concerned about risk of loss, not how much something moves up and down (volatility). Also, volatility fails to take into account the probability and magnitude of potential losses. To illustrate, consider two investments. One produces a gain of 5% in Year 1, 35% in Year 2, and 15% in Year 3 (see Figure 5.2). This investment, which had no losing years and gained 63% over three years, has a relatively high volatility (standard deviation) of 12.5%.

Figure 5.2: In this chart, a portfolio has a very high standard deviation, reflecting high risk, but never has a loss

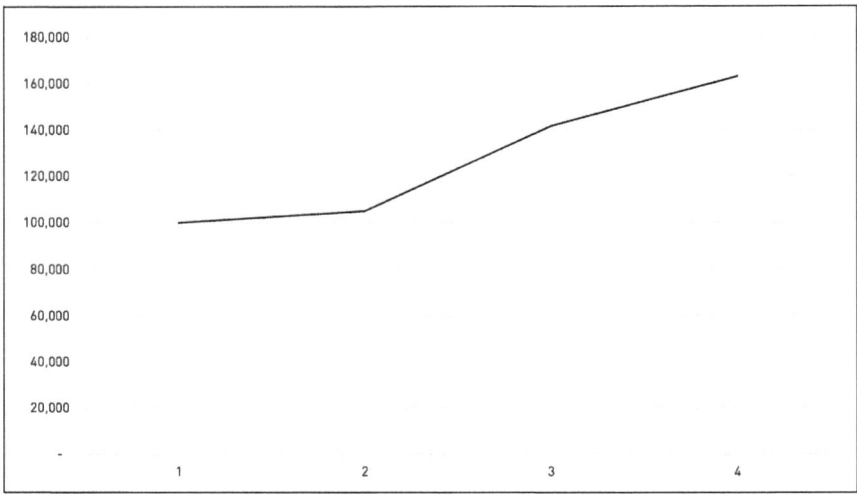

A second investment loses 15% per year for three years, resulting in a loss over the whole period of 38.5%. This investment has a standard deviation of 0%, or "no risk" (see Figure 5.3).

Figure 5.3: If an investment has exactly the same significant loss each year, its standard deviation will be zero, suggesting very low risk

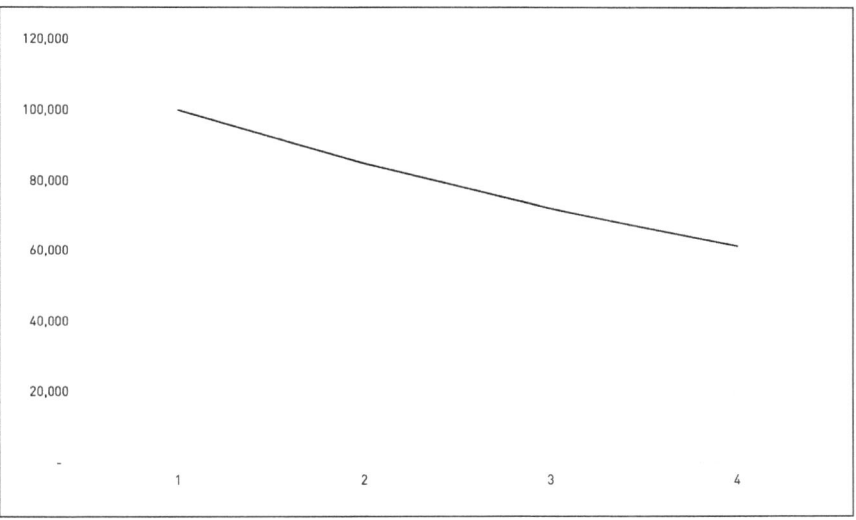

This example helps illustrate a "blind spot" that volatility has as a risk measure: high valuations and commensurate elevated levels of risk are not necessarily revealed by long-term volatility measures. An almost perfect example of this is the credit default swaps written on triple A rated mortgages that got blown to smithereens during the Great Financial Crisis. For years, these swaps showed very low volatility in pricing, helping to justify significant positions in them by banks across the globe. The standard deviation of these instruments helped obscure the enormous risks the products had due to flawed ratings.

A balanced portfolio has had a standard deviation of 13.38% over the past 80 years. Although volatility can fluctuate over shorter periods of one year or one quarter, many who build portfolios consider primarily the long-term volatility of an asset class for the purposes of portfolio construction. In January 1999, stocks were wildly overvalued, at 32.9 times trailing earnings. That valuation placed stocks higher as a multiple of earnings than in any prior period in US history. Between 2000 and 2002, the S&P 500 lost over 50% as a consequence. Alternatively, in January 1942, the trailing P/E ratio of the S&P 500 was near its all-time low of eight times earnings. At that level, the probability of losses was low and the possibility of gains was super-high. In the following years, the S&P 500 surged higher as a reflection of the undervalued market. Neither of these extreme markets was evident to advisors who used long-term standard deviation to assess portfolio risk.

I recall visiting a number of large advisory practices in 1999 which constructed portfolios using software that produced efficient portfolios according to modern portfolio theory. The allocation decisions that they made were identical to those of five years earlier when stocks were more reasonably valued. Their clients suffered greatly as a result when markets turned lower in 2000.

What about shorter-term trends in volatility? Have increased shorter-term volatility measures been predictive of turbulence ahead? To answer this question, let's look at prior volatility surges. The Chicago Board Options Exchange's Volatility Index (VIX) is a measure of implied volatility on the S&P 500 index. One might assume that as volatility increases, risk increases, leading to greater losses. In fact, as volatility increases (as reflected by VIX), it is predictive of less risk of losses ahead and greater gains. I looked at VIX from its inception in 1990 through December 2023. When VIX was very low, at less than 10 (indicating very low risk), returns in the S&P over the following year averaged only 7.96%. When VIX was elevated at between 30 and 40, gains averaged 20.13%. And at very high levels of implied volatility, when VIX was above 80—suggesting that risk was through the roof—gains averaged 48.8% during the following year (see Figure 5.4).

So not only do surges in volatility not indicate potential losses ahead; increased volatility historically can be an indicator that gains lie ahead.

In summary, volatility—our industry's primary risk measure—is blind to overvalued markets and fails to indicate the magnitude, frequency, or probability of losses. Economists needed a mathematically elegant way to define risk. In doing so, they chose a measure of risk that, if relied upon to limit losses, can be perilous to investors.

It's not unlike assessing the risk of a car driving off a cliff by measuring how rough the ride is, without looking to see what lies ahead. As volatility increases over the short term, it is predictive not of increased risk, but of increased returns.

Figure 5.4: Although one might assume that when the VIX is high, risk is higher, this chart shows that after times when VIX was elevated, returns increased—sometimes significantly. When VIX is off the charts, it suggests potentially huge returns

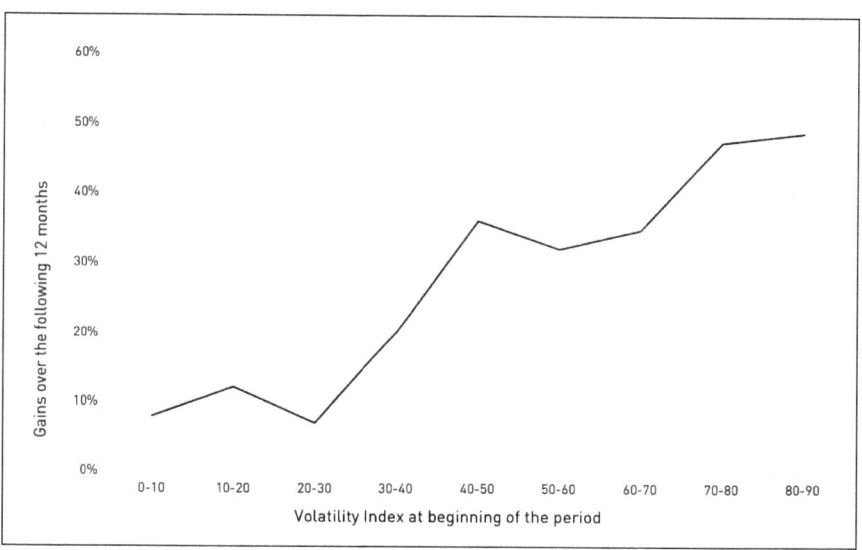

Our interest lies in measuring the risk of investor failure. Investor failure probability for retired investors that are drawing from portfolios increases when drawdowns in portfolio values are both large and lengthy.

Comprehensive risk management methodically assesses and develops strategies to mitigate all the risks to an investor of *not achieving their goals or becoming super-poor.*

Like Cornelius, all advisors have an inherent conflict between the need to convey confidence about the potential for market growth and the need to inform investors about the possibility of severe market declines. We believe that advisors can do both. We advocate building portfolios that assume worst-case scenarios could happen and attempt to temper or even capitalize on significant market dislocations. But we simultaneously believe that portfolios should be built to maximize returns during positive or even best-case scenarios, allowing investors to achieve gains along with the markets.

So, what do I mean when I say that advisors need to be comprehensive in their approach to risk management? I mean embracing your role as your clients' primary risk manager. I also mean removing some industry-wide recency bias when making portfolio decisions and considering all possibilities for market disruptions.

One way to add tremendous value to our investors is to force ourselves to admit that outcomes from the past can happen again, even when industry norms suggest that this is unnecessary. Bringing people to the outer bounds of what has happened, let alone what could happen, prevents us from being vulnerable to recency bias.

It's not your job to shield your eyes from unpleasant possibilities or to try to reassure investors that these things won't happen. The reality is that your clients are already ignoring the breadth of market history. As a way of coping with a complex world, humans naturally assume positive outcomes in order to avoid being in a constant state of anxiety (although some people are still in a constant state of anxiety despite this mechanism).

Your job is exactly the opposite. You need to *assume worst-case scenarios will happen*. To do that, it is necessary to define worst-case scenarios in a way that is comprehensive.

Behavioral economists define "cognitive dissonance" as the conflict between the truth and what people want to believe. This often occurs when we are confronted with new and credible information that challenges long-held beliefs (e.g., when we are shown that modern portfolio theory as an approach is challenged unless advisors find and deploy non-correlated assets). For many advisors, we are presenting new information—or, at the very least, reframing ways to think about risk.

It's the (complex) economy, stupid

A common perception for many of us is created by our training in traditional economics. Traditional economics frames the economic world as one of balance. Supply and demand, for example, tend to balance toward equilibrium. If demand for a good or service increases and prices rise, producers will increase capacity and produce more goods, and prices will return to normal levels. Think of it as a guitar string that is stretched and, when released, oscillates until it returns to its normal state. This framing of our economic system is limiting in the sense that it conveys a sense of mandated normalcy, as if preordained limits and order are imposed on us.

As your clients' chief risk manager, it is important to embrace the perspective conveyed by complexity economics. Eric Beinhocker, the author of *The Origin of Wealth*, explains the difference between complexity economics and traditional economics: "Traditional economies are closed, static, linear systems in equilibrium. Complexity economies are open, dynamic, nonlinear systems far from equilibrium."[26]

Complexity economics views economies as like natural systems. Nothing is certain in nature. It is constantly evolving and changing. Things follow regular cycles on the Earth today; but one day in the future, the sun will expand, the oceans will boil, and things will get really unpleasant. In complexity economics, the guitar is run over by a train.

Are we limited to losses of 84% in the stock market or a 36-year decline in bonds because that's the worst that the US markets have experienced in the past 100 years? Absolutely not. The markets are not like a swing that moves up and down, but is limited to how far it falls by ropes or chains. The markets are unbounded. Stock or bond portfolios can lose everything. If you don't understand this, you are missing out on a fundamental truth about investing. Once you *do* understand it, you have a strategic advantage over your competitors in the financial markets.

What we are all trained to understand about the stock market is that if you hold stocks for a long enough period, your returns will always be positive. As Figure 5.5 shows, for investors that held stocks for 20 years, there were no negative periods (if you look at total rather than price return of the S&P 500).

Yet it's easy to find evidence that this is not always true, as we illustrated in our discussion about Japanese stocks. Changing your perspective about risk will dramatically change how you approach portfolio construction. This book will establish a framework for building portfolios that attempt to address significant risks.

Figure 5.5: One way in which advisors convey stock market invincibility to investors is by reciting the statistic that if investors held and never sold stocks for 20 years or more (total return), they would have never realized a loss

Price Return S&P 500: 1927 - 2023			Total Return S&P 500: 1927 - 2023		
Time Frame	Positive	Negative	Time Frame	Positive	Negative
Daily	52%	48%	Daily	53%	47%
Quarterly	63%	37%	Quarterly	68%	32%
One Year	67%	33%	One Year	73%	27%
5 Years	76%	24%	5 Years	87%	13%
10 Years	86%	14%	10 Years	93%	7%
20 Years	96%	4%	20 Years	100%	0%

To help broaden our scope of possible risk events, it is worth both looking outside of experiences in developed countries and looking back further than just the last century. Carmen Reinhart and Kenneth Rogoff took a huge step in helping us gain perspective about the history of financial crises in *This Time Is Different: Eight Centuries of Financial Folly*. The book asserts:

> The essence of the this-time-is-different syndrome is simple. It is rooted in the firmly held belief that financial crises are things that happen to other people in other countries at other times; crises do not happen to us, here and now. We are doing things better, we are smarter, we have learned from past mistakes.

What are the "past mistakes" to which they refer that would apply to the mindset of developed country investors today? Well, for one, we might be inclined to believe that the Great Financial Crisis was a one-time, aberrant historical event. In the US, banking crises have been rare; but globally, they haven't been. Banking-related financial crises have occurred with enough frequency to allow us to create a history of how such events typically unfold.

One common financial phenomenon that is largely absent from the conventional risk management landscape is the possibility of a currency crisis, defined as a currency debasement of greater than 15% per year; or related hyperinflation, defined as inflation greater than 20% per year. Much of the rest of the world, including other developed economies, have experienced these risk events. Although the US has experienced high inflation, it has been fortunate enough to avoid significant currency devaluations or hyperinflation since 1800. So why worry about those now?

In a word, debt. Over the past two decades, government and private debt in advanced economies have both increased and today stand at unprecedented levels when compared to global GDP[27] (as shown in Figure 5.6). Reinhart and Rogoff assert that when individual countries' government debt exceeds 90% of their GDP, they become much more vulnerable to financial crises. And as debt mounts globally, we collectively become more vulnerable to financial crises. If countries continue to increase debt levels, there comes a point at which the debt is no longer sustainable. The solutions at that point are defaults or inflation. Current global debt levels present extraordinary risks that could adversely affect investors. These risks include increased vulnerability to and severity of financial crises and recessions, lower projected economic growth, and the possibility of high or even hyperinflation.

Let's summarize our discussion on reframing risk:

- Diversification among conventional assets is a mirage. Ultimately, most conventional assets will correlate lower in an imploding economy.
- Volatility measures how much assets move up and down, not the risk of loss. It also fails to assess the probability or severity of future market declines.
- Markets are unbounded. Stocks and bonds can lose all of their value.
- Perhaps the greatest value an advisor can provide is helping their clients understand and address risks that they were unaware of and assume the role of their chief risk officer.

Figure 5.6: When public, household, and non-financial corporate global debt are combined, we are at or near unprecedented levels

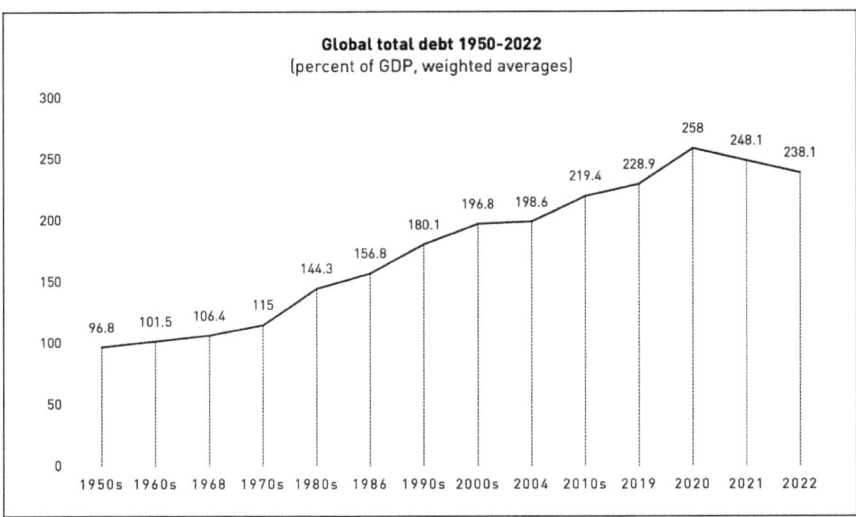

Source: International Monetary Fund (IMF) 2023 Global Debt Database and IMF staff calculations. The estimated ratios of global debt to GDP are weighted by each country's GDP in US dollars.

Comprehensively addressing risk in investor portfolios is the first step in taking a behavioral portfolio approach. In Chapter 6, I'll begin laying out specific criteria for building and managing behavioral portfolios.

CHAPTER 6
Building Behavioral Portfolios

THE INCORPORATION OF investor behavior into portfolio construction is not our invention. It was first introduced by Hersh Shefrin and Meir Statman in a 2000 paper entitled "Behavioral Portfolio Theory." The authors of this foundational paper were among the first to question the assumption that the ultimate motivation for investors is the maximization of the value of their portfolios. They suggested that investors have varied aims, and that they create investment portfolios that meet a broad range of goals. Statman continues to speak and write about behavioral portfolios, suggesting that investors have three types of needs from their portfolios: utilitarian, expressive, and emotional.[28]

Our work develops this concept into pragmatic portfolio prescriptions based on actual advisor and investor explorations. It addresses both risks and the desire that investors have to participate in (not miss out on) gains when they are produced by markets.

Now that I have reframed and redefined risk and laid out the basic principles behind building behavioral portfolios, I will start getting into specific parameters and help guide you toward their construction.

I'll begin by outlining the criteria that advisors will want to consider when building behavioral portfolios; and will then create a quantitative framework for expressing, measuring, and building these portfolios.

The criteria for building behavioral portfolios

The criteria to consider when building behavioral portfolios are as follows:

- Comprehensively address tail risks.
- Provide long-range, above-inflation growth.
- Capture gains during rising markets.
- Preserve gains.
- Attempt to maximize return consistency.
- Include primarily reliable, understandable sources of growth and/or income.

Address tail risks

Our lengthy discussion on risk was a necessary starting point to help advisors avoid "skating beautifully on thin ice." Addressing tail risk is the most important of our criteria for building behaviorally designed portfolios. Tail risk exists for both the equity and fixed-income allocations of portfolios. Stocks are at risk of significant losses during recessions or depressions, and bonds can lose purchasing power and principal when interest rates rise and inflation is high (or hyper!).

In a 2022 survey, we asked investors if they had a plan for bear markets. Of those that said they did, 69% indicated that the plan was to "ride it out." For those investors that will need to take distributions from their portfolios soon, this "plan" suggests a lack of understanding about the potential severity of market declines. Or the plan is actually "no plan." Although Gene Fama would be happy with "no plan" (he probably has a decent financial cushion!), your clients could be demolished. The portfolio should be built to assume that significant market dislocations will occur, and should be designed to attempt to buffer losses and potentially even profit from market dislocations.

Provide above-inflation growth

The second criterion for building behavioral portfolios is investing in assets that provide investors with above-inflation growth. Most (but not all) investors require this in order to achieve their life goals.

In my early experience in the financial planning field, when I was working at a small firm on the Main Line outside Philadelphia in the 1980s, we completed analyses for hundreds of mostly affluent retiring investors. In very few instances did an analysis reveal that investors with a long time horizon could achieve their retirement goals with investment returns from bond or fixed income-based portfolios that had expected returns that were only barely above or equal to inflation.

While above-inflation returns are essential for most, full stock market returns are generally not required. The mean return provided by balanced portfolios (assuming that the behavioral gap is minimized) is sufficient to provide growth and income to investors … on average. However, as I have shown here at great length, "on average" excludes those times when markets are overvalued or when there are significant economic disruptions or inflation (see "Address tail risks" above).

Stocks should be the prevalent asset class that provides above-inflation growth. Other potential sources of assets that can achieve above-inflation growth include growth-focused real estate investments and fine art or private equity. However, these asset classes have limited liquidity and require specific knowledge or high minimums in order to invest. Selling volatility, which has been formulated into indices and marketed and sold by ETF providers, is another way to access above-inflation growth that we will discuss later in the book.

Capture gains during rising markets

Didn't we just cover this by discussing the need for above-inflation growth? Sort of. Investors don't just desire growth; they want it when other people and the broader market are realizing gains. If markets rise by a lot and your clients don't participate, it's *no bueno* for you and your practice.

Portfolios should be positioned to attempt to capture market gains when they occur, with as high a degree of reliability as possible. Investors find missing out on gains painful, especially if this occurs over several years. In our story, Prudence made the decision to fully invest her portfolio in the markets again near the end of 2017, when stocks were clearly overvalued. She did this even though she had lived through steep losses during the Great Financial Crisis. We also told the story of an advisor in Chapter 1, Dylan, who saw his clients react violently to market underperformance and move assets into stocks at the top of the internet bubble. The effect is not unlike a herding phenomenon. Missing out on gains that others are getting, or being "wrong alone," is one of the best ways to crush your financial practice. After the Great Financial Crisis, we saw some financial advisors go completely defensive after losses were already realized (again, like Prudence). That meant missing significant gains during the rebound, along with having scores of unsatisfied clients.

Preserve gains

It's not enough to help investors preserve their invested principal. When they have gains, they want to keep them. Gains can occur over many years. Investors book gains and consider them part of their asset base. It's not okay to see a $100,000 investment increase to $300,000 and then fall back to $100,000, especially if the gains were realized over a long period. Such a loss provokes the same sense of panic as the loss of principal amounts. These losses can also jeopardize investors' goals.

Some investment products assume that preserving principal, and not gains, is sufficient. These include certain insurance-backed investments and structured products. If these products have a short enough term that they can be rolled up, purchased again, and lock in gains, that will satisfy this criterion. But if the protections offered by these products provide only principal protection for the life of the investor, and the products make up a sizable portion of an investor's portfolio, that fails to meet this criterion.

Maximize returns consistency

Of the six criteria for building behavioral portfolios, consistent returns are the most difficult to manufacture. Despite levels of diversification, there will inevitably be times when portfolios have lackluster returns (and we have behavioral strategies for addressing this). Theoretically, it would be possible to structure products that delivered returns every year. However, the cost of guaranteeing such returns would significantly lower investment returns and would jeopardize the objective of achieving above-inflation growth.

This doesn't mean that advisors shouldn't strive to increase the consistency of returns in how they construct portfolios. The best solutions include durable sources of above-inflation growth that have low correlations. This, combined with loss-avoidance strategies, can potentially significantly reduce recovery times when there are losses and deliver gains to portfolios more consistently.

Include primarily reliable, understandable sources of growth and/or income

For core allocations to growth or income, avoid strategies whose primary source of returns is manager talent. There is significant data to show that, net of fees, managers trail market benchmarks. If a manager outperforms over any one period, they are likely to underperform the next.

When evaluating assets, a simple question to ask is: what is the underlying asset that the manager is investing in, and is that a valid source of above-inflation returns or income? If the answer is that the manager invests in long stocks or bonds, then the engine of growth or income is reliable and may be incorporated. If it is almost anything else other than what we have discussed above, the answer is likely no. One example that has appeal in certain markets but fails on this criterion is managed futures. Buying and selling commodities futures is a less than zero-sum game. Their success depends solely on hiring managers who can produce positive returns. Thus, they fail to meet the criterion above. Although possibly a satellite position in a portfolio, these should not be considered part of an investor's core holdings. Things that are largely Ponzi schemes, like cryptocurrencies, should be excluded unless you really hate your client.

In summary, these six criteria guide the process of building behavioral portfolios. The result may not create the portfolio with the highest return—or even the highest return for a given level of risk. It points instead to a recognition that an investment portfolio is a consumer product that, like any other, is designed to fulfill one specific objective: to provide investors with the safest, most consistent above-inflation growth possible.

Quantifying the behavioral portfolio

The best quantitative expression of the objectives of a behavioral portfolio is a modified return distribution chart.[29] A normal distribution has similar left and right tails, implying that investors will experience both extreme losses and extreme gains, albeit with low probabilities. Attempting to avoid principal losses and preserve gains is expressed by a left tail that is shortened (less risk of extreme losses). Yet ideally, behavioral portfolios should not significantly alter the right tail. This indicates that portfolios are positioned to potentially provide above-inflation growth and gains when markets are rising. Although there is a desire to mimic the right tail to provide market returns during rising markets, there is an assumed cost to shorten the left tail. This cost can also be thought of as a budget that can be used to help provide hedging or take other positions that lower the risk of extreme losses. This is represented by a shift of the right tail of the curve to the left (see Figure 6.1).

Figure 6.1: The best quantitative expression of a behavioral portfolio is a modified return distribution chart. Ideally, the right tail is similar to a conventional portfolio, but the left tail is cut short, reflecting less significant losses. It is assumed that mean returns are lower to reflect the cost of hedging against losses

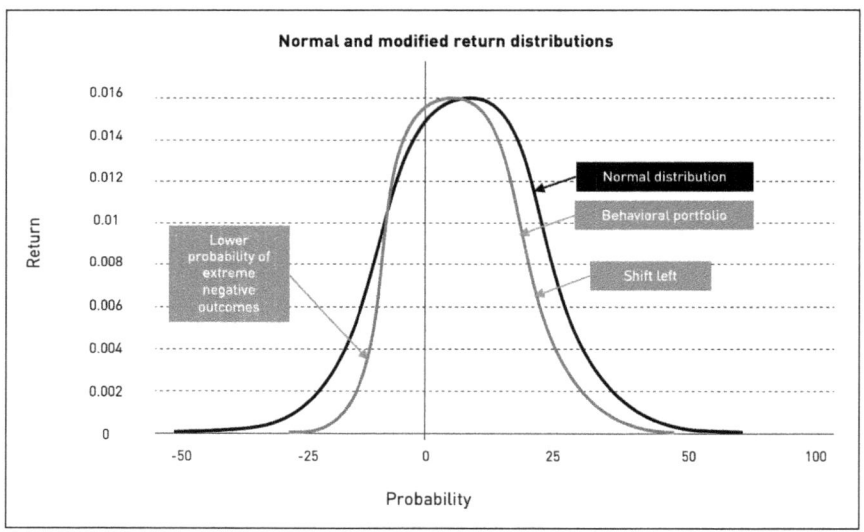

Managing both tails to match investor needs is important. Creating a portfolio that has a shorter left tail is an obvious objective for advisors when building investor portfolios. But managing the right tail is equally important. If the right tail of a portfolio's historical return distribution differs significantly from a traditional portfolio, this may suggest that the portfolio may not provide growth that exceeds inflation or, if it does, may not provide upside capture when markets are rising, presenting potential investor retention issues.

Consider downside and upside volatility independently

When building portfolios that have abnormal distributions, it is necessary to conduct separate analyses of upside and downside measures, instead of analyzing returns over all markets. For example, the objective is to match a market portfolio's upside volatility (good volatility) but reduce downside volatility (bad volatility), as shown in Figure 6.2.

It also may be helpful to conduct separate analyses of the equity and fixed-income portions of portfolios, to try to provide a clearer picture of the effects of managers or strategies on the potential ability to achieve a high up-market correlation and a low down-market correlation.

Figure 6.2: Instead of viewing all volatility as bad, view up-market volatility as "good" volatility and down-market volatility as "bad" volatility

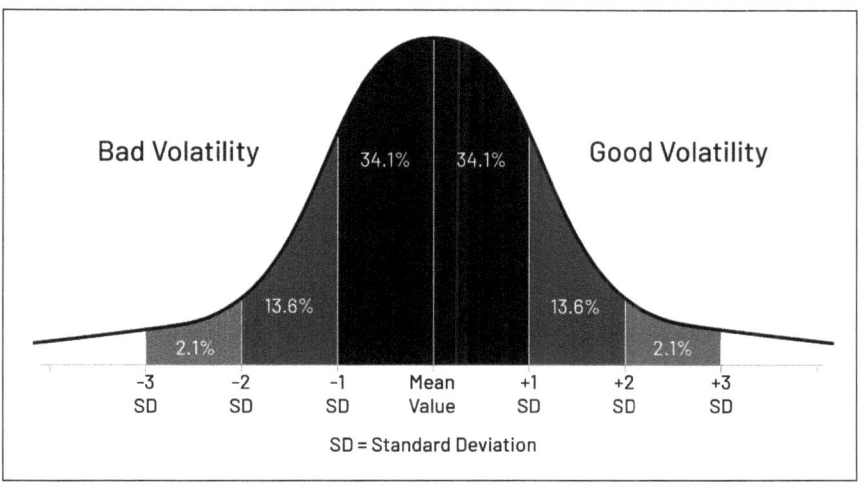

Measuring behavioral portfolios

Now that we have established a quantitative framework for defining behavioral portfolios, it is important to understand some basic means of measuring these portfolios.

Further quantifying behavioral portfolios

I have already shown how standard deviation measures volatility, but can fail to measure the probability and magnitude of losses that threaten portfolios. Because volatility can be good for portfolios if it is up-market volatility but bad if it is down-market volatility, building behavioral portfolios requires a separate evaluation of up-market and down-market measures. This represents the first significant change advisors should make when building a behavioral portfolio.

Down-market statistics

Just as homeowners virtually always have homeowners' insurance to address the improbable event of fire or flood, behavioral portfolios should include hedges against falling markets that can act to decorrelate from market losses and economic depressions. Behavioral portfolios include allocations to funds or strategies that explicitly attempt to limit losses. These include markets where virtually all asset classes are correlating at the peak of market turbulence. I will suggest a specific way to achieve this in a moment. But here, I'd like to establish how to help determine the level of downside risk management.

Obvious measures to include in attempting to complete down-market analysis are loss deviation and maximum drawdown. Loss deviation is among the best overall indicators of potential loss, but maximum drawdown may be the most effective way to communicate loss potential to investors. However, we recommend including a broader group of statistics to get a fuller picture of a portfolio's down-market exposure. Some of the most effective include time underwater (or the pain index), downside probability, and downside capture. Downside correlation is also an especially useful statistic, as it illustrates the experience portfolios exhibit during market declines. We recommend that advisors attempt to expand historical data to include at least the Great Financial Crisis and, if that's not possible for all investments, attempt to use best-fit indexes or other proxies to help evaluate returns.

Here is a summary of ways to measure down-market characteristics of a portfolio:

- expanded historical data (to include at least the Great Financial Crisis);
- evaluation of both absolute and real returns;
- maximum drawdown;
- time underwater/pain index;
- downside deviation;
- downside probability;
- downside capture; and
- downside correlation.

Up-market statistics

Consistent with our objective of mimicking the right tail of the probability distribution chart, up-market capture statistics are ideally similar to benchmark statistics.

As with down-market analysis, we recommend attempting to expand datasets to include a sufficiently long history to be meaningful and, if necessary, using proxies or best-fit indexes to estimate returns for instruments whose history is insufficient. Upside deviation and upside correlation may be among the most important statistics to evaluate when building behavioral portfolios.

Another statistic we have developed to help evaluate behavioral portfolios is a variation on tracking error that looks only at positive years. Up-market tracking error helps provide insight on the consistency with which portfolios participate in benchmark gains by measuring the standard deviation of the difference between investment strategies and a benchmark during rising markets.

Evaluate upside to attempt to reduce portfolio underperformance with the following:

- up-capture ratio;
- upside deviation;
- up-market correlation;
- upside probability; and
- up-market tracking error.

The behavioral portfolio—an execution example

Our iteration of the behavioral portfolio is built to change the focus of the portfolio to meeting what investors desire and need, rather than the arbitrary objectives of matching benchmarks or providing the best risk-adjusted returns. To this end, it attempts to meet the essential criteria that we have outlined in this book. It's important to point out that this is our way of building a behavioral portfolio. It is arguably not the only path to doing so. What's important is embracing the objectives of limiting losses and accomplishing the other behavioral portfolio objectives that we have outlined.

In this section, I will introduce the basic components of our behavioral portfolio and attempt to address a number of conceptual questions advisors are likely to have, as these ideas conflict with some long-held beliefs about investing. I will then show how this portfolio changes performance metrics for the better.

Our starting point for building behavioral portfolios is a conventional portfolio construct. If you have a balanced investor who is in a 60/40 stock bond portfolio (or 80/20, or 40/60), continue with that basic approach. This is probably a relief for advisors who may have been expecting me to leave the ranch of familiar portfolios and ask them to completely undo their education around what makes portfolios work. There is a reason for sticking with a conventional core construct.

Adopting the basic construct of a conventional portfolio honors two largely proven precepts: that markets are generally efficient; and that bonds can at times be an effective diversifier for stocks. This approach helps portfolios deliver returns that attempt to approximate the right tail of conventional portfolios. The key difference between conventional portfolios and the behavioral portfolio lies in how we invest in these two core assets.

The first significant change: hedging a portion of stock portfolios against significant losses

For stocks, the key is to hedge portfolios against significant downturns. This can be done by adding hedged equity funds or introducing hedges directly into individual portfolios. To accomplish the dual objectives of attempting to limit losses and having reliable up-capture, we recommend splitting stock portfolios between hedged equity and conventional stock allocations. If you have a balanced investor, place half each (30%) of a 60% allocation into both hedged and conventional equities. This allocation supports our behavioral portfolio objectives of providing market up-capture and attempting to avoid losses. If the allocation to hedged equities is too small, it exposes the portfolio to massive losses like the 84% loss in the Great Depression. If the allocation is too large, it could cause the portfolio to have poor market participation and fail to achieve sufficient above-inflation growth.

Although investment advisors are increasingly adopting hedged equity funds, 30% is a big allocation to an asset class that may be new to many advisors. For that reason, it's necessary to do your due diligence on funds added in this category.

Hedged equity funds are a type of fund that attempts to participate in rising markets but decorrelates from stocks during declining markets. The methodology for accomplishing this could be options contracts or in some cases trend following strategies that lower down-market correlation during market routs. At their core, they should:

- be constructed in a way that allows them to provide equity market participation sufficient to produce above-inflation growth for portfolios;
- have methodologies that potentially lower down-market correlation;
- address both sudden event and lengthy stock market declines; and
- avoid leverage or other exotic strategies that either amplify the risk of loss or lower the probability of up-market participation.

Due to the cost of hedging or time out of the market, there is an assumption that these strategies will have lower market up-capture than conventional equities. Their inclusion as a significant percentage of stock portfolios, however, is the primary tool for reducing investor losses during stock market downturns. As an example, during the Financial Crisis, if hedged equity strategies lost 10% when stocks were lower by 55%, this would have reduced a balanced portfolio drawdown from 33% to 20%. That's before any potential appreciation in bond portfolios. Under the hood of the strategies is potentially a truly negatively correlated asset. If hedged equity funds hold options contracts that can appreciate at times when stocks are falling, this is a source of appreciation with the portfolio that can lower the correlation between hedged and conventional stocks.

The second significant change: adaptive fixed income

By adding hedged equities to portfolios, we are positioned to achieve many of our investor criteria. The portfolio is poised to capture a majority of market gains and achieve above-inflation growth. It is also set up to help safeguard portfolios and preserve or lock in gains. The portfolio should additionally have greater return consistency by limiting losses during market stress events.

However, in the discussion of our behavioral portfolio recommendation, we have not yet addressed the significant but infrequent potential for losses in bonds. The rarity of big bond declines, and the amount of time since our industry has experienced losses, make their risks exceedingly difficult for investment advisors to grasp.

In order to address the history of bond market losses, the behavioral portfolio replaces a conventional bond allocation with what I refer to as adaptive fixed income. The resulting portfolio looks like the pie chart in Figure 6.3.

Figure 6.3: The starting place for a behavioral portfolio is a conventional construct such as a 60/40 stock and bond allocation. It is modified in two ways: half of the stocks are placed in hedged equities and bonds are allocated to adaptive fixed income strategies

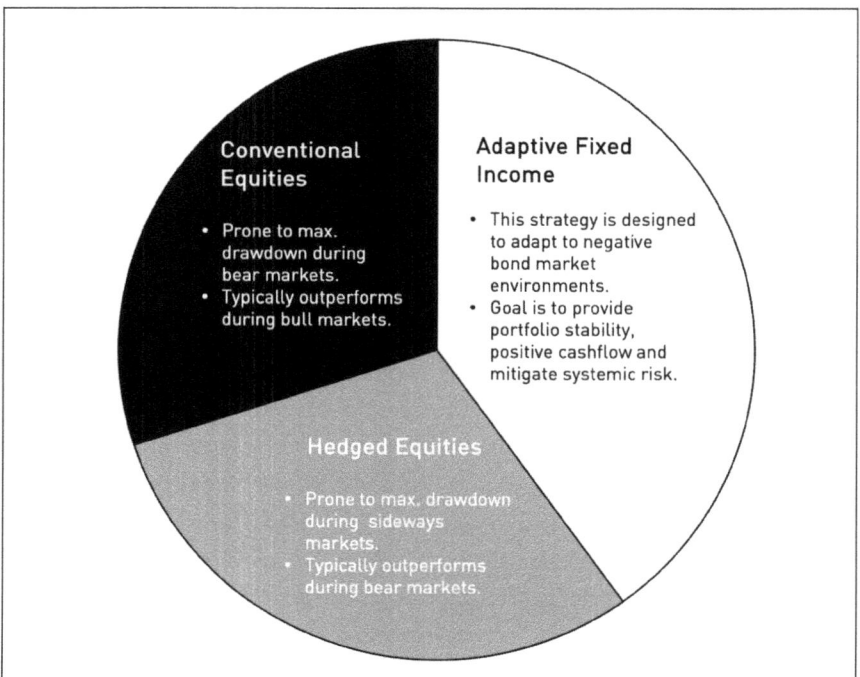

As previously discussed, the biggest decline in bonds to date happened over a 36-year period, from 1945 until 1981, during which they lost 18% of purchasing power. I believe that even that extreme loss understates the risk that bonds introduce into portfolios.

Why?

As we discussed earlier, we have had three episodes of high inflation in the US (see Figure 6.4).

Figure 6.4: The history of high inflation. Cumulative years of high inflation add up, totaling as high as 121% or a more than doubling of prices

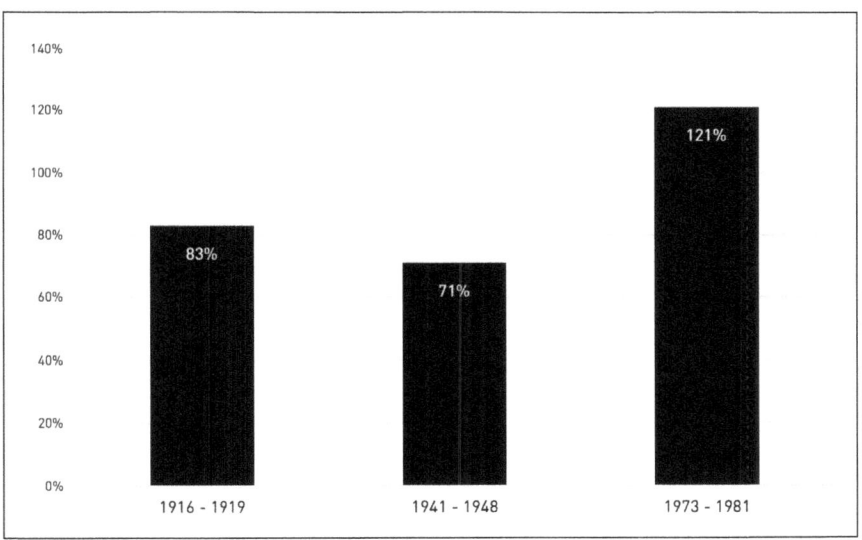

Inflation creates a double whammy for bonds. Inflation reduces the purchasing power of bonds. When inflation moves higher, the Federal Reserve raises interest rates to tame inflation. This creates the secondary effect of causing bond principal losses.

If, for whatever reason, the US enters a period of hyperinflation (greater than 20% per year) that could stretch upwards of 100% per month, a fixed-income investor would effectively be wiped out, as the purchasing power of their portfolio would largely disappear. Virtually all fixed investments would be at risk, including bank deposits, fixed annuities, immediate annuities, and bond portfolios.

We have discussed balanced strategies at length. However, more conservative investors can have allocations of 80% or more to bonds. Advisors should limit the size of fixed-income portfolios because of their vulnerability to real losses.

During the three episodes of inflation in the US, stocks held their own and kept up with inflation on average (at the same time as bonds showed significant real losses). During the massive bond bear market between 1945 and 1981, stocks did surprisingly well, showing cumulative gains of 738% even after inflation (see Figure 6.5). Another shocker: stocks did okay during the crushing inflation in the Weimer Republic in Germany. This means that a part of fighting inflation is keeping investors partially allocated to stocks. The use of hedged equities in portfolios may allow advisors to migrate more assets for conservative investors into stocks. This move simultaneously improves investors' prospects for realizing above-inflation returns and lowers their vulnerability to rising interest rates (or hyperinflation).

Figure 6.5: During the 36-year bond bear market between 1945 and 1981, stocks showed massive gains of 738% above inflation. This suggests that stocks can be a meaningful antidote to periods of high inflation and rising interest rates

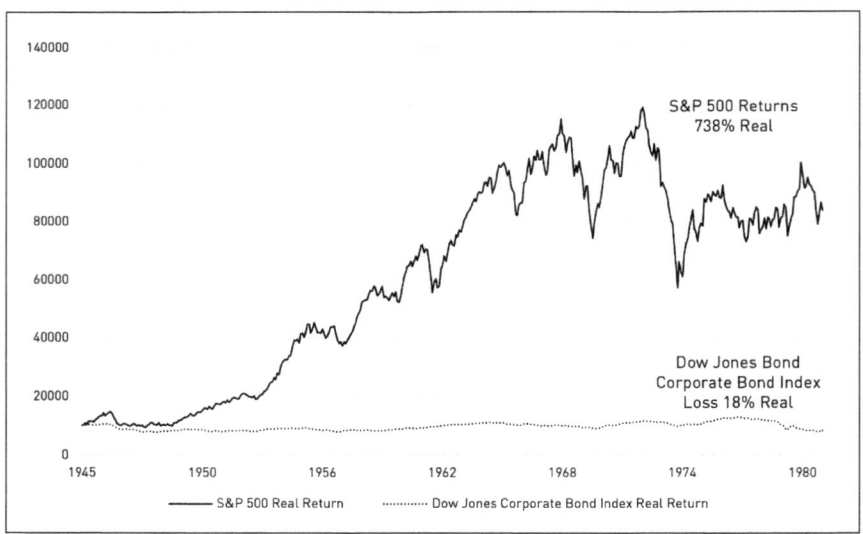

Further defining adaptive fixed-income strategies

Adaptive fixed-income strategies should have two objectives: to potentially increase yields above the potential negative real rates provided by conventional bonds, especially during times when yields are low or below inflation; and to help ameliorate potential losses as interest rates return to normal levels if inflation rises.

The conventional bond strategy of laddering helps accomplish the goal of lowering the risk of losses due to rising interest rates. "Laddering" means buying bonds with different durations and holding them to maturity. Bonds with a shorter duration typically have both a lower yield and a reduced vulnerability to losses when interest rates rise; while bonds that have longer durations tend to have higher yields and a higher chance of losing principal when interest rates increase. Instead of holding bonds that all have an average duration of five years, for example, an advisor can position investors in bonds with 10 different durations. Each of the bonds is held until maturity; so even though on a secondary market the bonds may have a lower value, at maturity they will pay out the full par value (assuming no default), so they are in a way immunized from principal losses. As short-duration bonds mature, they are reinvested in the longest maturity. If interest rates are rising, the new bonds are invested at a higher yield, allowing investors to increase yields—albeit at a slower pace than the market.

Laddering should be done with fixed holdings of bonds for each duration, not with open-ended mutual funds or ETFs that constantly change holdings and don't normally hold bonds to maturity. Unless you have a sizable portfolio and the ability and time to do due diligence on bond portfolios, I wouldn't recommend allocating to individual corporate bonds. Instead, deploy a strategy that incorporates bond unit investment trusts or funds that hold bonds to maturity.

The second type of adaptive fixed-income strategy that should be considered is unconstrained bond strategies or funds. These strategies can change allocations to bonds of different duration and quality based on the market environment. They might include high-yield (lower-quality) bonds, T-bills, longer-duration investment-grade bonds, or inflation-adjusted bonds. The aim is to:

- help lessen losses to principal when rates are rising;
- increase yields by taking exposure to lower-quality bonds when desirable; and
- position into longer-duration bonds to capitalize on bond appreciation when rates decline.

Unconstrained income funds might also include strategies to hedge against unfavorable interest rate moves.

Conventional equities

The final core component of our behavioral portfolio is plain old boring conventional stocks. These can be made up of passive indexing strategies or, if you wish to distribute some of your clients' wealth to asset managers, actively managed stocks. These strategies should have broad exposure to global equities markets. This is the portion of the portfolio that must be highly reliable at achieving our third criterion of facilitating up-capture during rising markets. The strategies or managers held in this portion of the portfolio should not be making big bets that might cause the portfolio to trail broad market benchmarks. If that happens and the hedged equity allocation also trails market returns, investor retention issues will mess up your world.

For example, overweight positions to sectors, value or growth, or cap over-concentrations should be avoided if possible. Any over-concentration in this part of the portfolio will inevitably cause it to at times trail broad market benchmarks and produce investor retention concerns.

The conventional equity portfolio allocation is an opportunity to keep overall portfolio fees low, as passive exposure to the markets can be next to free for most asset classes. More recent innovations that provide exposure to these passive indices through direct indexing is worth considering for the potential tax benefits for conventional stock exposure.

It is difficult for investors to maintain allocations to conventional stocks when markets enter severe declines, especially if other portions of the portfolio are avoiding losses. However, it is crucial that advisors keep a healthy portion of the portfolio in conventional stocks so that they participate in the opportunities for growth/profit when the market rebounds. Beginning in Chapter 8, I will discuss at length managing investor anxieties during market declines.

CHAPTER 6

Making the case for the behavioral portfolio

A significant proportion of the readership of this book may be experiencing heart palpitations at the mere suggestion that investors could ever include hedging strategies for stocks into portfolios, or that bonds should be anything other than a traditional bond allocation. No doubt, countless reviewers on Amazon will be rolling over in their beds at the senior citizens home at the very mention of anything other than a passive approach. However, emerging academic theory supports adding hedged equities to portfolios.

"What about the efficient markets hypothesis?" people will ask. Gene Fama's efficient markets hypothesis asserts that all information currently available is processed by markets to derive the correct price, making it impossible to outperform through security selection or market timing. The only way an investor can increase returns is by taking greater risk. And the only way to take less risk is to accept lower returns.

Although still the dominant theory supporting portfolio construction, the efficient markets hypothesis has not gone unchallenged. In his book *Adaptive Markets Hypothesis*, Andrew Lo concludes that markets are generally efficient, but that prices can diverge from perfect, rational equilibrium due to investor behavioral tendencies to buy when markets are rallying and sell when they are in freefall. Lo argues: "Investing in stocks in the long run may not always be a good idea, especially if your savings can be wiped out in the short run … the wisdom of crowds is sometimes overwhelmed by the madness of mobs."

The efficient markets hypothesis isn't wrong, according to Lo; it's incomplete.

What about times when markets have elevated or compressed price to earnings ratios? As we have already shown, studies reveal that valuations are predictive of future returns. A study by Robert Shiller and John Campbell supports this conclusion. In their 1998 study "Valuations and the Long Run Stock-Market Outlook," Campbell and Shiller conclude that initial price earnings ratios explain as much as 40% of future returns.[30]

A number of efficient markets proponents concede that market pricing is not always perfect, but believe that it isn't possible to take advantage of that mispricing and outperform the markets. Burton Malkiel, in his paper "The Efficient Market Hypothesis and Its Critics," writes that: "True value will win out in the end. And before the fact, there is no way in which investors can reliably exploit any anomalies or patterns that might exist."

Malkiel is skeptical as to whether:

> any of the "predictable patterns" that have been documented in the literature were ever sufficiently robust so as to have created profitable investment opportunities and after they have been discovered and publicized, they will certainly not allow investors to earn excess returns.[31]

Adherents of the efficient markets hypothesis will tell you that attempting to predict markets or capitalize on mispriced securities is a fool's game that, net of trading costs, will yield inferior risk-adjusted returns. So why bother?

What all of this focus on efficient markets fails to grasp, however, is that underperforming market returns over the long term in order to create a superior return path (that is more likely to create success for investors) is exactly what we're prescribing. I recently began comparing adding strategies to reduce left tail risk to taking out home fire insurance. Few people will experience a fire in their homes, but anyone who owns a home has fire insurance because the consequences of losing your home to a fire are so severe as to be unbearable. And yes, you will have less money if you pay for insurance than if you didn't.

For many, the consequences of devastating losses to their portfolios would be greater than the loss of a personal residence. Instead of ignoring the efficient markets hypothesis, we are accepting its conclusions and changing the focus away from maximizing returns.

Challenging the implications of the efficient markets hypothesis

Another widely accepted principle of economics is the law of supply and demand. This suggests that if the price of any stock is too high, there will be fewer buyers (or more sellers), until the stock arrives at an equilibrium price. It acts as a mechanism to bring efficiency to the markets by constantly repricing stocks based on all information available to investors.

But the idea of an absolute allocation to a passive (index) strategy, regardless of the price of any of the individual stocks in that index, causes a breakdown in the supply/demand construct. Why? Because, according to the efficient markets hypothesis, the price doesn't matter. If stocks are overvalued, there is no reliable means to take advantage of this. If you have money to invest, you should always buy because that yields the best results. The obvious problem with this is that if everyone uses this methodology, stock prices become untethered from their fundamental valuations. A company could become insolvent, with no revenues, but still be priced at a high valuation based on its historical weighting in indices.

As discussed in the introduction to this book, this produces a paradox. At one extreme, if nobody believes that the efficient markets hypothesis is valid, then there is no relation between stocks and their fundamental values. Under these circumstances, each investor has a strong incentive to research the fundamental values of assets before buying and selling, causing stock prices to reflect all information available and making the efficient markets hypothesis true.

At the other extreme, if everyone believes that the efficient markets hypothesis is valid, then stock prices already reflect all available information and investors have no incentive to research fundamental values. Everybody now purchases the index. Under this circumstance, stock prices will not reflect any available information, rendering the efficient markets hypothesis false.

One could argue that the markets started out efficient until we understood this to be true. As more people embrace market efficiency as the dominant principle, markets drift away from efficiency.

I agree with Andrew Lo. The markets are generally efficient. However, just as an individual is vulnerable to behavioral biases such as recency bias and fear, groups—or even a consensus of market players—can behave irrationally, causing aberrant or even extreme mispricing situations for investors.

I witnessed this when I watched advisors by the thousands walk into the buzzsaw of the 1999 growth/internet stock bubble. The law of supply and demand and the extreme valuations of stocks should have caused advisors to sell growth stocks to bring prices back to reasonable levels. But they didn't. Why?

Because advisors were trained that the markets were efficient. Buying and holding stocks was always superior to trying to predict market direction. So, they remained fully allocated and in many cases switched portfolios from value to growth stocks to increase exposure to the internet stock bubble.

Behavioral portfolios may position investors to profit from mispricing opportunities

Another sub-heading here might be, "How to capitalize on the inefficiencies of efficient markets." Let's juxtapose the wide acceptance of the efficient market hypothesis against the perspective of a hedge fund manager like Bridgewater Associates. Bridgewater has consistently produced significantly higher risk-adjusted returns than the market (something that the efficient markets hypothesis suggests is not possible). It accomplishes this through proprietary strategies.

While Bridgewater shares some of its overarching philosophy with the public, the specific strategies that it uses to earn billions of dollars of profits are carefully guarded secrets. The reason it is so secretive is obvious: if others learn the strategy and it is widely deployed, the market mispricing opportunity will vanish as the number of investor dollars deployed to the strategy expands. As strategies become more widely known, their ability to produce alpha is diminished.

Gene Fama believes that everyone should invest in the same way and has won a Nobel Prize for his work. But, unlike the Bridgewater Associates strategies, the ideas that support the efficient market hypothesis are transparent and available to all market participants.

The paradox of the efficient markets hypothesis applies to all investment strategies. The more widely accepted a strategy, the less valid it becomes. Once everyone in the market understands something to be true, and allocates on that belief, it is no longer true. From a trader like Bridgewater's perspective, when everyone believes that something is true, it is a trading opportunity—to do the opposite.

If the market believes that dogfood.com is worth $3 billion even though the company is made up of one employee with a PowerPoint presentation, that's an opportunity to create wealth. If the most sophisticated banks and traders believe that packaged mortgages held by borrowers without income or assets are triple A rated securities and you correctly identify this, that is (actually, it was) an opportunity to become very wealthy. And finally, if the whole world believes that buying and holding portfolios regardless of valuations is the only way to invest, that too is an opportunity.

If this seems confusing as it pertains to allocating your investor portfolios, that's because it is! For advisors, however, there is good news. The inherent complexity in financial markets virtually guarantees that you will have a career for decades into the future despite the oncoming force of artificial intelligence (AI) and robo-advisory services.

One of the tenets of behavioral portfolios is to do the opposite of, and take advantage of, the crowd's poor decision-making power. The behavioral portfolio recommendation overcomes the complexity of trying to bet for or against efficient markets by taking positions in both types of stock portfolios. The conventional stock allocation satisfies adherents of efficient markets by remaining fully invested at all times, regardless of market conditions. The hedged equities allocation capitalizes on market inefficiencies while still attempting to gain from the long-term growth in stocks.

Even if you are unconvinced by the efficient markets argument, the ongoing debate misses the point that I am making in this book. The purpose of deploying hedged equity strategies is not to outperform stocks over the long term, but to create investment products that reliably help investors achieve their goals. This means that adding elements of risk management to equities may indeed lower returns over the long term. But it also means that the risk of overwhelming losses is significantly reduced for investors, while the probability of meeting the investor's goals is dramatically improved. It also means that portfolios make more sense and are palatable to the investors they were designed to serve.

As a final point to address panic attacks among the conventional investing crowd, it may be helpful to frame the discussion about adding hedged equities to portfolios by talking about a risk reduction method that advisors already use: bonds. Advisors who are committed to buy-and-hold portfolios overwhelmingly support the idea of including bond allocations, even though this inevitably lowers long-term portfolio returns. I have shown that although bonds usually add stability and reduce risk in portfolios, there are times when bonds increase risks. To the buy-and-hold crowd, I ask: what if there is a more efficient way to create a stable return stream for investors than allocating between stocks and bonds? And if, while attempting to build that portfolio, we accept that hedged equities may trail the long-term returns of equities, how is that different than allocating a portion of equities to bonds, which also underperform stocks?

It's not. But acknowledging the wisdom of incorporating hedged equities into portfolios forces investment managers and the builders of investment products to enter the unfamiliar territory of understanding hedged equities.

During declining markets, the allocation of half of the stock portfolio to hedged equities has the potential to meaningfully reduce portfolio losses. During market distress, hedged equities cause the investor to understand that part of their portfolio is "smarter than the markets and potentially poised to thrive." This is an additional element that has led to the success of the behavioral portfolio recommendation.

Analyzing the impact of a behavioral portfolio

To articulate how behavioral portfolios might be built using the performance of historical funds/strategies, I will illustrate an execution of this portfolio built with data from the Morningstar database. I will discuss how it meets the different criteria that I have laid out, including the effects on down-capture and returns. Finally, and imperatively, I will use the return dynamics of this behavioral portfolio and illustrate how it can potentially directly improve the probability of success for retirees.

For the purposes of building this portfolio, a hedged equities category was created using Morningstar that found all equities funds/ETFs and strategies which were positively correlated with stock market gains (greater than .5) and had a low correlation with market drops (less than .5)[32] Similarly, for the adaptive bond allocation, I included bond strategies and funds that had a .5 or greater up-market correlation with the Barclays Aggregate Bond Index but a lower than .5 down-market correlation with the same index. More data on the construction of these portfolios can be seen in the notes below.

The point of selecting categories in this way is that I wanted to find stock strategies that met the criteria outlined above, meaning that they were positively correlated with markets when they were moving higher but had a relatively low correlation when they were moving lower. I included funds and strategies in the hedged equity category regardless of returns. In other words, there was no built-in bias toward higher-performing strategies; only that they moved in ways similar to hedged equity. The same is true for bond portfolios.

Because much of the conversation has focused on balanced portfolios, I chose to illustrate a 60/40 portfolio where half of stocks were positioned in hedged equities and bonds were allocated to an adaptive fixed-income approach (see Figure 6.6). Although I am illustrating a balanced portfolio, advisors should understand that behavioral portfolios should be built with the same risk profile approach as conventional portfolios. Younger investors will likely want to have a higher (even much higher) allocation to stocks. Investors that have less need for above-inflation growth could have a lower allocation to stocks. Strategies were included only if they had an inception date of January 1, 2008 or earlier, so that the impact of the Great Financial Crisis could be included in bear market stats. Conventional stocks were made up with an allocation to the MSCI World Index.

Figure 6.6: An example of a behavioral portfolio built with Morningstar data that included conventional equities, hedged equities, and adaptive fixed-income funds and strategies

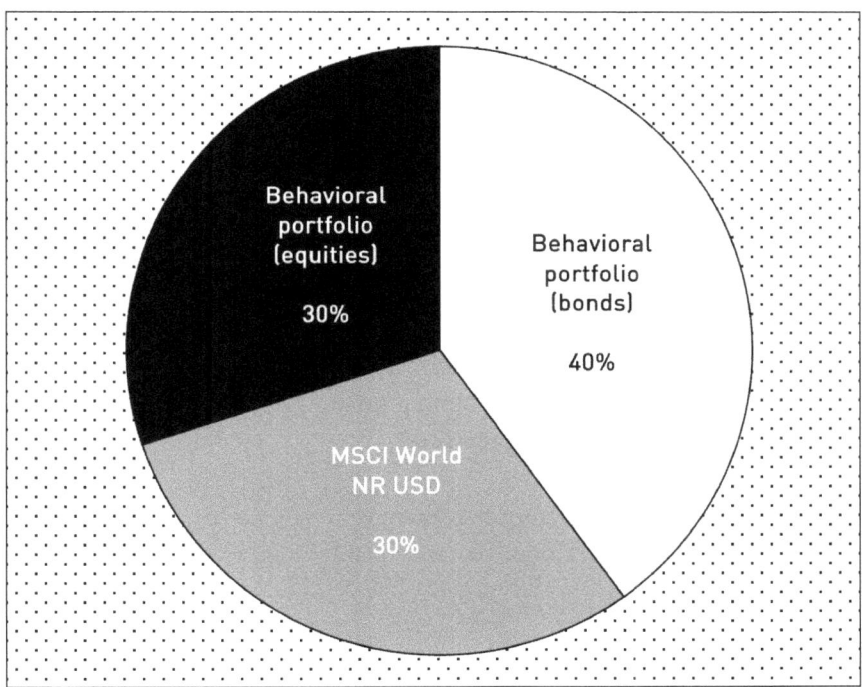

To evaluate the impact of introducing hedged equities and adaptive fixed-income returns on portfolios, let's return to our behavioral portfolio criteria, whose best quantitative expression is defined by a modified return distribution chart (see Figure 6.7).

Figure 6.7: The best quantitative expression of a behavioral portfolio is a modified return distribution chart. Ideally, the right tail is similar to a conventional portfolio, but the left tail is cut short, reflecting less significant losses. It is assumed that mean returns are lower to reflect the cost of hedging against losses

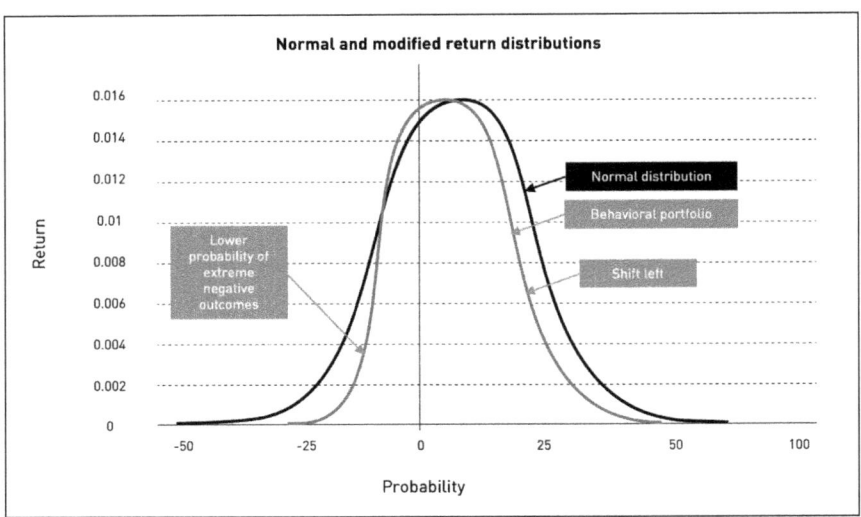

The criteria to consider when building behavioral portfolios are:

- Comprehensively address tail risks.
- Provide long-range, above-inflation growth.
- Capture gains during rising markets.
- Preserve gains.
- Attempt to maximize return consistency.
- Include primarily reliable, understandable sources of growth and/or income.

How well does the suggested behavioral portfolio meet our criteria? To evaluate this, I analyzed both the behavioral portfolio and a conventional balanced portfolio between 2008 (to include the Great Financial Crisis) and 2023. The behavioral portfolio that I built was compared to a 60/40 balanced portfolio constructed using a 60% allocation to the MSCI World Index and a 40% allocation to the Barclays Aggregate Bond Index.

Address tail risks

This criterion can be assessed by looking at the maximum drawdown of the behavioral portfolio, as shown in Figure 6.8.

Figure 6.8: The behavioral portfolio consistently reduced drawdowns relative to a conventional portfolio, with quicker recovery times

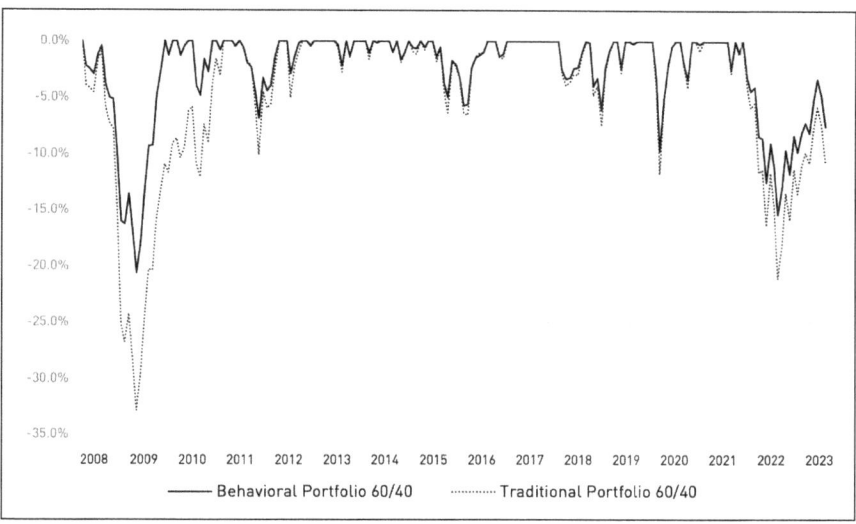

The maximum drawdown of the behavioral portfolio improved over a traditional balanced portfolio from 33% to 20.6%. The behavioral portfolio recovered from its largest losses experienced during the Great Financial Crisis in just 22 months, while the conventional balanced portfolio took 37 months to recover back to its original principal. Across a broad set of down-market metrics, the behavioral portfolio shows improved results, including loss deviation and market down-capture (see Figure 6.9).

Figure 6.9: In addition to a reduced maximum drawdown, other down-market statistics improve in the behavioral portfolio relative to a traditional portfolio, including the down-capture ratio and loss deviation

	Max drawdown	Loss std dev	Std dev	Avg drawdown	Worst quarter	Bear correlation	Down capture ratio	Down capture return	Down percent ratio	Down number	Down number ratio
Behavioral portfolio 60 / 40	-20.64%	5.41%	7.81%	-5.78%	-9.50%	0.97	71.86	-1.83%	0.92	70	0.94
Traditional portfolio 60 / 40	-32.89%	8.02%	10.51%	-7.96%	-11.59%	1.00	100.00	-2.54%	0.00	71	1.00

Notably, the behavioral portfolio helped reduce downside from both stock and bond declines. During 2008, 2018, and 2022, the behavioral portfolio experienced smaller losses than the traditional portfolio (see Figure 6.10).

Figure 6.10: In the three calendar years in our sample where the benchmark experienced meaningful losses, the behavioral portfolio shows lower drawdowns—which in some cases (2008) were significant

	2008	2009	2010	2011	2012	2013	2014	2015
Behavioral portfolio 60 / 40	-13.57%	17.72%	9.30%	0.89%	8.80%	12.11%	4.76%	-0.64%
Traditional portfolio 60 / 40	-24.28%	20.67%	10.30%	0.26%	11.29%	14.55%	5.36%	-0.14%

	2016	2017	2018	2019	2020	2021	2022	YTD 9/30/23
Behavioral portfolio 60 / 40	5.02%	12.40%	-3.44%	15.36%	13.06%	9.94%	-11.74%	4.80%
Traditional portfolio 60 / 40	5.61%	14.58%	-4.99%	19.93%	14.02%	12.08%	-15.90%	6.10%

Provide up-capture and above-inflation growth

Due to its adherence to a 60/40 stock and bond allocation, the behavioral portfolio also does a respectable job at providing up-capture when markets are gaining, suggesting that it would produce the long-range above-inflation growth that most investors require. The behavioral portfolio has a correlation of .97 to the benchmarked portfolio during rising markets and captures roughly 80% of increases at times when the markets are rising.

Figure 6.11: In our sample, the behavioral portfolio had slightly higher average mean returns, an 80% up-capture ratio and a .97 correlation to the benchmark during rising markets. This conforms to our objective of matching the right tail and providing gains when the markets advance

	Return	Bull correlation	Up capture ratio	Up percent ratio	Up number	Up number ratio
Behavioral portfolio 60/40	4.99%	0.97	80.14	0.15	119	0.97
Traditional portfolio 60/40	4.92%	1.00	100.00	0.00	118	1.00

Choosing a start date of January 2008 caused both the traditional and behavioral portfolios to have below-average annual returns of just 5%, or roughly 2.6% above inflation (inflation averaged 2.35% during this time).

Preserve gains and maximize return consistency

In each instance after gains were produced in portfolios, losses following those gains were smaller, suggesting that the behavioral portfolio helped preserve gains. The behavioral portfolio delivered positive returns slightly more consistently than the traditional portfolio, with gains in 119 out of 189 months. When there were losses in months in the behavioral portfolio, they were smaller, at 1.8% during any month, versus 2.5% in losing months for the traditional portfolio.

Include primarily reliable, understandable sources of growth and/or income

Our final criterion—that the portfolio include only reliable and understandable sources of growth and income—is clearly met due to the sole inclusion of strategies dominated by stocks and bonds.

Finally, the behavioral portfolio returns match the desired modified return distribution that I discussed earlier in the book. The left tail is cut shorter than that of the traditional portfolio. Mean returns were slightly higher for the behavioral portfolio in this example. However, as seen in Figure 6.12, the right tail shifted left commensurate with expectations from including a significant allocation to hedged equities.

Figure 6.12: The left tail of the behavioral portfolio, shown in the dark shade below, is much shorter than that of a traditional portfolio—although, as expected, the right tail is also compressed. The sample comes surprisingly close to matching our probability distribution chart objective

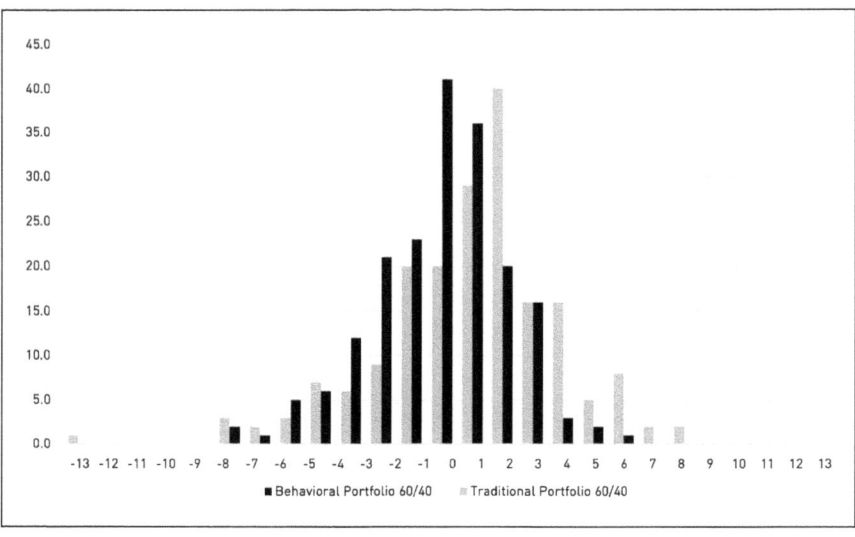

Key takeaways from the analysis of the behavioral portfolio

Before looking at how the behavioral portfolio changes the probability of success for retirees, I would like to summarize what we have done with this portfolio and communicate some essential changes that we've been able to achieve by making the alterations that we have.

Earlier in the book, I highlighted two generational historical periods over the past 100 years that would have derailed investors and threatened their livelihoods. During the Great Depression, stocks lost value over 14 years, drawing down as much as 84% along the way. Our visualization of this period showed that investors would have left stocks or run out of money (if they didn't leave stocks). From 1942 to 1981, bonds lost real value during a mega bear market that lasted for 36 years. As a consequence of these losses, along with inflation, balanced portfolios realized among their lowest real returns of any period that we examined.

Due to limitations in finding strategies that meet the criteria of our behavioral portfolio, I was only able to look at results going back through 2008. Thus, the results shown here—while compelling—don't tell the whole story, because they don't include significant multi-year declines for stocks and massive multi-year periods of inflation.

Although the results are desirable, due to this limited timeframe, they don't convey the full impact of the changes you would be making, which is that the behavioral portfolio could protect your investors—and you—from potential ruin. As an advisor, building contingency planning for extreme events into portfolio construction before and in anticipation of adversity, and where investors on their own likely would not do so, means that you have added value for your clients that transcends any other advice that you may ever give.

How the behavioral portfolio improves investors' chances of success

What if, in addition to addressing extreme risks and creating a more navigable return path for investors, the behavioral portfolio can be shown to improve the probability that investors will not outlive their income? In this section, I will deploy the data comparing the behavioral portfolio to a traditional portfolio and will plug it back into a Monte Carlo analysis to look at how this potentially changes retirement outcomes.

Let's return to the retired investor that we discussed in our examination of retirement distributions from traditional balanced portfolios. Our investor was 65, had $1 million in investments, and needed to draw 4% from their portfolio to meet their income needs (the assumptions for this investor are summarized in Figure 6.13).

The period studied produced low returns (due primarily to the start date correlating with the beginning of the Great Financial Crisis) relative to our longer-term study of the balanced portfolio. However, the effects of introducing the behavioral portfolio can still be seen. The arithmetic mean return of the traditional model during this time was 5.56%, and the standard deviation was 10.5%. Plugging this data into a Monte Carlo analysis engine shows that this investor would have a 75% probability of success at achieving their retirement distribution goal.

Figure 6.13: A summary of the assumptions for a retired investor drawing from a traditional portfolio, with a return of 5.56% and a standard deviation of 10.5%

Age	65
Investment assets	$1,000,000
Income drawn from investments	$40,000
Life expectancy in years	30
Assets remaining after death	0
Sample traditional portfolio return	**5.56%**
Assumed inflation	2.35%
Standard deviation	10.5%

Figure 6.14: The probability that an investor's portfolio will last through a 30-year retirement is 75%

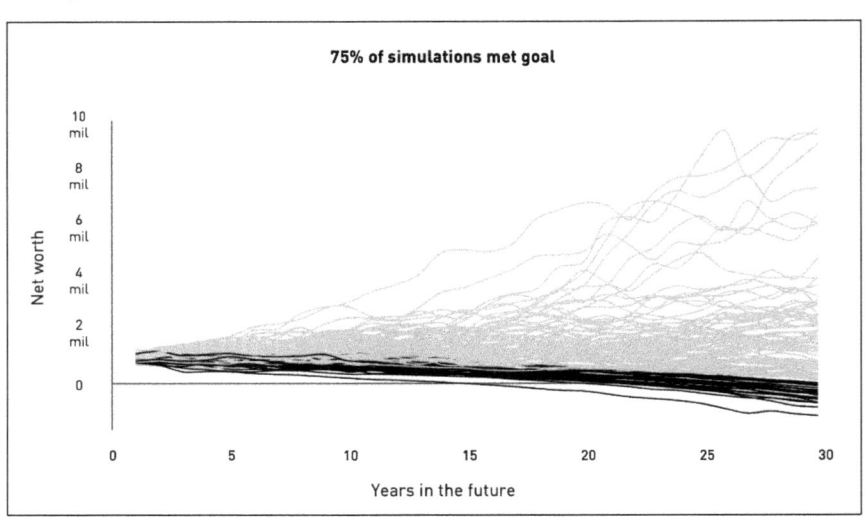

To compare: the arithmetic mean return of the behavioral portfolio is lower, at 5.29%; but the volatility (standard deviation) is also lower, at 7.7% (see assumptions in Figure 6.15). Despite having a lower return, the reduced volatility of the behavioral portfolio improves to an 82% chance of success—an increase of 7% on the probability of success of a conventional approach. It's worth noting that this comparison takes into account the fee differential between executing hedged equities and adaptive fixed-income funds, relative to the passive approach of the conventional portfolio, which is made up for our comparison of indices that are absent of fees altogether.

Figure 6.15

Age	65
Investment assets	$1,000,000
Income drawn from investments	$40,000
Life expectancy in years	30
Assets remaining after death	0
Sample behavioral portfolio return	**5.29%**
Assumed inflation	2.35%
Standard deviation	7.7%

Figure 6.16: The probability that an investor in the behavioral portfolio will last through retirement improves to 82%, despite a lower return

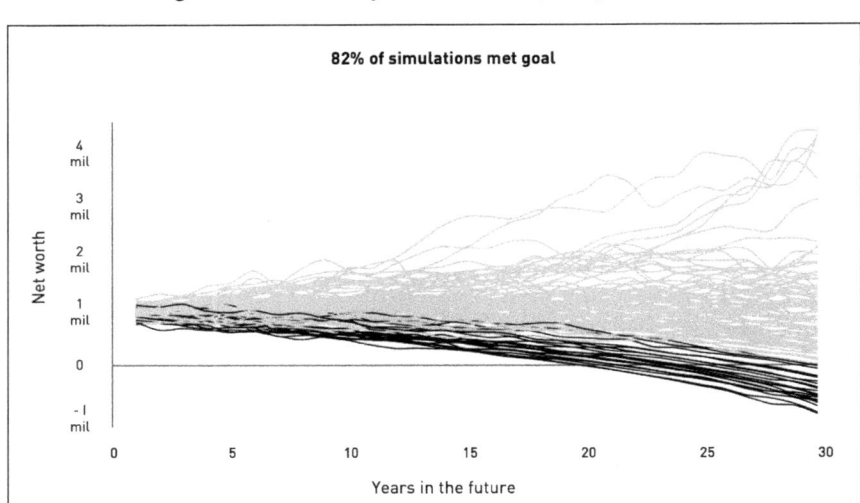

In addition to the improved probability of success suggested by this analysis, what if, through the use of the behavioral portfolio and investor training, we could reduce or eliminate the impact of poor timing on investor decision making?

The Morningstar *Mind the Gap* study that I discussed in Chapter 4 showed that the cost of poor decision making resulted in 1.7% lower returns per year. Some of that, it can be assumed, comes from investors fearful of market losses, who leave higher-returning assets during periods of market turmoil. Addressing that reality in portfolio construction creates the possibility that the realized returns of investors stretch higher. This could be another key factor in helping improve the probability of retirement success.

Wrapping up our chapter on behavioral portfolios

Stocks and bonds are combined into portfolios because they are the two core types of assets that exist and they help offset each other's weaknesses. The resultant portfolios, however, are at times fraught with risk and can have a low probability of helping investors achieve their goals.

Conventional portfolios are vulnerable to severe losses that can devastate investors. The return objectives and ways of managing risk are based on combinations of assets rather than on what produces the highest probability of investor success. These portfolios assume that markets are always reasonably valued, when we all know that at times they are not. Their primary risk management tool, diversification, fails if economic crises are severe enough. And finally, due to many of the factors described above and investors' inability to psychologically tolerate market gyrations, investors fail to correctly time decisions to buy and sell assets, further impairing their prospects of success.

Portfolios that are behaviorally designed are conceived by first establishing what investors both want and need from their investments. Investors want portfolios that are comprehensively safeguarded against severe losses, offer above-inflation growth, participate in market up-capture during rising periods, and preserve gains. By driving the product design process with clear investor objectives rather than arbitrary asset combinations, behaviorally designed portfolios can dramatically improve an investor's chance of achieving their financial goals.

Our behavioral portfolio recommendation still relies on the engines of growth and return provided by stocks and bonds. But it manages them in a way that dramatically changes their return paths across a variety of market environments. Adding components of hedged equities and adaptive fixed-income strategies helps safeguard portfolios and preserve gains. These portfolios address the possibility of extreme losses and diversification failure during turbulent economic crises. They also are inherently adaptive during overvalued markets, while increasing the chance of prospering through declining markets. This smoother return path with fewer declines, where contingencies have been addressed in advance, creates greater peace of mind for investors and improves their ability to navigate difficult markets.

Advisors who have been using these portfolios have a completely different perspective on the financial markets than those who adhere to conventional strategies. Instead of looking over their shoulders and worrying about market crises, they focus their efforts on communicating to their investors how their portfolio is adapting during different markets. Instead of shifting strategies in portfolios to address escalating dangers, they take advantage of mispricing opportunities by allowing strategies to buy after declines rather than sell and harvesting profits in conventional stocks into hedged equities as markets gain.

My focus thus far has been on the clients that account for the bulk of advisors' assets: older retiring or retired investors. In Chapter 7, I'll switch the conversation to focus on younger savers who have different needs from their portfolio and whose portfolios thus require different criteria. In the process, I'll make some important distinctions between behavioral portfolios for younger savers and conventional approaches.

CHAPTER 7
Behavioral Portfolios for Young(er) Savers

OUR PORTFOLIO RECOMMENDATIONS thus far have been focused on investors who have already accumulated assets. Intuitively, the bulk of the assets managed by advisors are for those clients who, well, have savings to invest. But I would be remiss if I didn't discuss behavioral portfolios for young savers. In this chapter, I will provide a brief summary of our recommendations for young savers, which includes some important deviations from conventional approaches used today.

For these savers, take everything that you've learned so far and turn it upside down. Let's look back at the criteria that we established for later-stage investors and juxtapose these against the needs of young accumulators.

Portfolio safeguarding

For retirees, the first and most important criterion is portfolio safeguarding. Young accumulators do not have significant savings that they need to safeguard. Instead, they are (or should be) adding to their investments periodically. Retired investors who are taking distributions from their portfolio are selling assets at a loss when they take distributions from portfolios after the markets have moved lower. For young savers, the opposite is happening. When the markets turn lower, these investors are buying shares at bargain prices. In other words, bear markets hurt retirees, but can help accumulators.

How extreme can this be? In early 2000, a friend of mine came to me upset about his stock option plan. At the time, his company provided a potentially significant percentage of his compensation via stock options. When stock options are issued, employees benefit only if the stock price increases above their price level when they were issued. He first started to receive options in 1995 when the stock price was 22. It had moved higher, but now was at 20—below the issue price of any options that he had received at that point. So, five years after he began receiving options, they had zero value. What, he asked, should he do?

My response was that this sounded just about perfect; and that, assuming the company was growing, it would be preferable for the stock to move even lower while he was accumulating options. Ultimately, I said, when the company stock price increases to reflect its proper value, his profit could be significant due to the low issue price on the options for all of those years.

It was a rough slog for the price of his options for a number of years. But in 2003, as stocks were recovering from the internet-related decline, the price began to increase. By 2007, it had tripled to 60. After the Great Financial Crisis, its ascent continued. On retirement in 2023, the total value of those options exceeded $10 million.

This story helps illustrate the fact that the best return path for young savers is losses or stagnating markets in the early part of their accumulation cycle, with gains late (as shown in Figure 7.1).

Figure 7.1: If savers contribute to their portfolios when prices are low, it improves their situation when assets increase in value closer to retirement

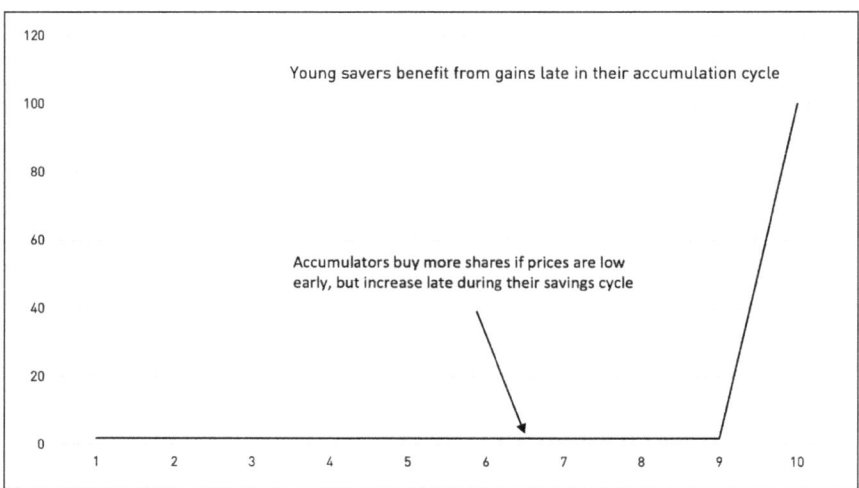

The reverse is true for retirees taking distributions from their portfolios, who prefer gains early in retirement, allowing them to sell fewer shares of their portfolios in order to fund their living needs (see Figure 7.2).

Figure 7.2: Retirees benefit from the opposite of young savers—they benefit from gains, not losses, early in their distribution cycle

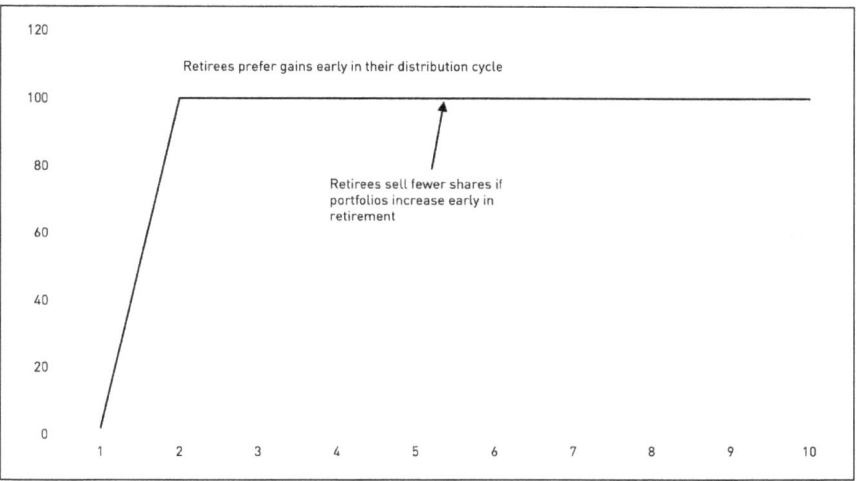

Along with the timing of returns, young savers fare best if their portfolios are—get ready—more volatile! Well, sort of. As many understand, young savers that dollar cost average (or buy at regular intervals) into the markets can do better—in some cases, *much* better—if the asset that they are dollar cost averaging into experiences significant volatility.

To illustrate, assume that an investor is saving $1,000 per year. In the first example, an investor experiences very low volatility. If a stock increases approximately 10% each year, a stock priced at $5 would increase to $77. Because the return is the same every year, the investment has a volatility (standard deviation) of zero. Over those 30 years, the portfolio would increase to an impressive $180,100, with only $30,000 invested (as shown in Figure 7.3).

Figure 7.3: In this figure, a saver invests $1,000 per year in a portfolio that is assumed to increase at 10% per year every year, with no variability. The portfolio grows to $180,100 in 30 years

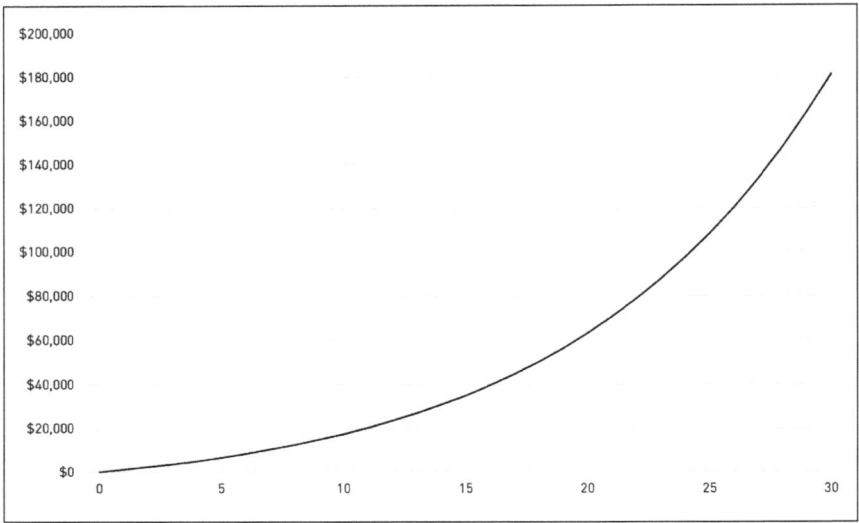

In the second example, our saver is still adding $1,000 per year and the stock still increases from $5 to $77. But, as shown in Figure 7.4, it gets there with extreme gains and losses each year. We used hyper-volatility reflecting a standard deviation of 290%. At the end of this period, instead of $180,500, our investor has accumulated $518,600—over three times as much! This is due to the benefit of dollar cost averaging. When the share price is low, investors buy more shares. When the share price is high, they buy fewer shares. As a result, the average price for shares is lower.

Figure 7.4: In this figure, an investor invests the same $1,000 per year for 30 years, but the returns are highly variable, with a standard deviation of 290%. At the end of the period, the portfolio has grown to $518,600

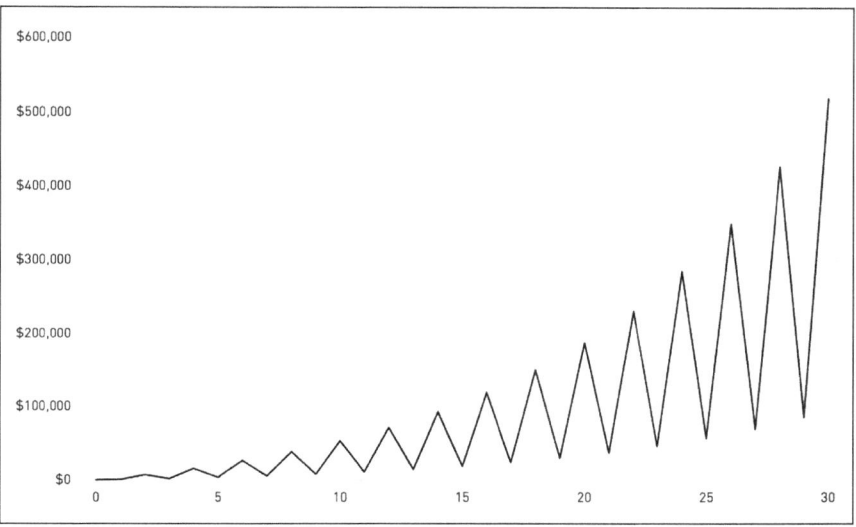

It's worth stopping here to discuss what would likely be startling conclusions for investors who are just starting to save:

- It's better if investments lose money during the initial years of saving.
- The longer that investments stay low and fail to recover losses, the better.
- It is preferable for young savers to experience volatility rather than a stable return path. The higher the volatility and the more significant the market swings are, the better the results will be for those investors.

As we seek to define the best portfolio dynamics for young savers, we need to add a level of complexity to address a change that happens as young savers build their portfolios which is largely absent from the thinking about young savers.

Early savers, in the very beginning, have no savings to protect. However, over time, as their portfolio grows, this changes. Our wildly volatile portfolio that grew to $519,000 was worth only $100,000 the year before. Losses to that level of $100,000 would be hard to grasp for most investors. Big losses to accumulated savings, even for young investors, have a negative impact that is both economic and psychological. While there are unlikely to be distributions from young savers' portfolios, when losses are realized, it takes time for them to recover and grow back to their original value. Also, even though there is a benefit for young savers if the asset that they dollar cost average into is volatile, there is still a negative impact to lump sums that have losses.

Accumulators' portfolios, then, can be divided into two categories. Monthly or quarterly savings should be invested into highly volatile, above-inflation investments. Periodically, however, assets can be swept into portfolios that are managed according to similar objectives as were discussed earlier in our behavioral portfolio recommendation. This second portfolio would see its return and drawdown parameters change over time as investors come closer to retirement.

Two factors help determine the timing for transitioning from volatile portfolios that are susceptible to losses to those that have more stable return paths: clients' risk tolerance and risk capacity. The first, risk tolerance, is determined by how much a client is willing to lose. Even though an investor might be young, any number of scenarios could cause them to have a fairly large portfolio. They might have been great savers from a very young age. They could have realized significant gains from an options grant from a company or received an inheritance. Regardless of the source, if investors determine that they are unwilling to expose portfolios to big losses, then their portfolios should be managed based on the maximum drawdown and target returns that they are comfortable with.

Risk capacity is determined by a means similar to what we discussed earlier. This determination considers all of an investor's available resources and anticipated earnings and distribution needs. It also looks at their ability to endure drawdowns and the return needed to help them accomplish goals.

In order to avoid making decisions based on market moves, which tend to expose an investor to bad timing, a plan for this transition must be made at the time that you build the initial accumulation portfolio for your investors.

Before moving on to outlining an investment plan for young accumulators, let's summarize our discussion about young savers:

- Above-inflation growth: The long time horizon and the effect of compound returns powerfully influence results for young savers. Helping accumulators understand this is an invaluable service that advisors can provide for investors.

- High-volatility investments for dollar cost averaging: By targeting the highest-volatility investments, young accumulators can improve their outcomes.
- Moving assets to more stable portfolios as their asset level increases and/or their risk tolerance or risk capacity dictates: Assets in these portfolios are guided by our earlier criteria for what investors want and need—portfolio safeguarding, above-inflation growth, preservation of gains, and consistent returns.

Finding high-volatility assets for dollar cost averaging

Because of the advantage provided by dollar cost averaging, we recommend that young investors always dollar cost average into highly volatile investments. But what should be up for consideration? Sneakers? Bitcoin?

No. An important criterion for these assets is that they should provide a reliable source of long-term above-inflation growth. The investments we choose must have an extremely high probability to be mean reverting after periods of losses. Let's talk about each of these things.

What do we mean by a "reliable" source of above-inflation growth? One example of a category that can have high volatility but is not a reliable source of above-inflation returns is managed futures. Managed futures are investments generally made up of futures contracts such as commodities or interest rates. These instruments by themselves may have a long-term growth expectation after inflation of 0%, minus fees. Gains realized in managed futures funds, if they come at all, come from manager talent. Managers create a strategy that attempts to take advantage of trends in commodities prices and potentially produce gains for investors. Because the underlying instruments fail to meet our criteria, they should be excluded from consideration for young dollar cost averaging investors, regardless of how well the category may have performed in the recent past.

Commodities and precious metals are instruments that tend to move higher over the long term along with inflation, but generally don't offer growth *above* inflation and should be excluded. What about bear market funds? Betting against stocks, which have moved up historically by 6% per year above inflation, would position investors to lose 6% per year more than inflation before fees. That would be a bad idea, so no.

What do we mean by "an extremely high probability to be mean reverting"? We highlighted two unexpected characteristics that help improve young investors' results: first, investments that lose ground early and stay undervalued, allowing investors to purchase shares for a low (compressed) price; and second, investments that are highly volatile. This all works because, ultimately, the bargain-priced or volatile asset will return to a more appropriate valuation at some point in the future. An example of an investment that does not have an "extremely" high probability to be mean reverting is a single stock.

Yes, my friend who invested in options that grew to $10 million had great results by owning just one company's stock options. In his case, the company didn't give him the ability to choose his investment vehicle. But for plan participants who have a choice about their investments, we would recommend against concentrating too much of a retirement plan into any one company. Why? Individual companies—even very large companies such as Chrysler and GM—go bankrupt. Even if a company continues to exist post bankruptcy, shareholders who hold equity during bankruptcies are usually wiped out. Dollar cost averaging works if share prices return to the mean. That can't happen if shares prices go to zero and your holdings disappear.

So where does that leave us? With mutual funds or ETFs, principally stock funds, that hold many securities and are not vulnerable to bankruptcies by any single issue. There are many different types of funds available and their volatility can vary greatly. We've included a Morningstar list showing all the US fund categories that have 20-year track records and ranked them by volatility (see Figure 7.5).

CHAPTER 7

Figure 7.5: Morningstar categories ranked from highest to lowest based on their standard deviation. Higher-volatility funds should be considered for dollar cost averaging by young savers

Morningstar category	Annualized return	Max drawdown	Standard deviation
Digital Assets	39.54%	-91.79%	99.46%
Muni Single State Short	9.33%	-17.59%	75.80%
Latin America Stock	6.66%	-74.70%	34.95%
Equity Precious Metals	5.92%	-77.79%	29.89%
Equity Energy	6.75%	-81.29%	29.32%
Energy Limited Partnership	5.58%	-74.68%	27.50%
India Equity	6.63%	-71.98%	27.45%
China Region	6.59%	-67.74%	25.04%
Real Estate	9.27%	-72.20%	24.71%
Communications	9.37%	-81.90%	23.15%
Derivative Income	10.23%	-72.90%	22.95%
Industrials	10.39%	-63.09%	22.88%
Consumer Cyclical	11.58%	-60.92%	22.09%
Technology	10.31%	-84.72%	21.76%
Pacific/Asia ex-Japan Stk	6.40%	-66.69%	21.49%
Natural Resources	7.18%	-61.42%	21.26%
Financial	9.16%	-70.01%	21.01%
Health	13.07%	-44.92%	20.94%
Diversified Emerging Mkts	6.26%	-65.56%	20.87%
Target-Date 2065+	8.25%	-32.68%	20.70%
Europe Stock	7.44%	-62.81%	20.44%
Target-Date 2055	6.41%	-55.17%	20.24%
Target-Date 2045	7.34%	-54.80%	20.18%
Global Real Estate	6.49%	-70.47%	20.07%
Target-Date 2050	6.26%	-55.05%	19.98%
Infrastructure	7.50%	-52.11%	19.73%
Commodities Broad Basket	0.50%	-69.16%	19.47%
Commodities Focused	2.89%	-56.85%	19.18%
Target-Date 2040	7.67%	-54.12%	19.00%
Small Value	8.51%	-67.91%	18.98%
Foreign Small/Mid Growth	8.68%	-63.03%	18.77%
Japan Stock	7.25%	-68.15%	18.67%

When looking at the list, a couple of funds appear to offer outstanding opportunities to satisfy our need to provide above-inflation growth and mean-reverting properties. Several funds offering the greatest volatility are single-country emerging markets funds. While investments in China or India may seem appealing, investing in any single country exposes investors to risks of a government or currency failure that may test our mean-reverting criteria. However, diversified emerging markets funds are also near the top of our list. Diversified emerging markets include stocks from countries like China and India and they may have a higher long-term expected above-inflation return than developed country stocks. Because the funds have exposure to many countries in multiple regions, they have higher mean-reverting properties than individual countries.

Other categories that meet our criteria include technology, communications, European, financial, and small company stock funds. Stock fund categories that have relatively lower volatility—such as large cap value, utilities, consumer staples, and healthcare—should be avoided in our search for optimal dollar cost averaging funds.

What other categories should be avoided for the dollar cost averaging funds for an investor? *Categorically*, fixed-income—including money markets, short, intermediate and long-term bond funds—or guaranteed investment options. These include strategies that have fixed-income allocations, such as balanced, target date, and asset allocation funds.

Your clients' long-term accumulation plan

I recommend discussing your dollar cost averaging and stable (behavioral) portfolio strategy at the time that you establish clients' plans, including deciding when assets will be transferred into more stable portfolios. For some clients who are highly risk averse, advisors may want to transfer assets each year into more stable portfolios. For investors who are both willing and able to tolerate greater losses, you may want to establish a level above which assets and gains are harvested and moved to more stable growth portfolios. As shown in Figure 7.6, an investor optimally will dollar cost average into high-volatility funds. Any amount over a hypothetical $100,000 (or an amount determined between you and the investor) will be transferred to a stable growth portfolio. During younger saving years, this could be made up entirely of stocks, but should include hedged equities as a portion of the allocation. Later, as an investor approaches retirement, that allocation can become more conservative and potentially include bonds.

Figure 7.6: A saver's portfolio should be bifurcated between a high-volatility dollar cost average portfolio and a more stable growth-oriented portfolio for lump sums already invested. Over time, assets can migrate from the dollar cost average allocation to the stable growth portfolio

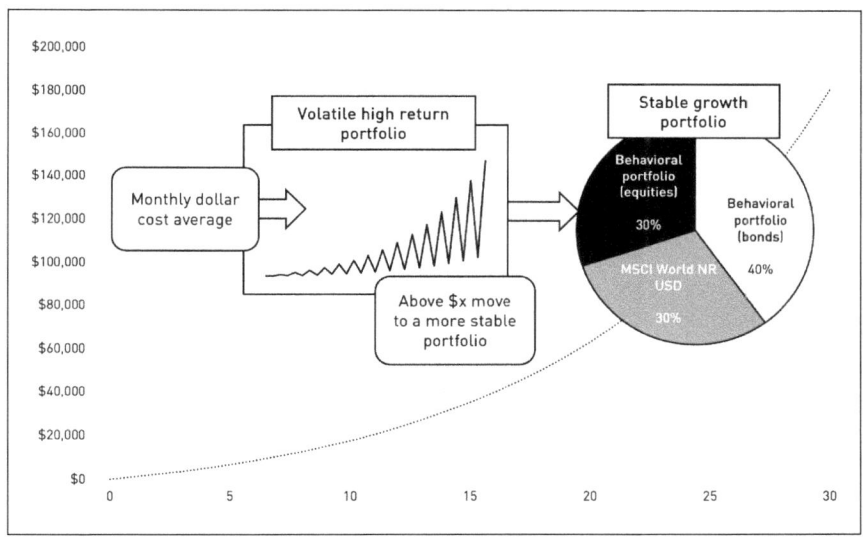

What investment companies or 401k providers are currently bifurcating portfolios according to dollar cost averaging and stable portfolios?

None that we know of. The reason, just as with the flaws in conventional portfolios for retired investors, is that our industry starts by looking at available investments and how they might be combined. Defined contribution plans typically come with a menu of funds available to participants, ranging from aggressive stock funds to very conservative fixed-income or money market funds. If there is a process to help participants—and there often is not—it resembles a standard risk profile questionnaire that attempts to guide them based on their time horizon and risk tolerance. The approach that we're advocating here both takes advantage of dollar cost averaging and addresses potential losses for larger retirement plan portfolios.

Building behavioral portfolios for older and younger investors is the foundation for addressing risks and managing investor behavior. In Part 3 of this book, I'll discuss the second major component in becoming a behavioral coach: creating a proactive decision framework that will allow you to transform your practice.

PART 3
TRANSFORMING YOUR PRACTICE WITH BEHAVIORAL COACHING

INTRODUCTION
A thought experiment about investing
by Blake Jordan

AT THE BEHAVIORAL INVESTING INSTITUTE, we have a simple thought experiment we run advisors through when explaining our position on behavioral finance: imagine a scenario where you have limited skills driving a car. You have a driving instructor who has taught you broadly about cars and has facilitated practice scenarios. Today, though, is your first big step driving further than the parking lot.

Now, fortunately, this side of the thought experiment we all have experiential knowledge of. We can all relate to the uncomfortable and clunky feeling of learning how to drive. Your right foot has to give just enough pressure; your hands are on the wheel turning with just enough force; your eyes are looking forward, behind, and to the side at the right moment. That is a lot of processing—and it all happens quickly. Still, the excited new driver has enough familiarity to wish to tackle the open road.

But, instead of going on roads that you and I are familiar with, imagine a scenario where the infrastructure for driving vehicles is non-existent. There are no traffic lights, stop signs, speed limits, or road lines. There is just pavement, and you dictate the rules to get from A to Z. There is also a lot of traffic and drivers with many different approaches. Some speed like crazy, others crawl; some stop at intersections, others don't. Some drivers stay on the right side of the road, others stay on the left, others both. (This actually sounds somewhat like New York!)

How does the new driver respond? Almost certainly with fear. The driving instructor can do their best to calmly guide the student on the road toward their destination. But the chaos—the unpredictable nature of the other vehicles, the speed, the honking—makes the new driver have an intense emotional reaction.

Drivers' behavioral responses to this intense stimulation will vary. A small handful may get a thrill from the uncertainty. They get a rush from the speed and don't seem to care much for the safety of their trip. The driving instructor in this scenario is with a driver who seems to relish the danger they find themselves in.

For the majority of new drivers, however, the scenario is traumatizing. No matter the instructor's plea, the student will refuse to drive again until some level of safety protocol is introduced to the road. The unpredictable nature of the environment seals many of these would-be drivers' fate: they will avoid driving altogether if this is what it means to drive.

In the thought experiment above, are the new drivers' emotions unwarranted? Would you view them as irrational for having such a flight response?

If you said they were acting completely rationally, I would agree with you. This rational-but-emotional state seems warranted given the circumstances. It doesn't sound unjustified at all to consider driving to be too fatal a hazard to pursue.

Back to the real world

Fortunately, in the real world, student drivers can take to the road and enhance their skills with practice. Over time, the anxiousness and decision fatigue fade. Eventually, we expect a fully competent driver at the wheel.

This leads to another question to ponder: in everyday life, how emotional are we when we drive?

In contrast to the lawless driving thought experiment, we all have experiential evidence to color our answer. While our individual answers will differ, I can tell you from a personal perspective that driving, on the whole, carries less emotional weight for me than most tasks in my life.

In my personal life, putting together a piece of Ikea furniture with many different parts or trying to fix my phone with advice from an internet forum are far more taxing emotional events than driving. I avoid them like the plague.

I would presume most of us follow a similar pattern in daily life. Mundane but inconvenient tasks like email replies and paperwork make us feel dread. The sheer emotional power of continuously repeating these behaviors makes us contemplate switching careers.

Contrast that to the task of driving. I barely think about it. I certainly don't feel trepidation or resistance to the act. It is emotionally neutral—or maybe even a net positive if I play a quality podcast or music in the car. This is baffling if you pause and contemplate for a minute.

Driving is inherently consequential. We each know that getting inside a vehicle poses a significant threat. If we have not been in an accident ourselves, we more than likely know someone who has. At the very least, we have been in a traffic delay because of a collision. Worse, the longer you drive, the greater the likelihood that you will be involved in an accident.

Whether at the back of our heads or at the forefront of our consciousness, the danger and seriousness of driving are always present. Yet even with this realization, I will get in my car again today with essentially the same indifference as the day before.

The most essential and powerful question to applying behavioral finance to financial advising is the following: how is it that driving, with its significant potential for bodily harm, is emotionally inconsequential, yet the act of investing has the threat level of nuclear fallout? That doesn't add up.

The smooth ride

Fundamentally, what is the emotional difference between our lawless driving thought experiment and real-life investing? Putting the question more analogously: when an investor is pulling up to the investment highway for the first time, is there a sense of infrastructure they can feel comfortable operating in? Not really.

The market environment seems to have no rules. It may go down, it may go up, and it may remain flat at times. Regardless, the market seems to follow no predictable format. It has no traffic lights, speed limits, or road lines in place to give a sense of order. Even worse, the market's only predictable quality is that it can subject its participants to turbulent conditions at a moment's notice without remorse. That is scary. An investor's livelihood is tied to a chaos agent. Even with that realization, the investor knows the market is the only feasible roadway to get to their financial destination. They must start driving, whether they like it or not.

Being forced to drive makes it worse. They are coping with the possibility that their transport system will dissolve half their money in an instant and refuse to let them retire on time. The investor's future life depends on a market that behaves volatilely and disregards their needs. Being partnered with such an actor is emotionally adjacent to being held against your will. Fear, frustration, grief run into helplessness and desperation. No control. No satisfactory answers. Just a relationship with an uncaring, eruptive saboteur. With all this instability, it isn't a surprise that clients sit in cash for extended lengths or pursue unwise investments. Luckily, they have you.

Instead of facing the unpredictable landscape alone, you are acting as the driving instructor in the front seat—providing comfort, feedback, assurance, and adjustments as the challenges of the transport system shift. This all feels great, and it defines how most advisors view their role. However, what is still missing are the rules of the road! By introducing these rules (adding lines on the road, noting which side we drive on, introducing speed limits, creating strategies for addressing stress), you are providing an investing infrastructure that attempts to make investors feel safe and in control. Under this premise, your main job is to ensure a smooth ride—not a fast, bumpy, and emotionally draining one.

Keeping with our driving instructor theme, imagine you have a student with an appointment set at 1:00 and you are well within the parameters to arrive five minutes beforehand. The driving student has a proclivity for the fast route. Would you choose to go as fast as possible, on the harshest road conditions, with large numbers of inattentive drivers, just to arrive at the appointment 30 minutes earlier than expected?

Of course not. The juice isn't worth the squeeze. As the instructor, you can sympathize with your student's plight to arrive early, but you have a broader perspective. Whether you arrive five minutes or 30 minutes early, the appointment is still at 1:00. The additional pain doesn't equate to a compelling reward. Similarly, you could select a financial vehicle that runs at 120 miles per hour and you may get to your financial destination faster—but for what?

Your main job isn't to capture upside or chase performance. Your client does not even prioritize that in the first place. Your job is to get your client to their main goal on time, with as much control as possible. That is how you minimize client emotion and assess your performance as an advisor. Client conversations centering around control and safety strive for maximum comfort, while being realistic about the ever-present "what if …?" that can run through a client's head. "What if the economy goes into a recession—a depression, even?" "What if we go to war?" "What if inflation continues?"

No matter how deep the relationship with the client, no matter how much they feel heard, they need you to answer the "how" question directly: "How does my advisor protect me from the 'what if …?'" Part 3 of this book will enable you to answer the "what if …?" and provide investing rules of the road.

In Chapter 8, I'll explain why and how advancing yourself as a behavioral guide is a vital part of the management and marketing of your practice, what your clients will like about it and how to communicate this to your investors.

CHAPTER 8
Communicating the Unique Value-Add of the Behavioral Portfolio to Investors

IN CHAPTER 3, I told the story of our firm's challenges in managing investor behavior. In 2006, we began offering our behavioral portfolio recommendations, built to attempt to navigate diverse market environments. The recommendations have delivered on the objectives that we outlined in Chapter 6. Despite having this portfolio, however, investors during those early years, and prior to building out the behavioral coaching strategy, failed to navigate the markets successfully. Investors left strategies that were included to attempt to be risk-off and moved into high beta strategies just as the Great Financial Crisis was heating up in late 2007 and early 2008. After the crisis, when most of the risk was already out of the markets, money poured out of high beta and into hedged strategies.

Prudence and Cornelius were similarly afflicted. Each time the markets moved, Prudence felt her portfolio needed to change. After each market move, she worked with Cornelius to change her allocation so that she would have done well had she had that portfolio in the previous year or two. What seemed like thoughtful portfolio management was instead performance chasing.

Adding components to portfolios like hedged equities adds a new dimension to managing client behavior as clients see some stocks losing money, while others are protected. One of the most important lessons to take from this book is this: *if you don't build an investor behavior component into your practice, you are Cornelius.* This isn't a prediction. It's a statement of fact made in advance.

Another point that absolutely cannot be missed. Morningstar's behavioral gap—the difference between what funds return and what investors realize—likely applies to most investment advisors. Through an evolved communications approach, reducing or eliminating that gap could add 1.7% annual to investor returns, or more, if investors are able to make counterintuitive decisions and buy (rebalance) after markets have declined.

Even though we have recalibrated portfolios to attempt to address virtually all types of markets, we're only halfway done. Our next step is to help you become a behavioral guide.

Building an investor behavior component is *imperative*. As we have shown, investors' chances of prospering through perpetually vacillating markets are severely challenged and are worse when compounded by poor decision making. But in addition, most areas of traditional financial planning—tax management, portfolio rebalancing, and selecting investments—can easily be automated and don't require an investment advisor.

Something that is not easily automated, and that can significantly boost investor returns, is investor coaching. In other words, your job in some parts of the marketplace is already being replaced by AI. Behavioral coaching brings real value in the form of potential increased returns and improved investor peace of mind.

Learning to be a behavioral coach for your investors sounds like a big change. It is, and it can have a profound impact on your investors' wellbeing. But executing our ideas doesn't require that you turn your practice upside-down. Instead, it means looking into the future to anticipate the behavioral challenges that your investors are likely to encounter, changing portfolios to address each challenge (we've done that!), and explicitly discussing courses of action, in advance, that you and your investors will take.

By talking with your investors about uncertainties before they happen, you remove uncertainty from market stress points and help them know that all is well with their portfolios, even when the financial markets enter chaos. You are laying out the rules of the road.

This part of the book comes with a complete toolset to use for many interactions with your clients, from the initial meeting through planning and portfolio implementation to portfolio reviews. By the conclusion of this part, you'll be armed to act as a behavioral coach for your investors.

In the following chapter, I'll help address investing decision challenges by discussing investor and advisor surveys that we've conducted over the past five years, revealing paths forward for increasing investor confidence and loyalty.

CHAPTER 9
What Investors Tell Us They Know about Investing, and What Can Help Build Confidence in Their Portfolios

What helps immunize investors from poor decision making?

THIS QUESTION IS one we have pursued for years. To gain insights, it's important to query and listen to investors. We have done that through extensive surveys of investors that work with advisors. I'll share with you significant lines of inquiry that we have explored with investors, and then follow that up with specific prescriptions for addressing the weak spots revealed in our surveys.

In the Spring of 2020, as the COVID-19 pandemic was approaching full velocity in the eastern United States and we began Cloroxing our kids' mac and cheese boxes before bringing them in the house, we conducted our first Investor Behavioral Survey,[33] and followed that with two additional surveys of investors and advisors in subsequent years. The surveys, which were conducted among investors who had investable portfolios worth $500,000 or greater and worked with financial advisors, adopted several lines of inquiry:

- Do clients understand the significance of past bear markets?
- What level of market losses are investors willing to tolerate?
- Would investors accept lower returns if they had a lower probability of experiencing significant losses?

- Finally, would having specific plans for market disruption create greater peace of mind regarding investors' financial future?

Do investors understand the significance of past market declines?

In our most recent survey, conducted between May and June 2022, we asked investors: "Looking back, we have experienced periods of significant market turmoil. To the best of your knowledge, what were maximum stock losses during the Great Depression, the Financial Crisis, and the pandemic?" (See Figure 9.1)

Figure 9.1: Investors were asked what level of declines was associated with the stock market losses during the Great Depression, the Great Financial Crisis, and the Covid-19 pandemic, revealing that they generally lacked accurate knowledge of these events

	No decline	Less than 10% decline	10-39% decline	40-59% decline	60-79% decline	80% or greater decline	I don't know
The Great Depression 1929-1933	2%	2%	16%	18%	20%	24%	19%
The financial crisis of 2008-2009	1%	7%	36%	29%	11%	3%	13%
The global pandemic since March 2020	7%	20%	39%	11%	8%	4%	11%

The results showed that only 25% of investors understood that the stock market fell more than 80% during the Great Depression; 33% correctly identified the loss during the Great Financial Crisis; and 36% identified the loss during the pandemic.

Although all of the investors in our survey worked with a financial advisor and all had investable assets of more than $500,000, most didn't understand how bad things can get in the markets and half felt that their portfolios would fail them if losses reached levels that we saw during the past two bear markets. Why does this matter? Because if investors believe that markets can fall by a certain amount and they later find that their own losses exceed that amount, it likely makes them feel off the rails. I wouldn't refer to this type of emotional decision making as "irrational," but rather "rational fear-based decision making."

CHAPTER 9

Do investors fear that they could outlive their money?

There are a number of behavioral challenges that investors face, including having low or flat returns for an extended period and not fully participating in a market bubble. But the most fundamental fear that investors have is that they will outlive their money. In our 2022 survey, we asked investors: "To what extent are you concerned that you might outlive your money?" Thirty percent (nearly one-third of investors) were somewhat or very concerned (see Figure 9.2).

Figure 9.2: In our survey, 30% of investors indicated that they were somewhat or very concerned about outliving their money

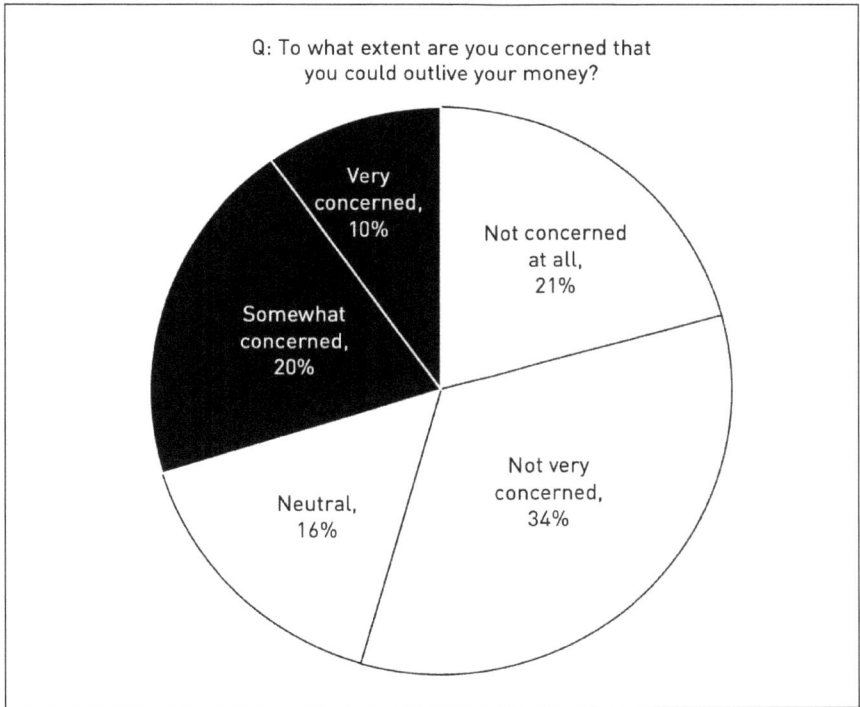

According to advisors, investors' assessments about their ability to be able to sustain themselves during retirement are too optimistic. When we asked advisors, "How concerned do you think your typical client should be about outliving his/her money?", they responded that 55% should be either somewhat or very concerned (see Figure 9.3).

Figure 9.3: When surveyed, advisors were more concerned than their investors that the latter would outlive their assets. Fifty-five percent of advisors felt investors should be somewhat or very concerned

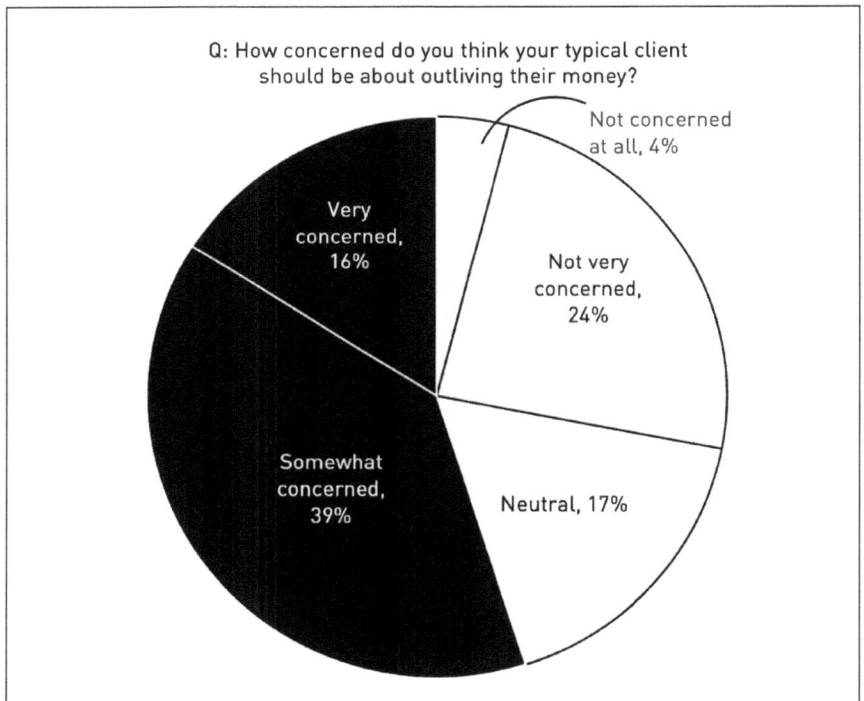

Or course, anxiety is directly related to what's happening in the markets. During bear markets, optimism decreases. In the same survey, we asked investors how a bear market would impact their level of concern that they might outlive their money. Seventy-eight percent indicated that they would be more concerned, with 60% saying that they would be somewhat to much more concerned about outliving their money (see Figure 9.4).

Figure 9.4: Investors' anxiety increases during market turmoil. When asked about the impact of a bear market, 60% said they would be somewhat to much more concerned about outliving their assets

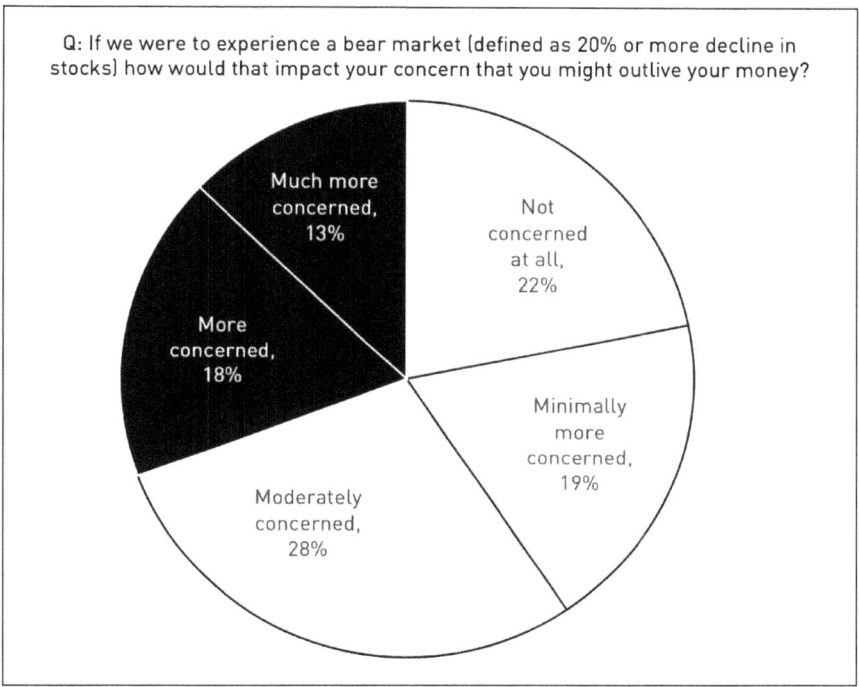

Blake Jordan, a practice management consultant at the Toews Behavioral Investing Institute, suggests the high-stakes issue of running out of money transcends the sphere of behavioral finance and becomes more like a form of grief. There are two forms of grief:

- Primary grief results from an event that causes major life changes to a person (typically death, but it does not have to be).
- Secondary grief relates to additional losses that arise as a result of the primary loss.

According to Blake, running out of money is a life-changing event that can disrupt an investor's entire life. In the event of an uncontemplated loss (a bear market), they may have reactions of shock and anger that constitute a primary grieving pattern around their lifestyle change. In addition to losing money, secondary losses might impact their potential roles in family life, their relationships, and their general level of optimism.

The high impact of preparing investors for inevitable market crises

When juxtaposing the high-stakes issue of investor fear about losses against the conventional approach some advisors take, a communication void the size of a black hole becomes apparent. If only around 25% of investors understand how bad markets can get, how is it possible for them to feel prepared for inevitable market crises?

Our surveys reveal that significant benefits derive from taking on crisis market preparedness. Our most recent survey revealed that 59% of investors had a formal plan of action in place should they experience a bear market (see Figure 9.5).

Figure 9.5: Fifty-nine percent of investors surveyed thought that their advisor had a formal plan of action for a bear market

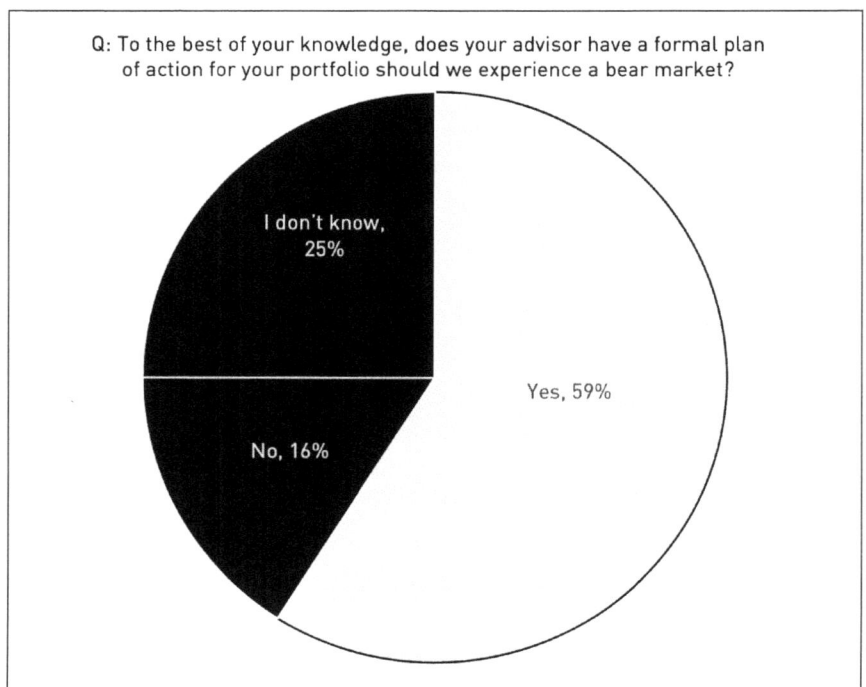

Investors who felt that advisors had an explicit plan in place for bear markets showed a significant increase in both their level of confidence that they would reach their goals and their loyalty to their advisors.

Figure 9.6: Those investors that had a plan of action for a bear market were significantly more confident about reaching their financial goals, with 84% saying they felt more confident

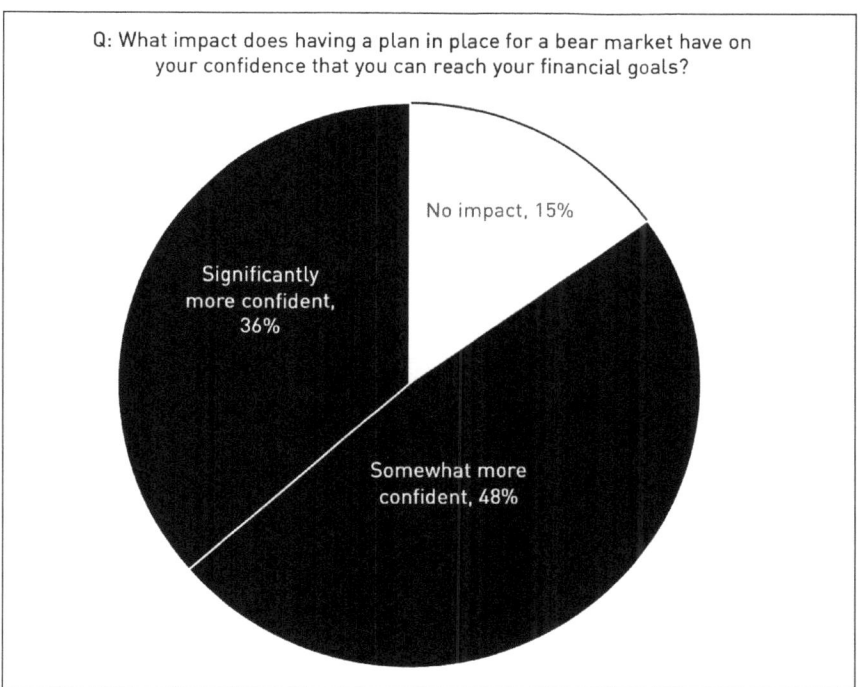

As shown in Figure 9.6, 84% of investors felt somewhat or significantly more confident that they would achieve their financial goals if they had a plan in place for bear markets. And 69% of investors felt increased loyalty to their advisors when they believed that the advisor had reduced the risk of them outliving their money (Figure 9.7).

Figure 9.7: Investors feel more loyalty to advisors that have reduced the risk of them outliving their money, with 69% saying they felt more loyal

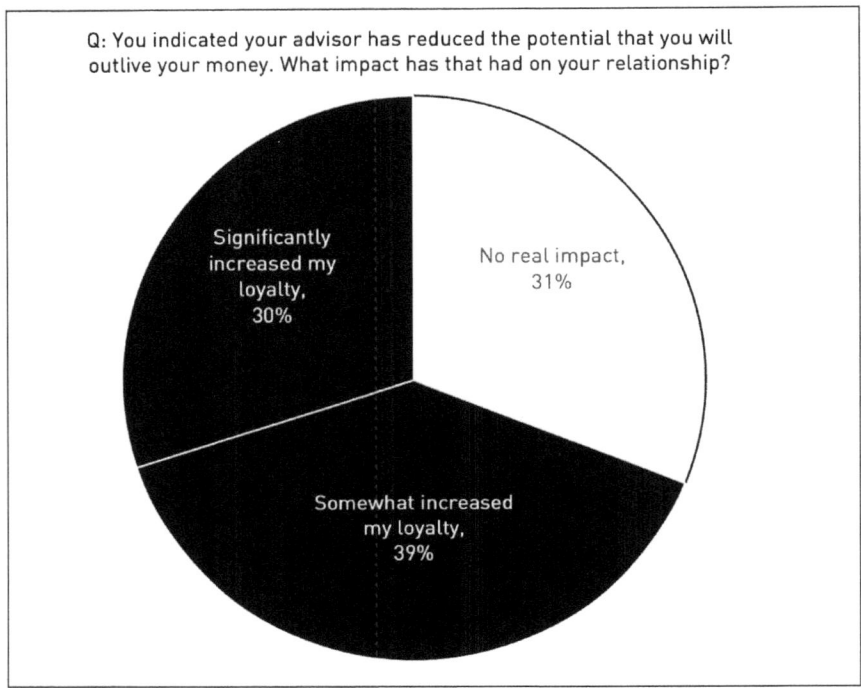

Q: You indicated your advisor has reduced the potential that you will outlive your money. What impact has that had on your relationship?

- Significantly increased my loyalty, 30%
- No real impact, 31%
- Somewhat increased my loyalty, 39%

Crisis preparedness: examining plans for bear markets

So, what's the plan for a bear market? In our 2022 study, we wanted to get more information about the exact plan that investors had for enduring a bear market which they referred to throughout the survey. As shown in Figure 9.8, 67% of investors said that the plan was to "wait it out."

CHAPTER 9

Figure 9.8: Unfortunately, of those investors that felt they had a plan for enduring a bear market, 67% simply planned to "wait it out"

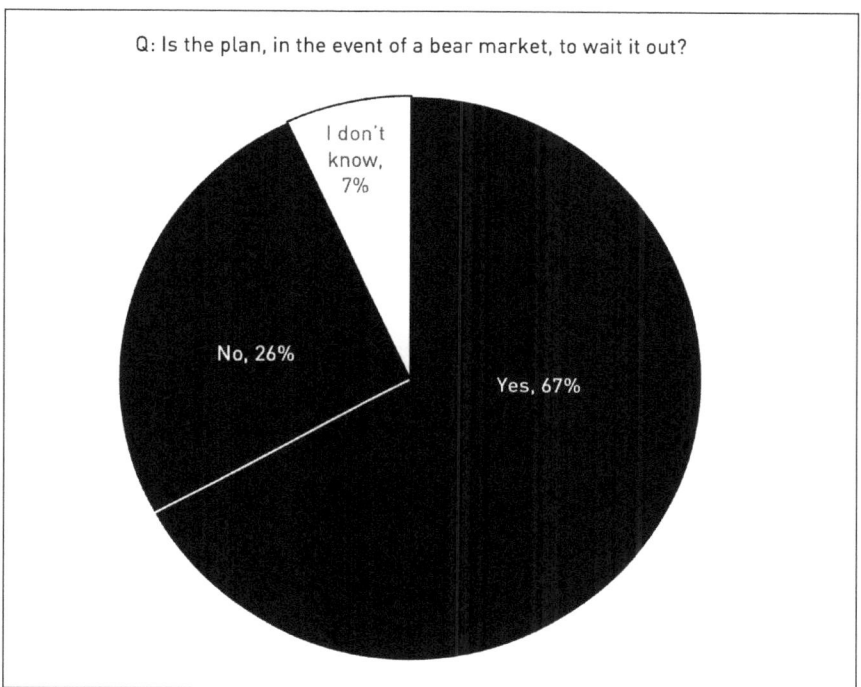

But as we illustrated earlier, "wait it out" doesn't always work, even if investors have a balanced portfolio. Investors who fail to understand the severity of market history also likely fail to comprehend the true historical risks to their portfolios and ability to avoid running out of money. Even those investors who could economically endure multi-year bear markets may be unable to psychologically tolerate those losses or may suffer greatly if they do.

Would investors accept lower returns if they had a lower probability of experiencing significant losses?

In our surveys in 2020 and 2021, we asked investors: "To what extent do you agree or disagree with the following statement? 'I would accept lower returns if I was confident that the probability of experiencing significant losses due to negative market events would be lowered.'"

Figure 9.9: Sixty-five percent of investors surveyed said that they would accept lower returns if they had a lower probability of participating in significant losses. Only 11% of respondents disagreed with the notion

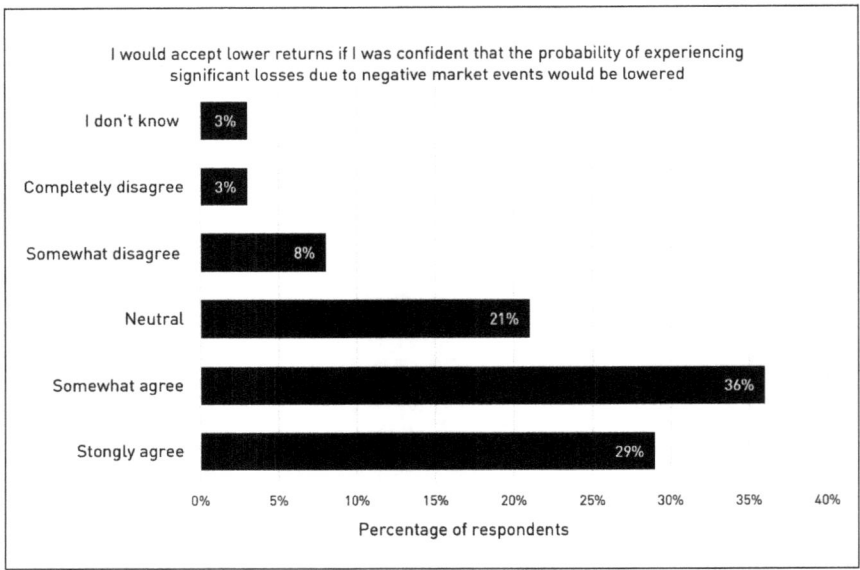

Sixty-five percent either agreed or strongly agreed with the idea of lower returns in order to reduce exposure to significant losses, with only 11% disagreeing and 21% saying they were neutral on the question (as shown in Figure 9.9).

Such a high level of acceptance of this premise—with only 11% disagreeing—confirms that investors support many of the notions of behavioral, all-weather portfolios that have explicit plans in place to attempt to avoid significant losses.

How do we turn investors from the uneducated who don't understand their plans for market turmoil into thoughtful clients who can navigate volatility with confidence? In Chapter 10, I introduce our process for helping clients avoid many of the emotional/reactive challenges of investing.

CHAPTER 10
A Process for Avoiding Emotional/Reactive Decision Making

IN CHAPTER 10, I will discuss specific ways to prepare investors for some of the most common behavioral challenges.

Two thousand years ago, remarkably few people were managing their stock portfolios—principally because stocks didn't exist. We have evolved into the marvelously well-adapted species that we are today. Yet our finely tuned emotions, logic, and intuition help guide us to make perfectly incorrect investment decisions, virtually every time.

Take, for example, the case of recency bias. Investors with recency bias (that would be all of us) assume that investments will continue to perform as they have in the recent past. So, after significant gains, investors pour more money into the same investments. But after investments have moved higher, they can be overvalued and set up for a decline. Big market drops scare investors away because investors assume that the losses will continue. But the best times to invest tend to be after the worst declines.

Much behavioral literature focuses on relatively short-term declines—like the 16 months of extreme losses experienced during the Great Financial Crisis—as a worst case for investor behavior biases. Yes, these types of moves are significant challenges for investors. But even worse than short-duration trends are longer market super-cycles that can last for a generation. These market super-cycles trigger what I have called "Corona Bias," where investors' attitudes to an asset class fundamentally change.

Evolution has taught us to employ experiential learning. If we have a concrete or observed experience, it informs our understanding and beliefs about that phenomenon. If we have repeated experiences over a long period, our confidence in our beliefs increases until, in some cases, we are immovable.

Thirteen years after the 1929 stock market crash, an S&P investor who paid average fees would have had 23% less than they began with. They would have experienced two significant bear markets and witnessed widespread economic despair. During that time, they "learned" that stocks don't help investors. Once they were absolutely convinced, the stock market began the biggest bull market in the past century. During that same period of the Great Depression, when stocks were being pummeled, bonds fared well, helping buffer against losses and providing positive returns to investors. If investors had moved from stocks to bonds near the end of the Great Depression, they were setting themselves up for the longest-duration bond bear market of the century—the 36-bear market that we discussed earlier in this book. Applying our intuitive, experiential learning process to environments like the Great Depression and its aftermath would devastate investors.

Advisors refer to the tendency to make decisions about investing along with the crowd as "irrational behavior." We prefer the perspective of Massachusetts Institute of Technology finance professor Andrew Lo, who writes that "a more accurate term for such behavior might be 'maladaptive'. The flopping of a fish on dry land may seem strange and unproductive, but under water, the same motions are capable of propelling the fish away from its predators."[34] In other words, the experiential learning that benefits us in so many parts of our lives makes us terrible investors.

There are other aspects about how we think that short-circuit our ability to make wise investment decisions. In James Montier's exceptional *Little Book of Behavioral Investing*, he talks about two types of thought processes that we have. Our reflexive thought process is what we automatically engage when we trip and catch ourselves or make instantaneous decisions. This type of thought process is reactive and can be emotional (think Scotty on the Star Trek Enterprise). The second type of thought process is reflective and analytical. To engage in this type of thought process, we need to focus as we might when doing a math problem. This process tends to be less emotional (think Spock). According to Montier, we are most likely to rely upon our Scotty-like reactive thought process "when the problem is ill-structured and complex; when information is incomplete, ambiguous, and changing; when the goals are ill-defined, shifting, or competing; and when the stress is high, because either time constraints and/or high stakes are involved."[35] This list describes investing, as shown in Figure 10.1.

Figure 10.1: The characteristics of investing create a tendency for investors to utilize reactive rather than contemplative thought processes

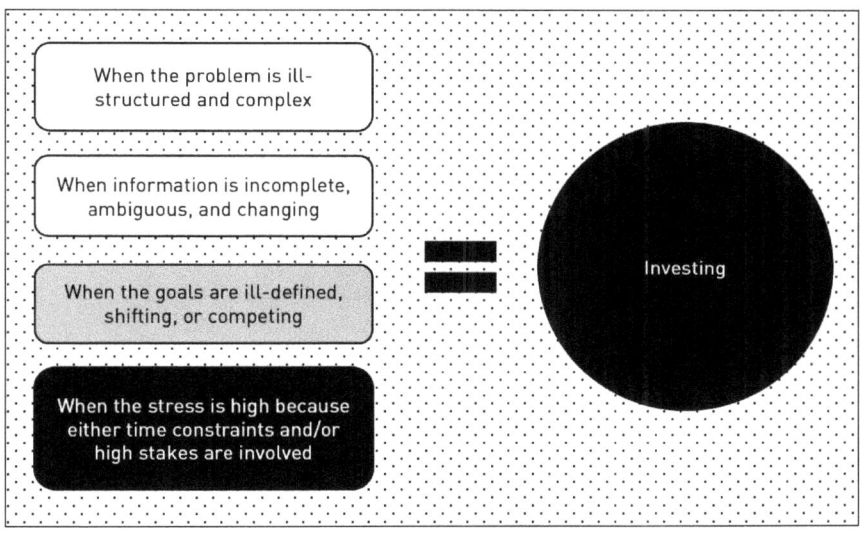

To be a good investor, you must acknowledge your inner Scotty (recognize your decision-making biases) and embrace your inner Spock (make rational, often counterintuitive choices). How?

We recommend that advisors lay out a decision-making process for investors:

- Identify the market or behavioral challenge.
- Look at the data behind similar occurrences from the past.
- Determine probable outcomes of the situation based on the evidence.
- Review pre-commitments regarding the issue.
- Make decisions based on data/probable outcomes.

What just happened when you read that? If you're like me, you were put into a Spock state of mind! This process asks investors to make decisions based on data and plans that you have predetermined for when market disruptions occur. Another way of describing these thought processes is the quick brain (the hare) and the slow brain (the tortoise).

Figure 10.2: There are two types of thought processes that we use: the quick brain (the hare) and the slow brain (the tortoise)

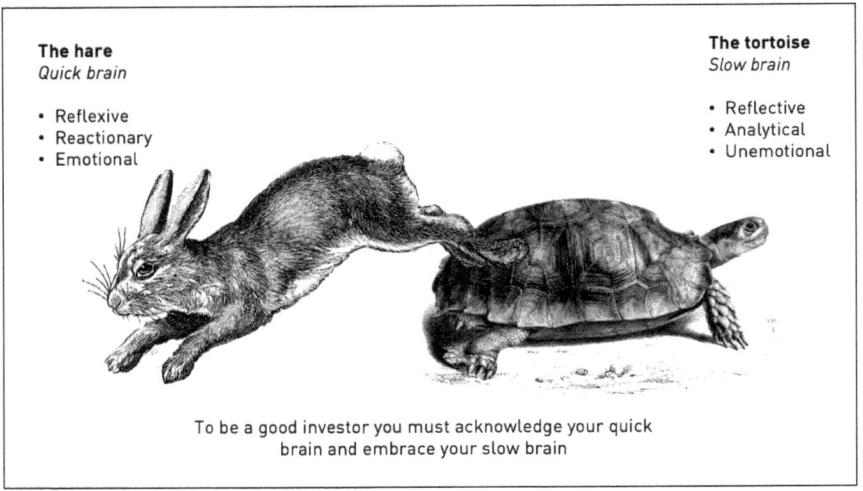

To be a good investor you must acknowledge your quick brain and embrace your slow brain

Solutions for investors' biggest behavioral challenges

In this section, I will introduce the Investment Owner's Manual (Figure 10.3)—a core tool for advisors to use in their practices in an attempt to proactively communicate solutions for market challenges that investors will likely face.

Early on in our efforts to manage investor behavior, we struggled to find a way to communicate our investor behavioral framework to clients. We were interested in a simple way to introduce our ideas. We also wanted to have a document for clients to refer to when behavioral challenges emerged.

Our first step toward solving this challenge was a series of workshops on behavioral finance that were designed for investment advisors. Through these workshops, and with the help of investment advisors, we identified the six biggest investing challenges for investors, as well as a suite of solutions to address them. The workshops also communicated that investors' intuition served them poorly when making investment decisions and proposed a process that advisors and their investors should use to make investment decisions.

Our next step was to reformat this material to make it investor appropriate and compile it into a document that we now refer to as the "Investment Owner's Manual."

Figure 10.3: The Investment Owner's Manual is a proactive tool for helping investors make investment decisions

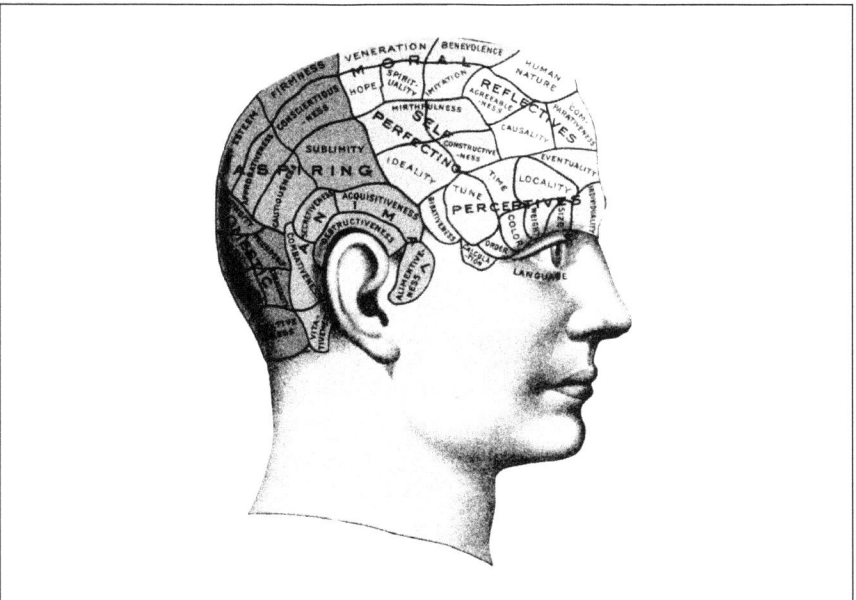

The Investment Owner's Manual is an anchor investor behavioral tool for your clients. It talks about the two types of thought processes that investors use and the need for Spock-like thinking. It lays out the decision-making process that we discussed. It provides an overview of how you build portfolios based on the concepts of the behavioral portfolio that we discussed. It then moves on to explain to investors what we have identified as the six biggest behavioral investing challenges.

To create this list of investors' biggest behavioral challenges, I drew upon literature discussing investor biases. We also surveyed the 1,200-plus advisors who work with our firm and weighed our own challenges over the past two decades. The list of behavioral challenges, shown in Figure 10.4, is not comprehensive. Instead, we were most interested in tackling the major obstacles produced by the markets that could potentially cause investors to derail from their plans.

Figure 10.4: There are many behavioral challenges for investors. Six of the most significant are shown below. The Investment Owner's Manual outlines a decision-making process for each

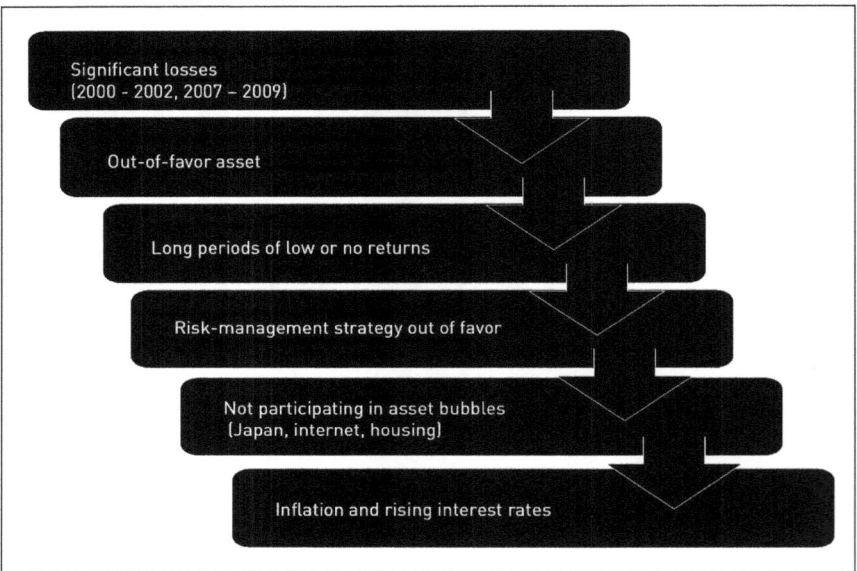

Conventional portfolios are built by advisors who hope that bad things don't happen. When they do, these advisors ask investors to ride them out. Clients taking a conventional approach require that markets perform well (or at least not horribly) in order to succeed. It follows, then, that these advisors must lean optimistic when discussing possibilities for their portfolios in order to attract business. When market challenges emerge, these advisors and their clients can only hope the trajectory changes. But hope is not a strategy.

And beyond that, what is most disorienting for investors who have not fully contemplated negative market events is the unknown. "When will the trajectory of the markets change to my advantage?" "How bad will it get?" "How long will this last?" "If it gets worse, or lasts longer, will I be destitute?" When fearful minds are confronted with overwhelming media pessimism, they panic.

The Investment Owner's Manual guides advisors to take the opposite approach. During the process of acquiring an investor, an advisor should expressly discuss worst-case scenarios. Instead of telling clients that markets *may* move against them, we suggest that advisors tell their investors that—especially for those with long-term investment horizons—investors *will* likely experience all six of our behavioral challenges, some of them multiple times.

By considering worst-case scenarios during portfolio planning, explaining to investors what has been done to anticipate negative markets, and elucidating a plan of action that you and the investor will take during negative markets, most of the "unknown" of market events is removed.

As we have mentioned throughout this book, however, our guidance may go even further than just curbing investor biases. Investors who are trained to understand the counterintuitive nature of investment decision making, and who have a plan laid out in advance—as we do—may *improve* performance above the return of the markets. Let me explain.

In April 2009, days from the bottom of the second-worst stock decline in the past 100 years, I wrote in a letter to our advisor community that it was "a good time to invest in stocks due to their bargain prices." The commentary went on to argue the case that stocks were poised to rally strongly. I got a call from an advisor who was surprised by our message. "As an asset manager who avoided most of the recent losses, shouldn't you be focused on current risks?" he asked.

I defended our commentary with a simple message: "Our job is to unveil for investors what their emotions aren't letting them see, not reinforce their own preconceptions, and currently investors are failing to see that stocks are a screaming buy." That message, if delivered by advisors at the time, could potentially have added significant value for investors who heeded their recommendation. From April 2009 through the end of 2017, the S&P 500 rose 303%—a tripling in value in less than nine years.

This wasn't a brilliant market call. It was simply reverse thinking the markets. Think about what everyone will typically do in your situation. Then do the opposite. The more compelling the crowd's behavior, the more compelling the investment case for doing the opposite.

So what if, in addition to removing market unknowns and laying out a plan in advance, we were able to show investors how they could benefit from market disruptions? We believe that we can, and I have outlined a six-step process for making decisions to achieve this for each behavioral challenge (see Figure 10.5). The logic will become clearer as we talk about the specific solutions for each behavioral challenge.

A suite of solutions to address behavioral challenges

Figure 10.5: For each investor behavior challenge, there is a six-step decision-making process designed to reduce biased decision making

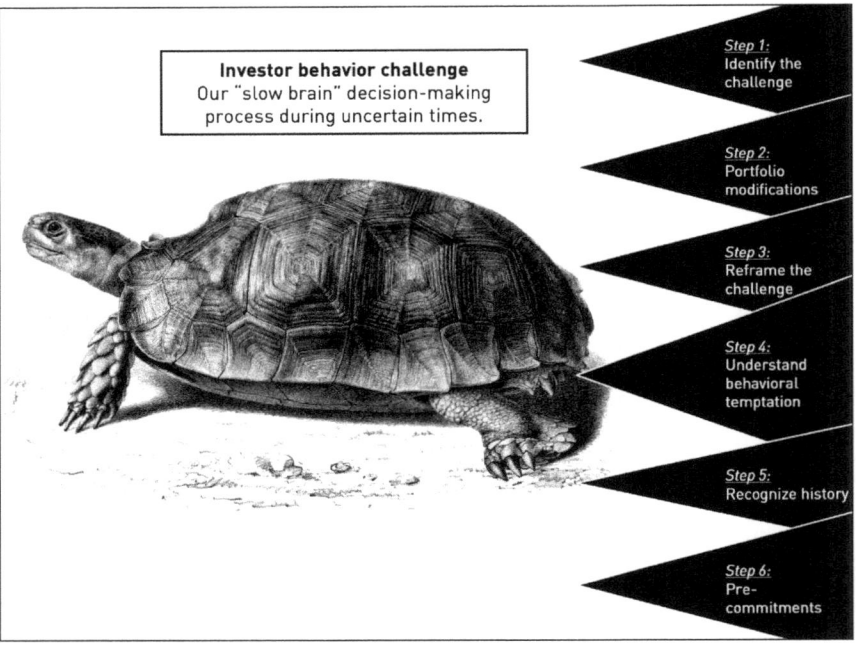

Investors don't love the idea of being told that their behavior needs to be managed in order for them to avoid making decisions that will compromise their plans. Instead, think of the best behavior management as invisible and built into the structure of your practice.

When you want to avoid eating Oreos late at night, is it better to set up some elaborate reward and punishment system for yourself, or simply not have the Oreos in the house in the first place?

That's how you should think of managing behavior. Build a communication, investment, and planning strategy where the Oreos are not in the house to eat. By avoiding significant drawdowns and communicating why avoiding drawdowns has such positive implications on the upside, you are naturally building an avoidance to performance chasing and recency bias.

I'll discuss these behavioral challenges individually. But first I need to explain the concept of an investor pre-commitment. The way you have curated the portfolio to address the possibility of each behavioral challenge helps investors understand what you have done to anticipate each challenge. The investor pre-commitment tells clients what action both you and the client will be taking when the behavioral challenge emerges. By using the term "pre-commitment," we want to convey to the investor that they need to understand and accept the plan in advance of it happening. Another way of thinking of this is conveying "our action plan."

The first behavioral challenge: significant losses

We have talked a lot about losses, and these are the first challenge that most of us think about when considering the behavioral obstacles our clients face. Our discussion on comprehensively addressing risk changes the way that advisors approach risk management.

The Investment Owner's Manual elucidates your plan for significant losses. Don't downplay the potential for and size of losses that the markets can produce. Be radically transparent. Discuss the 84% stock market loss during the Great Depression, which took 14 years to recover from. Highlight the more recent 50% stock market decline during the dotcom bust and the recent 50%-plus stock pullback during the Great Financial Crisis. I suggest making the statement to each client that: "During your investing life, the markets likely *will* produce losses of greater than 50%, potentially more than once."

To help make this point to your investors, the figure presented in Chapter 2 and reproduced again below (Figure 10.6) showing that every decade dating back to 1900 has produced bear markets of approximately 20% or greater is included in the Investment Owner's Manual.

Figure 10.6: Every decade since 1900 has seen a bear market of nearly 20% at least once, with an average of two bear markets per decade and average losses of 36%

	Years	Number of bear markets	DJIA percentage decline				
Significant declines are part of the fluctuations of the markets	1900s	3	-49%	-46%	-32%		
	1910s	2	-47%	-40%			
	1920s	1	-47%				
	1930s	5	-89%	-52%	-37%	-23%	-22%
	1940s	1	-24%				
	1950s	1	-19%				
	1960s	2	-37%	-27%			
	1970s	2	-45%	-27%			
	1980s	2	-36%	-24%			
	1990s	2	-21%	-19%			
	2000s	2	-54%	-38%			
	2010s	1	-19%				
	2020s	2	-37%	-22%			
	Average number of bear markets		**Average loss**				
	2		**-36%**				

Solutions

Portfolio modifications

Portfolio modifications made to address significant loss involve including hedged equities in a sufficiently significant allocation to help lessen declines (see Figure 10.7). The key is to position portfolios to defend against the momentum of the markets and seize on opportunities presented by the crowd's poor decision-making ability. By avoiding market downturns, you not only lessen losses, but may create an opportunity to benefit by positioning the portfolio to possibly gain during market rebounds. Should that strategy play out, the uncorrelated portion of the portfolio may realize a net benefit from the market drop.

Figure 10.7: The portfolio modification to address significant losses is to allocate a portion—or as much as 50%—of stocks to hedged equities.

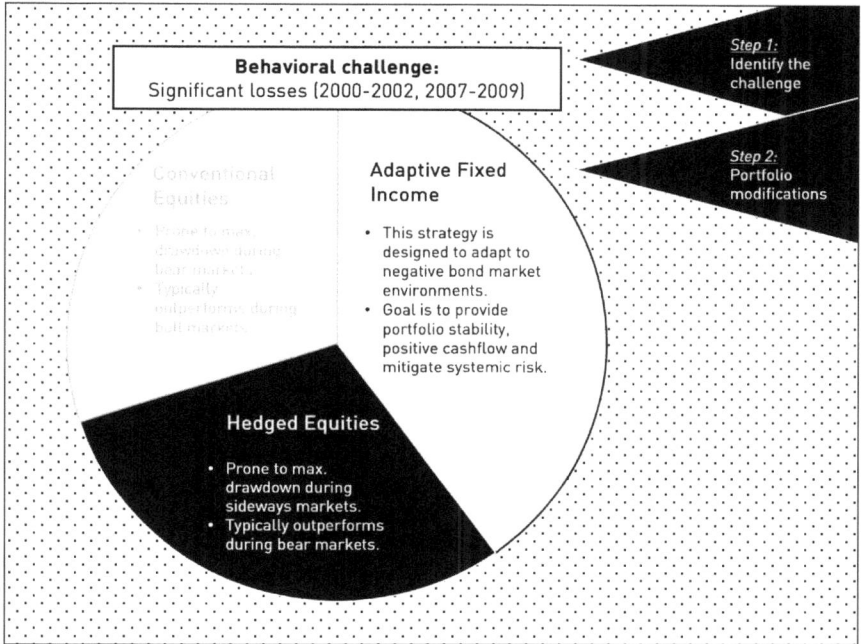

Recognize history

What has been the outcome in the past when markets have made significant declines? As shown in Figure 10.8, extreme market declines are likely to be followed by extreme market gains. In the eight prior instances of declines of 30% or more in the Dow Jones Industrial average, the average rebound was 91% over an average duration of 2.1 years.

Figure 10.8: Extreme market declines have historically been followed by extreme market gains (average 91%)

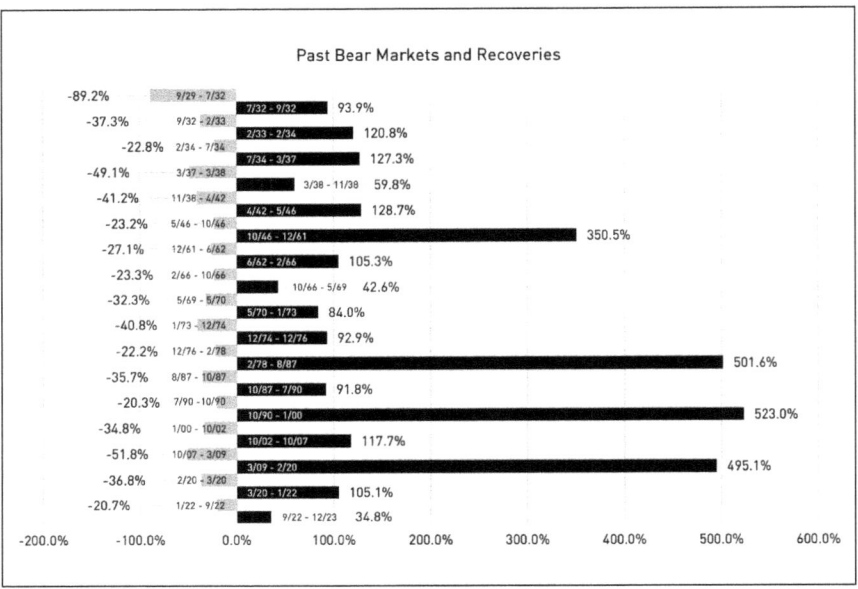

Understand the behavioral temptation and reframe the challenge

Due to the near-universal tendency toward recency bias, the temptation is to leave stocks during or after significant declines under the assumption that they will continue to move lower. One way to reframe this challenge is to think of stocks as being "on sale" (see Figure 10.9). Any time other products have drastically reduced prices, as they do on Black Friday, we rush to buy more. It should be the same for stocks. This is the time to think not about selling, but about buying.

Figure 10.9: The temptation for investors after significant losses is to exit stocks. This behavioral challenge can be reframed as a chance to buy stocks at bargain prices, like on Black Friday!

Pre-commitments

As shown in Figure 10.10, as an advisor, your job is to rebalance the portfolio into assets with steep declines to take advantage of Black Friday prices. Likely, this will be done on a systematic basis that prevents your own recency bias from being triggered. For investors, they must be able to embrace the opportunity presented by steep declines and avoid selling at the bottom.

Figure 10.10: The pre-commitment agreed with investors should allow you to rebalance portfolios into assets with steep declines

When markets face steep declines

Us: Systematically re-balance portfolio into assets with steep declines and take advantage of "Black Friday" sales prices

You: Embrace potential opportunity

Step 6: Pre-commitments

How big has the opportunity to take advantage of bargain stocks been? Let's look at the worst decline in the past 100 years in the US: the Great Depression. Investors tend to think of the period between 1929 and 1942 as one dismal economic experience. Instead, it was two severe declines, each followed by fierce market rallies. The heart-stopping decline of 86% between 1929 and 1932 was followed by a rally of 354% over the following five years. Markets turned lower again between 1937 and 1942, but then gained 1253% over the subsequent 14 years (see Figure 10.11).

Stock declines during the Great Depression caused severe economic losses to many investors. Although the potential for future profit was there, one could argue that many investors could never have psychologically persevered and held stocks throughout these gyrations to realize eventual gains. On the other hand, if a portion of portfolios is poised to potentially benefit from declines, it may cause a psychological shift for investors.

Figure 10.11: Illustrating the potential gains from buying at bargain prices, stocks soared higher after declines during the Great Depression, increasing 354% between 1932 and 1937, and 1253% after 1942

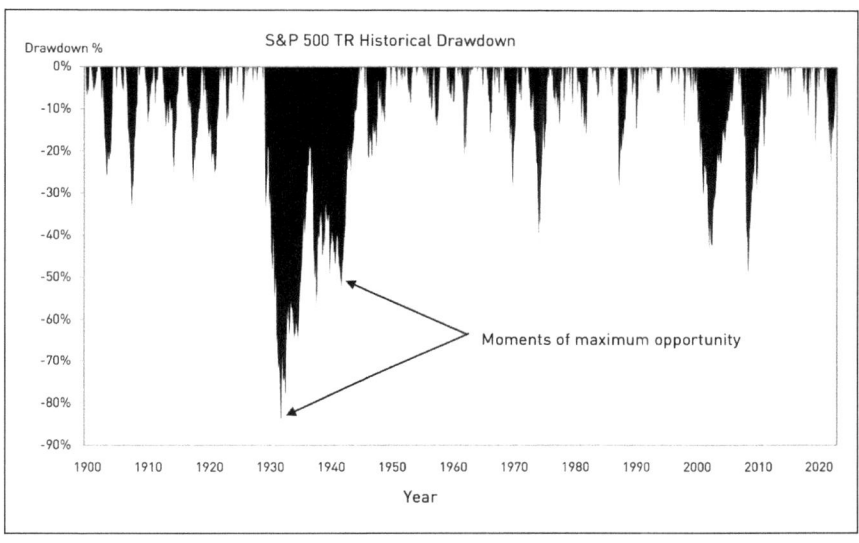

When almost everyone believes something and they are mistaken, this can be an opportunity for the few who believe otherwise. Advisors who adopt a conscious pattern of opposing the crowd through investor training and pre-commitments are positioned to prosper in that market environment, when everyone else is struggling.

The second behavioral challenge: long periods of low or no returns

People not in the investment industry might find this a non-issue that is easily overcome. Investment advisors know otherwise. When markets make big declines, investors understand why they're not seeing their portfolios increase in value. When there are no headlines about market disruptions and portfolios go nowhere, investors tend to blame their advisors and look for places where they can get at least some gains. This is especially true if a widely watched benchmark like the S&P 500 is gaining, but diversified portfolios that hold small/mid-cap stocks and international stocks are stagnant.

There is the added factor that novice investors who understand that stocks have moved up 11% per year on average have the expectation that this will happen every year. While 11% is the average, it turns out that stocks rarely move up exactly 11%. As is illustrated in Figure 10.12. advisors may be surprised to learn that over the past 100 years, the S&P 500 has only returned 11% (with rounding) twice!

Figure 10.12: Despite averaging 11% per year since 1984, stocks have only returned exactly that amount (with rounding) twice

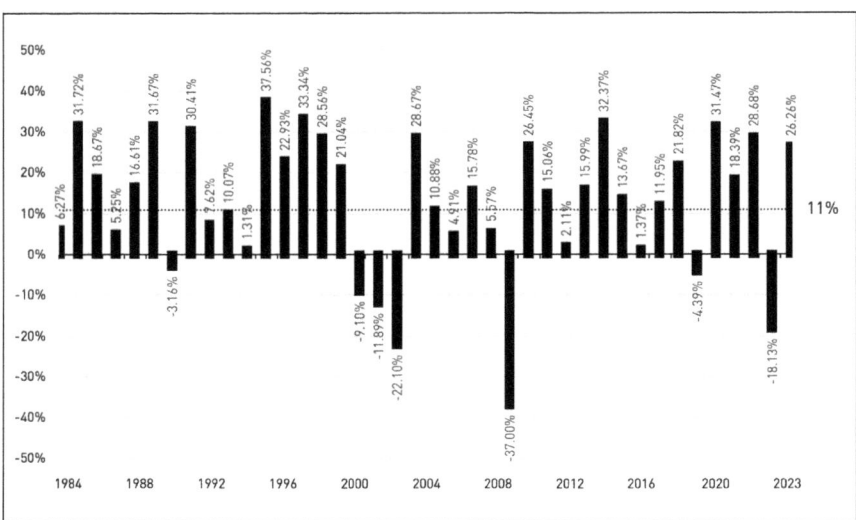

When portfolios languish, investors are vulnerable to *action bias*. James Montier illustrated action bias by citing a study on soccer goalkeepers:

> Imagine you're a goalkeeper facing a penalty kick. As the striker hits the ball, is it best to dive left, right or stay in the centre? In research, goalkeepers have been found to dive one way or the other a massive 94 percent of the time. Yet the optimal strategy is to remain unmoved in the middle of the goal.[36]

We have an innate desire to act to give ourselves a sense of control. We are hardwired to seek instant gratification. For investors, the outcome of taking action tends to mirror the performance-chasing results illustrated by the Morningstar *Mind the Gap* study: lower performance.

Just like declining markets, stagnant markets are pervasive throughout history. Since 1915, the chance that any three-year period of the S&P 500 will return less than 3% per year is one in six. Similarly, the odds that investors will experience five-year periods with less than a 3% per year return are one in six. The message to investors should be that portfolios going nowhere is not uncommon.

Solutions

This doesn't mean that all parts of a portfolio will be stagnant at the same time. As is illustrated in Figure 10.13, my portfolio recommendation is to hold and maintain exposure to uncorrelated assets and management styles. This differs from conventional portfolios in that strategy diversification potentially adds another type of return stream that may not correlate with conventional asset classes.

Figure 10.13: My portfolio recommendation to address long periods of low or no returns is to hold and maintain exposure to uncorrelated assets and management styles

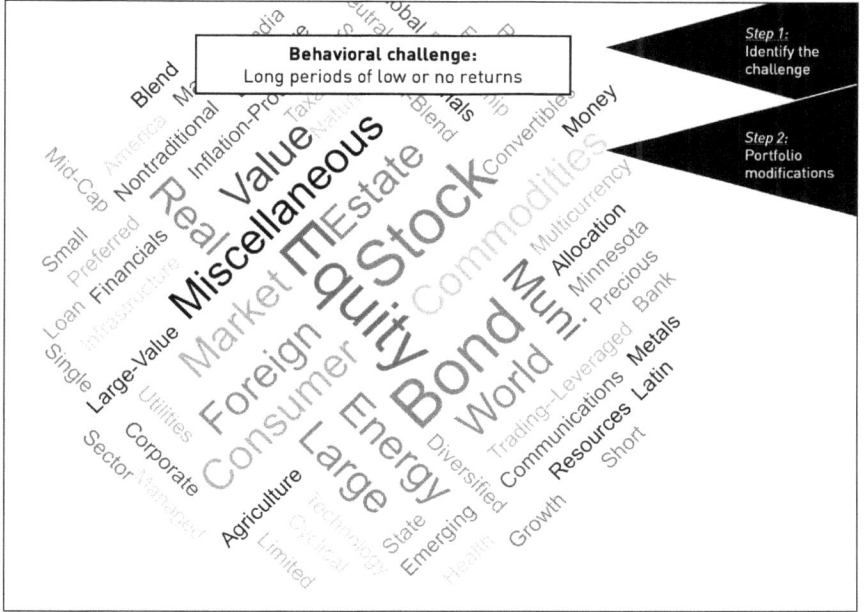

For significant declines, we were able to lessen fears by removing the unknown aspects about them. We were also able to frame certain strategies as potentially benefiting from declines. In a similar vein, by creating a strong expectation of stagnant markets, investors may be less likely to be surprised when they occur.

Recognize history

Stagnant markets, just like declining markets, generally point to sizable gains ahead. Looking all the way back to 1860, we asked the question: what gains typically follow sideways markets?

When stocks have returned less than 3% per year for any three-year period, the average gain over the following three years was 43%, or 11.6% per year. If stocks moved nowhere and gained less than 3% per year for five years, the average gain over the next five years was 83%, or 12% per year. And in the rare instances when stocks earned less than 3% per year for 10 years, the average gain over the next 10 years was 219%, or 12% per year (see Figure 10.14).[37]

Figure 10.14: When stocks go sideways, they can have powerful rebounds in the following years. The longer that they go nowhere, the bigger the gain at the conclusion of the period of stagnation

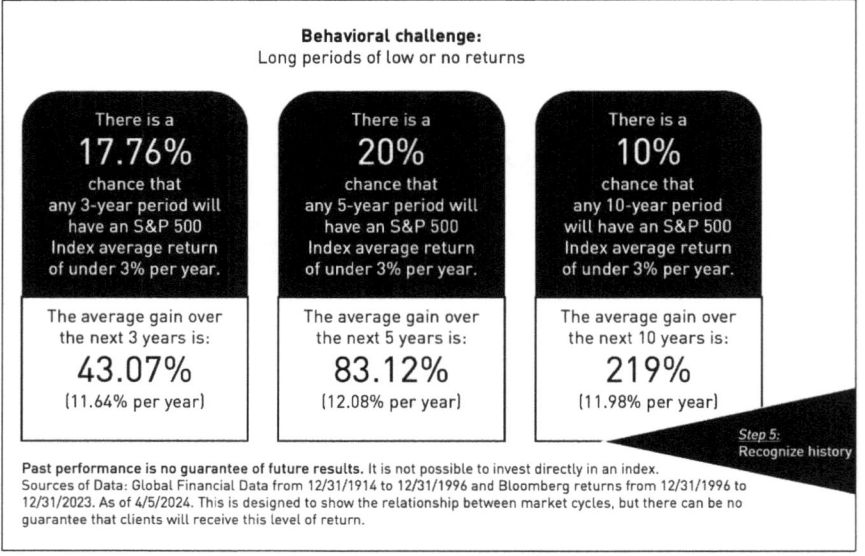

Understand behavioral temptation and reframe the challenge

Long periods of low or no returns are an exceedingly difficult challenge for investors and may require a Vulcan mind-meld—in part because they can last for such a long time. The temptation to seek any gains, even if minimal, may cause investors to leave the rails of a long-term growth-based plan without any realized means of returning to a growth-based portfolio. As shown in Figure 10.15, help investors understand that long-term stagnant periods in asset prices are normal and are typically followed by high-return markets. One device that has worked for advisors is to think of long-term stagnant periods as a spring: the longer the period, the more compressed it becomes, until ultimately it springs much higher.

Figure 10.15: The behavioral temptation after a period of long or no return is to leave a well-planned portfolio. Reframe the challenge by thinking of stagnant periods as a spring that will eventually propel markets higher

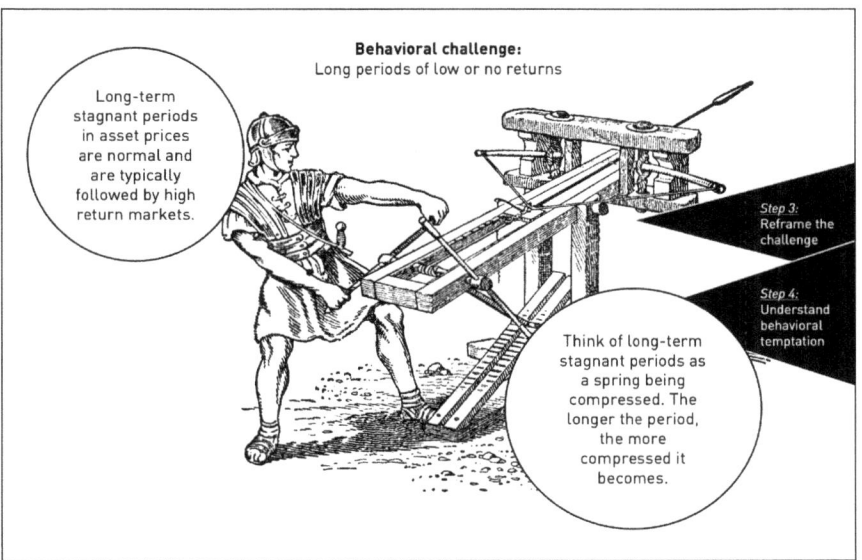

Pre-commitment

The pre-commitment that you will make as an advisor is to monitor and maintain a portfolio blend that aims to help investors meet their goals (see Figure 10.16). The pre-commitment of investors is to practice rigorous patience and do nothing, *nada, niente*!

Figure 10.16: During periods of low or no returns, the action to take is no action at all. Practice rigorous patience

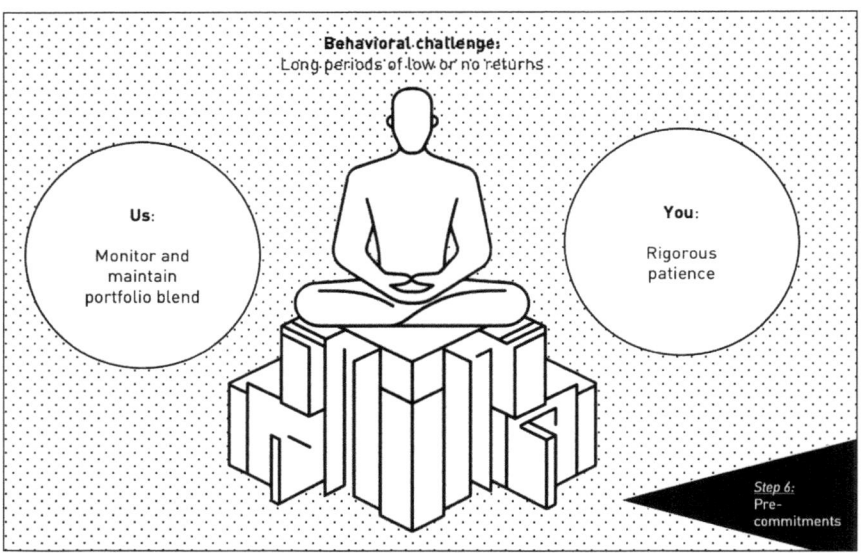

The third behavioral challenge: underperforming strategies, managers, or assets

Ask any investment professional who advises clients about investor behavior and this topic will likely rank high on their list of disruptive investor biases. Both conventional and behaviorally modified portfolios inevitably create situations where one manager or one asset class does well, while others show no gains or even losses.

Behemoth investment consulting firm Callan updates its Callan Periodic

Table of Investment Returns annually. For the purposes of this book, we recreated a table based on the data shown in Figure 10.17. The table breaks down performance by asset class each year over the past 20 years and the disparity between different asset classes can be stark.

Figure 10.17: This table shows how extreme the variations are between asset classes from one year to the next.[38] The emerging markets category is highlighted to show the dramatic variations in ranking that are possible

2014	2015	2016	2017	2018	2019	2020	2021	2022	2023
Real estate: 15.02%	Large cap equity: 1.38%	Small cap equity: 21.31%	Emerging market equity: 37.28%	Cash equivalent: 1.87%	Large cap equity: 31.49%	Small cap equity: 19.96%	Large cap equity: 28.71%	Cash equivalent: 1.46%	Large cap equity: 26.29%
Large cap equity: 13.69%	U.S. fixed income: 0.55%	High yield: 17.13%	Developed ex-U.S. equity: 24.21%	U.S. fixed income: 0.01%	Small cap equity: 25.52%	Large cap equity: 18.40%	Real estate: 26.09%	High yields: -11.19%	Developed ex-U.S. equity: 17.94%
U.S. fixed income: 5.97%	Cash equivalent: 0.05%	Large cap equity: 11.96%	Large cap equity: 21.83%	High yield: -2.08%	Developed ex-U.S. equity: 22.49%	Emerging market equity: 18.31%	Small cap equity: 14.82%	U.S. fixed income: -13.01%	Small cap equity: 16.93%
Small cap equity: 4.89%	Real estate: -0.79%	Emerging market equity: 11.19%	Small cap equity: 14.65%	Global ex-U.S. fixed: -2.15%	Real estate: 21.91%	Global ex-U.S. fixed: 10.11%	Developed ex-U.S. equity: 12.62%	Developed ex-U.S. equity: -14.29%	High yield: 13.44%
High yield: 2.45%	Developed ex-U.S. equity: -3.04%	Real estate: 4.06%	Global ex-U.S. fixed: 10.51%	Large cap equity: -4.38%	Emerging market equity: 18.44%	Developed ex-U.S. equity: 7.59%	High yield: 5.28%	Large cap equity: -18.11%	Emerging market equity: 9.83%
Cash equivalent: 0.03%	Small cap equity: -4.41%	Developed ex-U.S. equity: 2.75%	Real estate: 10.36%	Real estate: -5.63	High yield: 14.32%	U.S. fixed income: 7.51%	Cash equivalent: 0.05%	Global ex-U.S. fixed: -18.70	Real estate: 9.67%
Emerging market equity: -2.19%	High yield: -4.47%	U.S. fixed income: 2.65%	High yield: 7.50%	Small cap equity: -11.01%	U.S. fixed income: 8.72%	High yield: 7.11%	U.S. fixed income: -1.54%	Emerging market equity: -20.09%	Global ex-U.S. fixed: 5.72%
Global ex-U.S. fixed: -3.09%	Global ex-U.S. fixed: -6.02%	Global ex-U.S. fixed: 1.49%	U.S. fixed income: 3.54%	Developed ex-U.S. equity: -14.09%	Global ex-U.S. fixed: 5.09%	Cash equivalent: 0.67%	Emerging market equity: -2.54%	Small cap equity: -20.44%	U.S. fixed income: 5.53%
Developed ex-U.S. equity: -4.32%	Emerging market equity: -14.92%	Cash equivalent: 0.33%	Cash equivalent: 0.86%	Emerging market equity: -14.57%	Cash equivalent: 2.28%	Real estate: -9.04%	Global ex-U.S. fixed: -7.05%	Real estate: -25.10%	Cash equivalent: 5.01%

Among the easiest divergent paths to spot are emerging market stocks. Emerging markets are part of many portfolios. Their inclusion is due to a possible higher long-term return when compared to developed country stocks. But they also provide a level of diversification to portfolios. For years, some of the most respected market prognosticators have argued that emerging markets stocks are undervalued and have the highest likely returns when compared to other types of stocks. Inexplicably and dramatically, however, emerging markets over the past three years have ranked near or in the bottom half of asset class returns. Meanwhile, large cap US stocks—considered to be overvalued and set up for a fall by many—have ranked at the top for two of the last three years. It's one thing for an investor to see one part of their portfolio earn slightly less than another. It dismays investors, however, to see one fund or category of funds lose money when other stocks are making substantial gains.

Advisors will tell you that, for clients that pay attention to detail and like to understand all aspects of their portfolios, the underperformance of one asset—even if it only makes up a minute percentage of an overall portfolio—can dominate an entire quarterly or annual review meeting. What's going on?

Figure 10.18: Emerging markets stocks between 2013 and 2016 illustrate how challenging underperforming assets can be. They returned -9.9% cumulatively during a time when the S&P 500 earned 72%. The following year, in 2017, emerging stocks were the top return asset class, with a gain of 37%

Year	Emerging Markets Stocks	S&P 500
2013	-2.60%	32.75%
2014	-2.19%	14.89%
2015	-14.92%	5.52%
2016	11.19%	6.89%
Cumulative Return	-9.9%	72.0%

Looking at Figure 10.18 with the benefit of hindsight, it might seem obvious that emerging markets stocks, which trailed the S&P 500 severely over three years, might be poised to rebound and do very well. However, investors living through this level of underperformance can experience extreme frustration, especially if it plays out over multiple years.

Each year, during reviews with their advisor, clients make a mental note that one investment has done poorly. Each year, the advisor states something like: "Yes, but we expect it will do better than average in the coming years." But then the asset fails to deliver.

At some point in their communications, the client finally asserts: "I want out of that investment." From their point of view, if the advisor had just listened to them during their previous visits, they'd be much better off. Advisors who are entrenched in their views will counter: "Let's give it six more months to see if it turns around." This proclamation sets the advisor and client on a path for conflict and bad decision making if things don't turn around quickly.

One of my favorite biases is the "turkey illusion": the tendency to extrapolate the past to predict the future. A turkey sees the farmer as a source of food—and never anticipates Thanksgiving.[39] That's exactly what happened with emerging markets stocks at the end of 2016. One of the most respected market prognosticators is iconic firm GMO, which manages $60 billion for institutional investors. Each year, it issues a seven-year forecast. At the end of 2016, just as clients might have been forcing their advisors to exit an emerging markets position, GMO was predicting that the real (after inflation) returns over the next six years would be higher than those in any other major asset class. And the returns in 2017? Before considering inflation, emerging markets stocks gained 37.3%, while US stocks returned 21.1% that year.[40]

And so it has gone for emerging markets stocks. For years, they will be either the best or the worst asset class, only to reverse course and whipsaw investors who are tempted or tortured by their returns.

Keeping investors in underperforming *asset classes* is a constant challenge for advisors. But as difficult as that may be, keeping investors with underperforming *investment managers* is even more difficult.

Asset class underperformance can be explained by pointing to fundamental data. Emerging markets may have low P/E ratios or greater projected growth, which is persuasive enough to justify continuing to hold them despite long periods when they trail broader markets. Rarely, however, is there quantifiable data that supports staying with a poorly performing manager. In many cases, investors own an asset manager because an advisor recommended them. If the average emerging markets manager earned 37% in 2017 but the emerging markets manager that *you* recommended only grew by 20%, it reflects poorly on your choice. When underperformance extends over several years, advisors may be quick to change to avoid looking foolish.

It's virtually guaranteed that top-performing managers will fail to stay in the top performance quartile all of the time; and it's probable that any fund or strategy will spend some time in the bottom quartile of performers at some point during a five-year period.

Solutions

Our suite of solutions includes how you have addressed the possibility of asset class or manager underperformance through portfolio construction, as well as the action that you and your investor will take when managers or assets trail. As shown in Figure 10.19, the portfolio solution is to ensure that multiple managers and asset classes are used within the portfolio. When one manager underperforms, another may outperform.

Figure 10.19: Portfolios should hold multiple assets across a spectrum of different managers and asset types in order to reduce the effects of the underperformance of any one investment

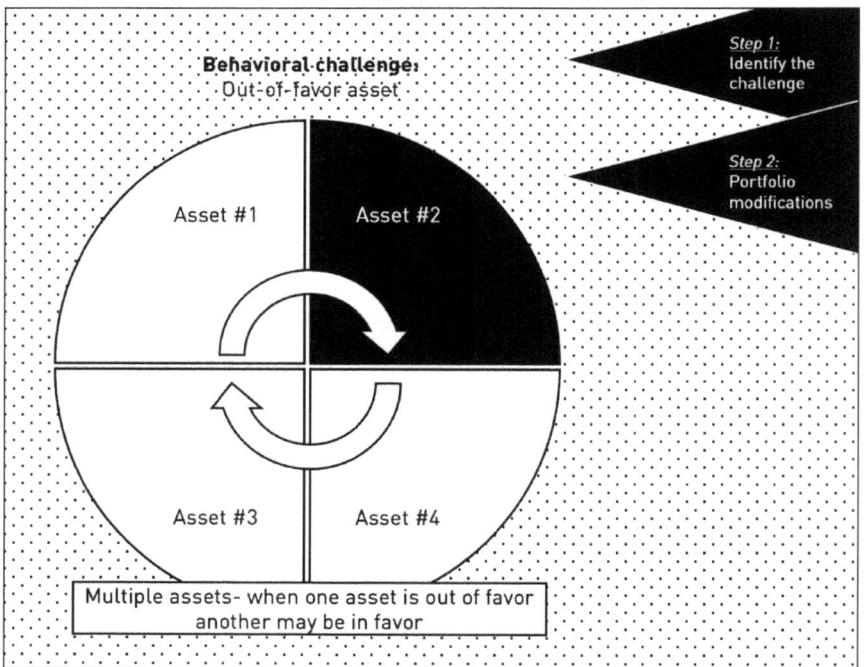

CHAPTER 10

Recognize history

Research shows that managers who trail over three to five years outperform during the following period. One of the starkest examples of this is illustrated by an ongoing study by S&P. In its Persistence Scorecard, S&P evaluates how well top-performing funds are able to remain in the top quartile of funds. In its scorecard in December 2022, it concluded that in five out of six equity fund categories and three out of four fixed-income categories, not a single manager whose performance was in the top quartile for the 12-month period ending in 2018 managed to remain in the top quartile for the next four years.[41]

The data also shows a strong likelihood that the best-performing funds will become the worst-performing funds and vice versa. As is illustrated in Figure 10.20, in S&P's 2017 study of 371 funds that were in the bottom quartile, 14.56% moved to the top quartile over the five-year horizon, while 23.45% of the 371 funds that were in the top quartile moved to the bottom quartile during the same period.[42]

Figure 10.20: The temptation when one asset is out of favor is to move out of that asset, potentially just before it is set to outperform. History shows that underperformance tends to be followed by outperformance and vice versa

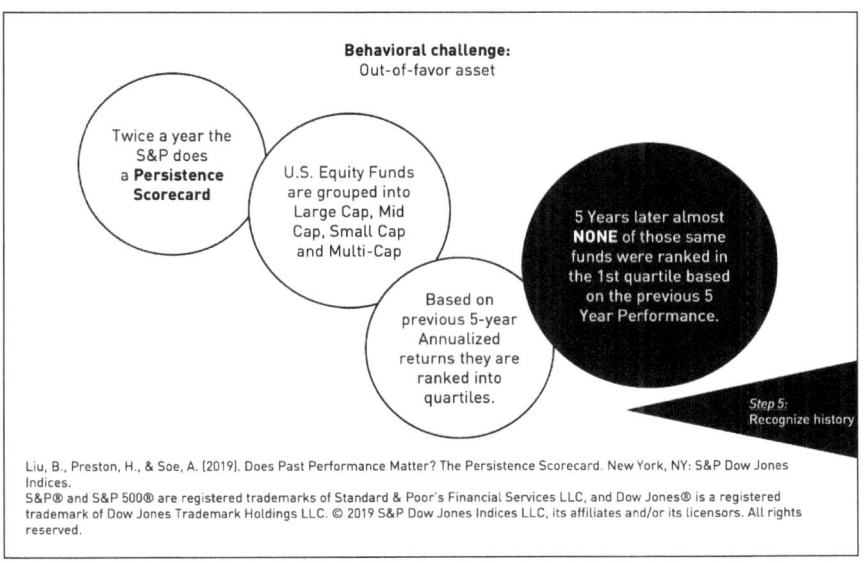

Understand the behavioral temptation and reframe the challenge

The temptation for investors is to exit what has done poorly and allocate to what has done very well. Sharing the history about the S&P scorecard and the Callan periodic table allows you to illustrate how these can move counterintuitively. One of the best rhetorical devices that advisors have used is to explain that if each asset in the portfolio is going up at the same time, they may all go *down* at the same time too (Figure 10.21). That something is doing badly—maybe even very badly on a relative basis—can be used as evidence that the portfolio is actually diversified.

Figure 10.21: Reframe the challenge to help investors understand that there may always be some assets that appear to be lagging, but that if everything is going up at the same time, it may go down at the same time too

Pre-commitment

When an asset is out of favor, your course of action as an advisor is to realize profits from in-favor assets and transfer them into the out-of-favor assets—to rebalance (see Figure 10.22). This is the opposite of the crowd's behavior and potentially allows you to sell high and buy low on an individual asset basis. For your clients, their job is to anticipate that an out-of-favor asset may be more likely to do well than other parts of their portfolio.

Figure 10.22: The pre-commitment to address out-of-favor assets is to agree in advance to make the contrarian move to allocate more assets into the out-of-favor asset through a rebalance, in an attempt to have more assets participate in a rebound

Like other investor challenges, our pre-commitment attempts to do the opposite of the crowd.

Adding some color to buying out-of-favor assets

Some years ago, I met the chief investment officer of a firm with over $2 billion under management. The core strategy for his company's investors was investing the bulk of their assets that it managed not just into asset classes, but into managers who were in the bottom quartile of performers over the prior three years. It had great success with this approach. By motivating your investors to take a similar tack, you stand to be among the *very few* that actually take advantage of the return to the mean tendencies of manager performance. You are also likely to streamline review meetings and avoid excessive investor angst when managers or asset classes trail markets.

The fourth behavioral challenge: not participating in asset bubbles

For our discussion of bubbles, I will turn to iconic economist Robert Shiller. Professor Shiller's seminal book *Irrational Exuberance* comprehensively discusses the history of bubbles, with a focus on the extreme stock market bubble produced by internet stocks in the late 1990s. He wrote this book with perfect timing *before* internet stocks collapsed over the nearly three years following its release. If you haven't read it, pause now to buy the latest edition.

Throughout much of 1998 and 1999, I spoke at advisors' conferences to discuss what I felt was an extremely overvalued market. When the first edition of *Irrational Exuberance* was published in 2000, I began bringing a copy and strongly recommending it (as I do to this day) to investor audiences.

When they're not dominating the news, bubbles may seem to many advisors like something that is unlikely to happen and equally unlikely to affect their practice. This attitude, however, runs counter to the long-term history of bubbles and even recent events. There is virtually always some bubble that is inflating or peaking in the financial markets. Making plans for the inevitable occurrences and potential effects of bubbles on your practice is a crucial part of establishing a behavioral framework for your investors.

To better understand bubbles, Shiller points us first to Ponzi schemes. In a Ponzi scheme, a fraudster creates a plausible means of making a profit and collects small amounts of money from an initial group of investors. As the conman acquires funds from newer investors, he then pays out sizable gains to the initial group. Other investors gain confidence in the scheme after seeing people making significant profits. Although the source of profits is false, positive feedback loops propel the scheme to sometimes fantastic heights. In *Irrational Exuberance*, Shiller writes:

Charles Ponzi attracted 30,000 investors in 1920 and issued notes totaling $15 million, all within seven months. The recent Bernie Madoff Ponzi scheme, carried out from the 1970s until its collapse in 2008, is considered to be the largest financial fraud in U.S. history, estimated at almost $65 billion. Neither experience nor sophistication seems to effectively immunize investors against falling victim to this type of fraud.[43]

As Shiller points out: "[T]he process that generates a speculative boom is in some dimensions analogous to these Ponzi schemes."[44] The math behind some of the companies that inflated to insane valuations are not that unlike the fraudulent stories told by Ponzi schemers. As written in *Forbes*:

> grocery delivery service Webvan went public in late 1999 on little more than hope. The stock doubled on its first day and the company quickly earned a $6 billion valuation, even though the company had less than $5 million in revenue, and it cost over $27 to fulfill an order. The company flamed out quickly and went bankrupt in 2001.[45]

I personally recall visiting my brother in Highlands Ranch, Colorado, and having dinner with several of his friends who had become involved in internet startups. Their strategy was to build a PowerPoint and go get the cash (from bankers).

During market bubbles, the news media—far from tempering irrational markets—instead create an environment in which bubbles flourish. Major market moves don't occur in a vacuum. They require consensus among many people. News outlets are the perfect way to make that possible. As many advisors likely recall, during the housing boom, news stories constantly reminded us that there had *never been* a meaningful decline in home prices and, as a result, such a decline from the housing boom was not worth considering.

The news media also can distort arguments by presenting two sides of an argument, both of which are biased toward current and irrational market trends. I recall in 1999 watching a CNBC interview where two money managers were debating the valuation of a stock. One, a value manager, was arguing that an internet stock was fairly valued at 75 times earnings. The other insisted that a much higher valuation, in the range of 100 times earnings, was justified. I was pulling my hair out, as the valuations were mainly based on non-traditional metrics like webviews and media hype.

As Shiller points out: "[S]peculative market expansions have often been associated with popular perceptions that the future is brighter or less uncertain than it was in the past. The term new era has periodically been used to describe these times." During the internet boom, there was a palpable sense that the internet had changed the rules of the game. There was an old way to price stocks and a new way. Limitations to the speed at which companies might grow revenues and profits no longer applied.

Associated with this "new era thinking" was a new way to price stocks. Instead of looking at revenues and profits, a number of firms began to value companies based on company web visits. In Chapter 1, I talked about price/earnings ratios. The mean historically for the S&P 500 is around 16, with an all-time high set during 2000 of 43. "By the end of the 1990s, the NASDAQ Composite reached a price-earnings ratio of 200, dwarfing the peak price-earnings ratio of 80 for the Japanese Nikkei 225 during the Japanese asset price bubble of 1991."[46]

In recent years, access to investment platforms on mobile phones, Reddit messaging about surging meme stocks, SPACs, and cryptocurrencies have created bubbles that dwarf the internet bubble. To address this, I decided to create a way to call out what's happening and publicize this nationally.

A new holiday: National Investment Risk Day

When it comes to speculative investing insanity, we haven't just left the ranch; there is no more ranch. As self-perceived leaders in hedged equity portfolios, my company and I took it upon ourselves to create a new holiday to focus investors and advisors on the *folie de l'année* (lunacy of the year), and created National Investment Risk Day (NIRD): an honest-to-god holiday, celebrated on January 19, that is registered with the National Archives.

The internet stock bubble was stark raving crazy. However, at least investors had some rationale and believed that one day, some of the stocks they were investing in would be highly profitable. Recent bubbles no longer appear to require an expectation of future profit. In the next few paragraphs, I'll review some recent examples to show how far from the gravitational pull of reality we have come and outline the possibility that has been created for what may be massive systemic risks to the economy and the financial markets.

Let's start with the relatively new phenomenon of meme stocks. In January 2021, a surge of messages on Reddit highlighted large short positions held by hedge funds in the company Gamestop (GME). Investors began "gaming" this position with massive purchases of the stock. As a result, the total value of GME increased from around $250 million in early 2020 to over $21 billion—nearly 100 times its starting value. This is remarkable because there was little doubt at the time that GME was not only experiencing net losses, but possibly on a trajectory for bankruptcy, which would zero out the value of its stock. A key distinction between this rally and the dotcom stock bubble is that, unlike those internet stocks that investors at least plausibly believed would one day become great companies, investors in Gamestop had no belief that the company value would ever be justified by profits. It was effectively a known Ponzi scheme, where investors intended to jump in early and jump out before a crash. Meme stock purchases continue today. At the time of writing (February 2024), GME has a total value of $4.2 billion, yet it is still losing money. Bursts of prices moving higher and lower continue due to the one-time glory of its valuation. Other meme stocks over the years have included AMC, Rivian, BlackBerry, and Virgin Galactic. In December 2021, one fund company even launched an ETF with the symbol MEME that specifically targeted meme stocks, providing access to speculative, sometimes worthless stocks (the ETF eventually closed in 2023).

SPACs—also known as "blank check companies"—are another example of the modern evolution of speculative bubbles. SPACs hold a special place in my heart for crazy ideas due to the relative unknown of the ultimate companies that will be merged with or invested in at the time that the SPAC raises funds. Investors are often motivated by the credibility of the individuals of firms that are sponsoring the SPACs. Let me distill this down for you: people are investing in something, but they don't know what it is.

Prior to a merger or acquisition by a SPAC, a vote by common stockholders is typically required to approve the deal. So, there is some level of insight that investors have before money is put to work. However, this does not justify the volume of money that is invested. In 2021, SPAC initial public offerings raised more than $160 billion, according to Statistica Research.

The bubble prize, however, goes to the world of crypto—both currencies and non-fungible tokens (NFTs). In 2021, a work of art titled "The Merge" sold as an NFT for over $92 million to over 28,983 collectors (see Figure 10.23). Fifteen months later, in March 2023, CoinCodex estimated that "The

Merge" had a total outstanding value of about $3.2 million, representing a loss of 96.5% (it has declined by another half since then).

Figure 10.23: One iteration of the NFT titled "The Merge." Collectively, "The Merge" NFTs brought in $92 million. You can photocopy this page for free, however

NFTs create plausible value because the owner can potentially capitalize on holding the digital rights of an artwork. If a media company at some future date wishes to license the rights to use the image in an NFT for commercial purposes, that could produce income. However, the reality of the ownership of most NFTs is hard to comprehend. How, for example, could a holder of "The Merge" NFT ever capitalize on this ownership if there are 28,000 other owners of units who might also wish to commercialize their units?

Cryptocurrencies are the current reference standard for speculative excess, however. They possess the trifecta of qualities for bubblicious investing: no income, no potential income, and no assets or tangible value. If cryptocurrencies are *currencies*—that is, systems of money that can be used in exchange for goods—they might be able to hold their value or fluctuate slightly relative to other currencies; but they should not be viewed as investments that can provide significant appreciation over time. Potential appreciation, however, is clearly why people buy cryptocurrencies. Bitcoin is so successful because it has appreciated—wait for it … 6.9 *billion* percent, from $.00099 per bitcoin at its first pricing in 2009 to an all-time high of $69,000 in late 2021. One dollar invested in Bitcoin at its inception would be worth $690 million today—enough to buy a decent Manhattan apartment. Yes, you missed out!

A number of factors are working to support the price of Bitcoin—chief of which, I believe, is its adoption by established investment managers and banks. In January 2024, as I was finishing the final draft of this book, a crucial next level of legitimacy was achieved by Bitcoin when the SEC approved Bitcoin ETFs—an event which I have labeled the "democratization of idiocy." Now, living on virtually every investment custodian and platform are ETFs that investors can allocate into, just like any other stock or bond ETF. I believe that this unprecedented access to cryptocurrencies, along with the limited supply of Bitcoin and possible dramatic appreciation now that it is in ETF form, may create systemic financial market risks. You read it here first, folks.

At the prior high of $69,000, Bitcoin—along with other cryptocurrencies—reached a total market capitalization of nearly $3 trillion, according to statistica.com. To put that value into perspective, the GDP of the UK is roughly $3 trillion. All other countries' GDPs (other than the five largest globally) are below $3 trillion.

A better comparison to frame potential economic risks, however, is the subprime mortgage fiasco, which was squarely responsible for creating the Great Financial Crisis. There was less than $1 trillion in subprime mortgages outstanding in 2007, according to the Federal Reserve.[47] Losses in subprime mortgages created cascading losses more broadly in real estate and stock market wealth far in excess of that amount as systemic pockets of vulnerability were exposed in the banking and insurance system.

The value of crypto already exceeds the amount of outstanding subprime mortgages leading into the Great Financial Crisis. Cryptocurrencies fell dramatically in 2022 from their high of $3 trillion, causing the failure of a number of crypto exchanges and losses of billions in wealth of crypto owners. The total market value of cryptocurrencies declined by over $2 trillion to approximately $850 billion. In 2023, however, cryptocurrencies rallied again, with Bitcoin recently reaching $52,000. The market capitalization of cryptocurrencies surged back to $2 trillion. I believe that the new legitimized status of Bitcoin through ETFs has created the possibility that the total value of cryptocurrencies could soar far above the prior high of $3 trillion in the coming years.

What happens if cryptocurrencies reach a total market cap of $10 trillion or $20 trillion? During the Great Depression, thousands of banks failed and money held in those banks evaporated, dramatically impacting people's wealth and ability to consume, and causing the economy to go into freefall. Banks and stocks are safer today because of the FDIC and the SEC. However, the FDIC and the SEC can do nothing to prevent the evaporation of wealth if Bitcoin—the world's largest Ponzi scheme, with no income or asset to justify any valuation whatsoever—creates trillions of dollars of losses.

The point of establishing NIRD is to call out current investor lunacy. Each year, a panel of experts votes on January 19 on the three dumbest investments of the prior year. Stay tuned as the situation with current bubbles plays out!

Solutions

To return to our Investment Owner's Manual and its suite of solutions, acknowledge to your investors that bubbles will occur numerous times during their lifetime. Emphasize to them that there will be temptations to allocate assets to the bubbles; and the bigger those bubbles are, the harder it will be to avoid temptation.

Our portfolio solution is to maintain broad diversification across asset classes and management styles (see Figure 10.24). This will create a scenario where investors are likely to have some exposure to assets that are rapidly inflating if those bubbles are being created in conventional assets. Where possible, point out to them which portions of the portfolio are benefiting from a rapid rise.

Figure 10.24: Portfolio modifications aim to maintain broad exposure to equity assets and avoid allocating excessive dollars to specific assets in a bubble. This may allow investors partial exposure to assets that are increasing in value as a result of the bubble (as with AI stocks)

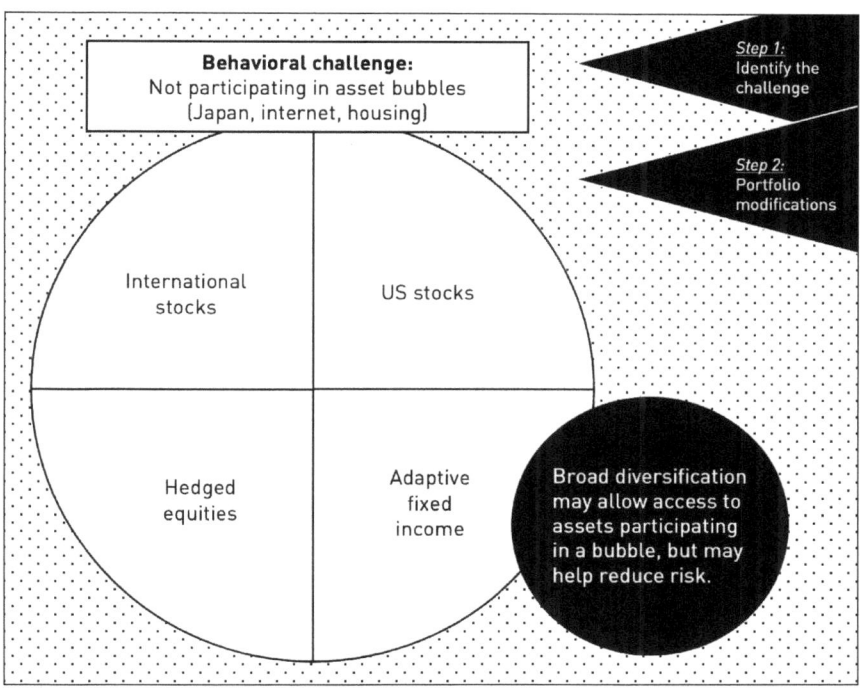

Recognize history

Remind clients that, from internet stocks to real estate to tulip bulbs, bubbles always pop! (See Figures 10.25 and 10.26.)

Figure 10.25: As a way of helping investors internalize the nature of bubbles, refer to past bubbles

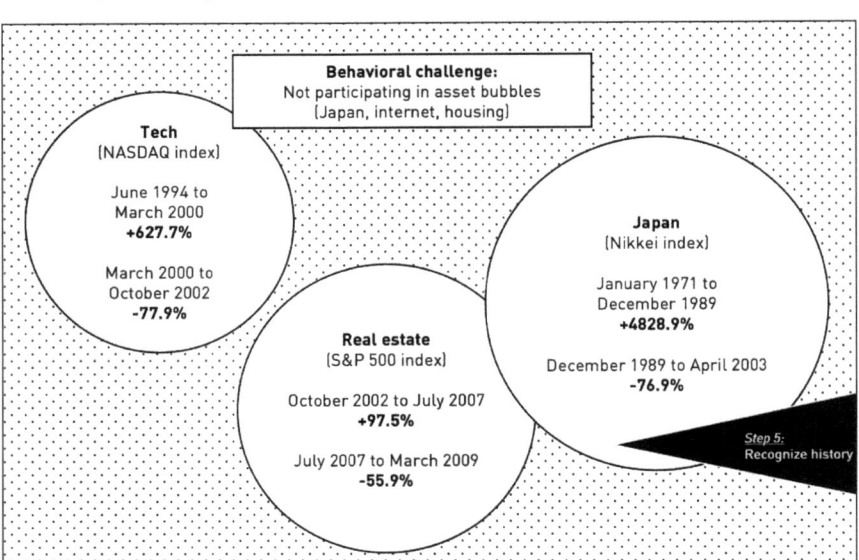

Understand the behavioral temptation and reframe the challenge

Pointing to the history and outcome of past bubbles makes clear that the cause of price increases during bubbles is nothing other than crowds buying something and pushing up the value. Ask the simple question: "What is creating the fundamental value of the asset?" Tell them that if compelling potential income or assets can back up the price, you will always consider it.

Figure 10.26: Historically, bubbles have always popped, resulting in huge losses!

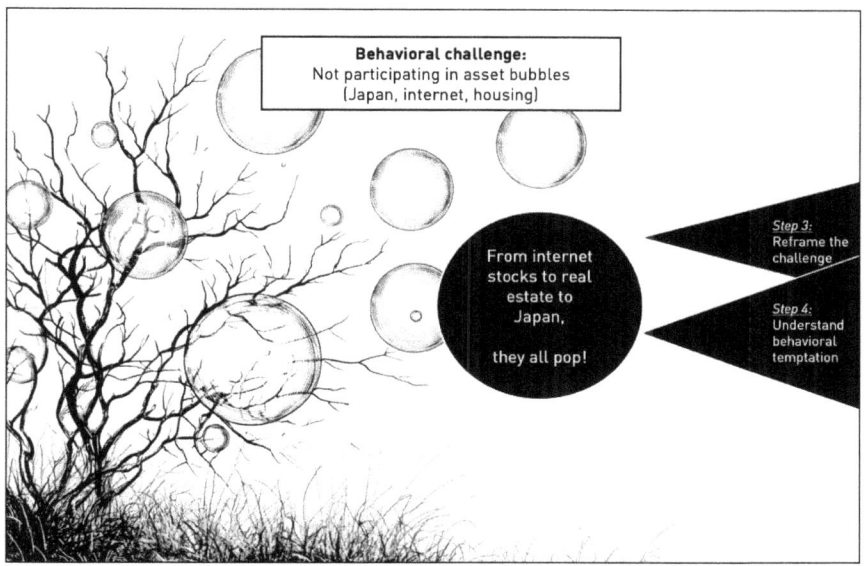

Pre-commitment

As bubbles reach the point of bursting, your pre-commitment is to rebalance away from assets that have experienced bubble-like appreciation (Figure 10.27). Your client will want to disengage from the crowd and watch in amusement as the bubble mania plays out. As bubbles inflate and others invest more, your investors will be harvesting gains in inflated assets and rebalancing them into other parts of the portfolio.

Figure 10.27: The investor pre-commitment for bubbles is to rebalance portfolios out of assets that are increasing dramatically, potentially locking in gains and attempting to avoid losses from the top

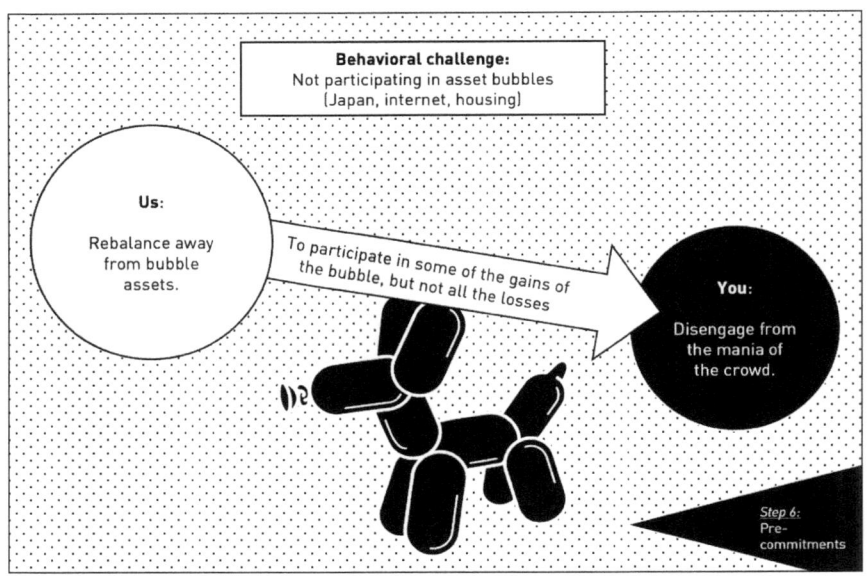

The fifth behavioral investing challenge: underperforming hedged equity strategies

Advisors that utilize hedged equities in their portfolios are likely to encounter some resistance among their clients when these strategies trail the markets. Deploying hedged equities is one of the only ways to address the behavioral risks associated with significant portfolio losses. But utilizing these solutions generates its own behavioral investment challenges. Although we have already discussed the behavioral challenge of underperforming strategies or managers, there are a few extra wrinkles that have caused me to highlight hedged equities.

One wrinkle is that hedged equities are such an essential component in addressing market risks. If an investor exits an emerging markets fund that was 5% of their portfolio, the consequences might be that their returns are slightly lower. If an investor leaves their hedged equity allocation, the consequences could be dire if markets plummet over multiple years. The behavioral effect of owning hedged equities isn't always negative. It's bipolar. Either investors are elated that they have outsmarted the markets, and even profited as a result, or they are despondent that this part of their portfolio has trailed benchmarks.

In the aftermath of the internet stock crash in 2003, we saw huge interest in our hedged equity strategies *after* they had helped avoid losses during the prior three years. However, after markets rallied and our strategies trailed during the bull market between 2004 and 2007, investors left. Once again, when the stock market bottomed in March 2009 and investors looked back at how well hedged equity strategies avoided the decline, we saw significant interest. This is Cornelius and Prudence on full display. Addressing the probability of the issue improves your ability to navigate hedged equity underperformance.

Solutions

Just as hedged equities are part of a portfolio to address market drawdowns, conventional equities are part of the portfolio to attempt to provide reliable market up-capture. This portfolio approach (see Figure 10.28) embraces the fact that markets are generally efficient, but there are times when investors as a group become irrational and price stocks unrealistically high.

Figure 10.28: Hedged equities are bound to trail during rising markets and may provide relatively strong returns during rising markets

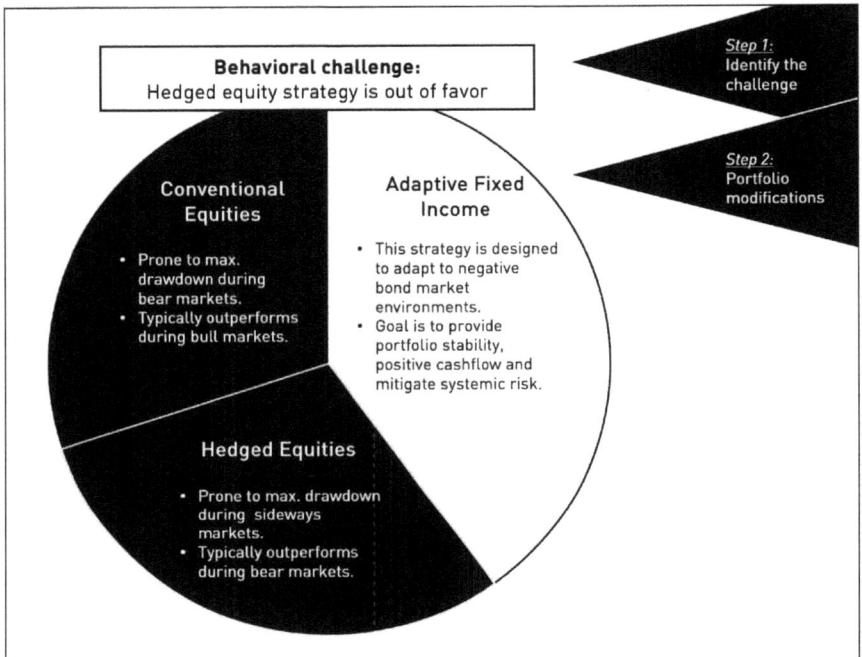

Recognize history

After long bull markets, stocks are more vulnerable to declines. That's when hedged equities are the most important part of portfolios (see Figure 10.29).

Figure 10.29: After long bull markets, when stocks have higher valuations, they are more vulnerable to declines and hedged equities become more important

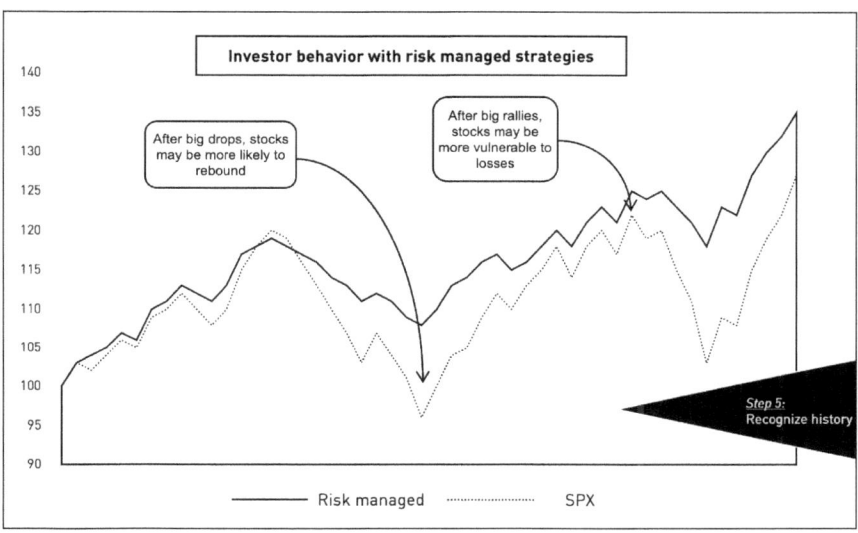

Understand behavioral temptation and reframe the challenge

The target returns and maximum drawdown that you establish with each client help investors stay committed to their portfolios when hedged equity strategies underperform. As we have discussed, at the outset of the relationship, you will establish each investor's necessary return and maximum drawdown. As a part of that conversation, we strongly recommend that you show investors how increasing the drawdown of their portfolio lowers their probability of success. If investors understand that they're okay if their portfolio loses as much as 20% but are in serious jeopardy of running out of money if they lose 40%, they're unlikely to want to deviate from strategies that have lower drawdowns.

Ask investors who are disgruntled with hedged equity performance and want to add more to conventional strategies if it's okay to increase the maximum target loss of their portfolio from, say, 20%, to 40%. At the same time, show them a mathematical calculation of how this might lower their chances of success. The conversation is pretty straightforward. Investors understand the implications and tend to stay with the behavioral portfolio recommendation that includes risk-off strategies.

Figure 10.30: The behavioral temptation is to leave hedged equities after bull markets and buy hedged equities after market routs—the opposite of what would be the most desirable. Reframe the problem by showing investors how their probability of success may decline without hedged equities

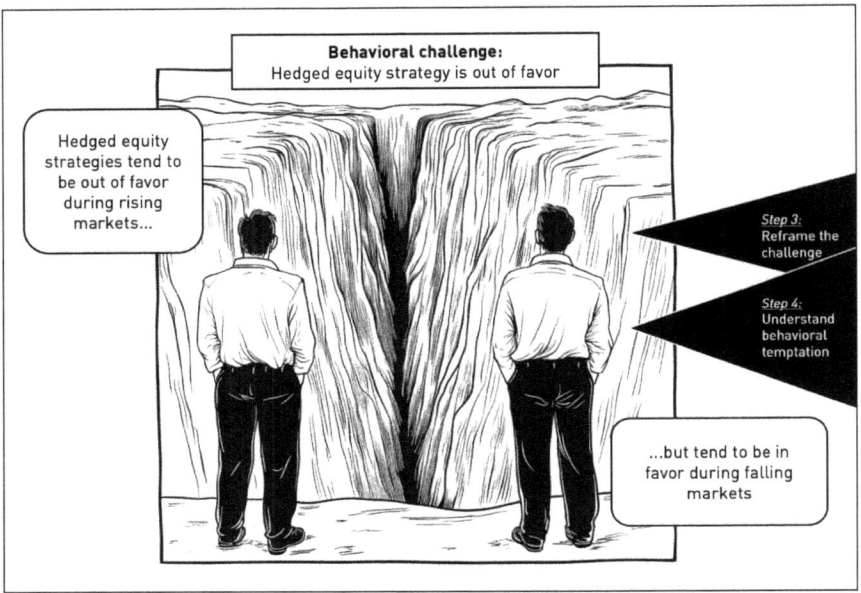

Pre-commitments

When our hedged equity strategy underperforms the market, our plan as advisors is to systematically rebalance from unprotected assets to hedged equities (Figure 10.31).

This strategy has the effect of harvesting gains during rising markets and investing them in more stable strategies. So, in addition to helping achieve investors' needs to fully participate in market rises and reduce the risk of loss, it helps to achieve investors' desire to lock in gains. It also positions investors to allocate out of hedged equity positions into conventional stocks after market routs, potentially positioning them to more fully capture rebounds.

In addition to rebalancing, advisors should look to evaluate the effect of market declines on levels of income. If assets have fallen sufficiently to break the lower barrier of asset levels, income may need to be adjusted lower in order to address market downturns.

Figure 10.31: The pre-commitment is to make the contrarian trade. Harvest gains from conventional equities into hedged equities after bulls and move from hedged equities into conventional equities after market routs through rebalances

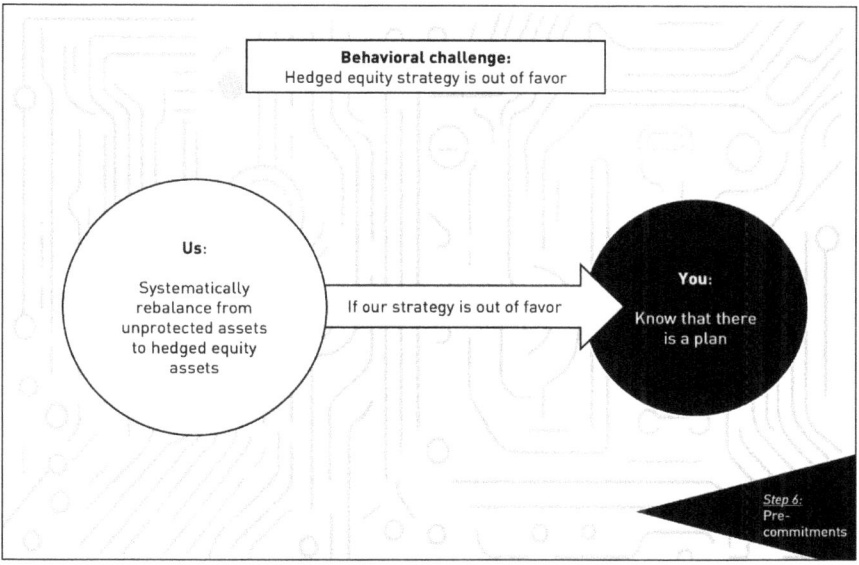

For investors, perhaps the most important thing to understand is that there is a plan; and that market declines not only are not a surprise, but were explicitly planned for during the portfolio construction phase.

The sixth and final behavioral challenge: inflation and rising interest rates

We have spent a lot of time talking about the risk that inflation and interest rates pose to portfolios. Inflation and interest rates can also move in market super-cycles, where they behave one way for a generation or more, only to change course and behave in a completely different way for the next generation. Because we rely on experiential learning, super-cycles perplex entire populations—and investment professionals are not immune. Add to that the fact that inflation produces losses that are not shown on investment statements but are gradually felt over time in an investor's ability to purchase goods and we have what may be the most vexing investor behavioral challenge of them all.

Figure 10.32: The portfolio solution to address rising interest rates and inflation is to hold adaptive fixed-income strategies and maintain an equity allocation commensurate with an investor's risk profile

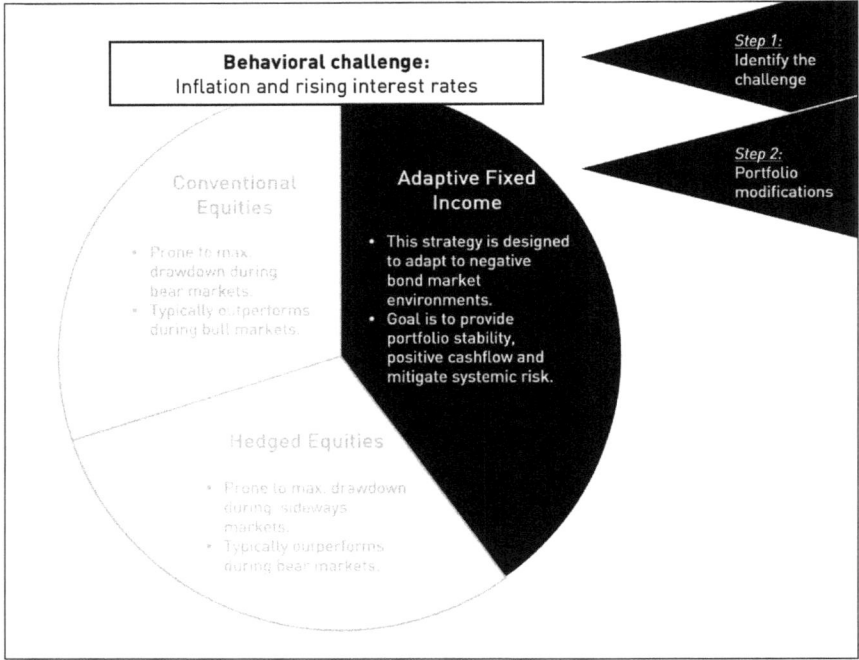

Solutions

In order to address the possibility of rising interest rates and inflation, advisors should build in allocations to adaptive fixed-income strategies in the form of ladders or unconstrained bond funds or strategies (see Figure 10.32). Adaptive fixed-income strategies are designed to move to defensive short-duration positions if interest rates rise or to inflation-protected bonds if inflation increases. A message that is implicit in the behavioral portfolio pie chart (which includes an allocation to stocks), but is not expressly stated, is that a portion of the portfolio should be allocated to asset classes that are not invested in fixed income. We have shown that stocks tend to act as a pass-through for rising prices during times of high inflation. The combination of allocating a portion of portfolios to stocks, which can rise along with inflation, and a portion to adaptive fixed income, which may lessen losses during a bond bear market, addresses the very real risks that can arise when bonds enter a bear market.

Figure 10.33: Recognize history by acknowledging the very real risks to fixed income that can last for decades

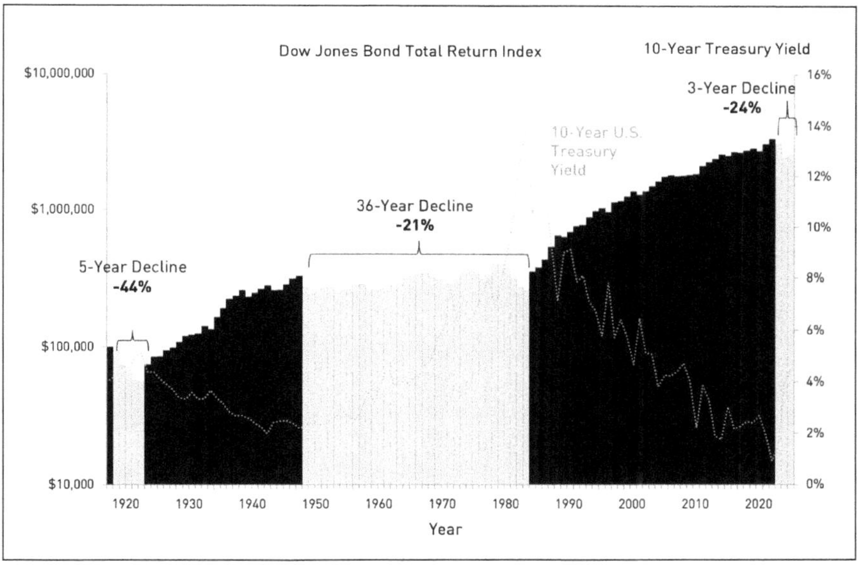

Recognize history

The starting point for advisors who wish to address this challenge is to educate clients about the history of inflation and its potentially corrosive effects on their financial wellbeing.

Introduce the graph in Figure 10.33 to help illustrate its effects on bond investments that have produced real losses over as long as 36 years. We also recommend that advisors discuss the possibility of even higher—in some cases, much higher—inflation that other countries have experienced. The message is that inflation and rising interest rates are either nothing to worry about, or something to worry about, or the only thing to worry about.

Understand the behavioral temptation and reframe the challenge

For both investors and advisors, the temptation is to ignore the inflation threat. Mention to investors when you review portfolios what has been happening with inflation and remind them what has happened in the past. There is virtually always a country experiencing high inflation that can keep it real for investors. In January 2024, Argentina's annual inflation soared to above 250%.

Figure 10.34: The behavioral tendency is to ignore inflation if it has not been an issue recently. Reframe the challenge by talking about how certain assets, such as stocks, may do well during times of high inflation

Reframe the challenge by pointing to ways in which your portfolio can benefit from high inflation (see Figure 10.34). Stocks, which are a form of real asset, are backed by companies that can increase prices along with inflation. As a result, they can and have increased significantly during periods of high inflation. Also, other holdings such as real estate or other hard assets can appreciate and improve an investor's net worth as inflation drives up the prices of those assets. That's not real above-inflation growth, but it's a lot better than renting during a high inflation period.

Figure 10.35: The pre-commitment is to emotionally untether from the past success of strong bond performance and maintain an allocation to adaptive fixed-income strategies

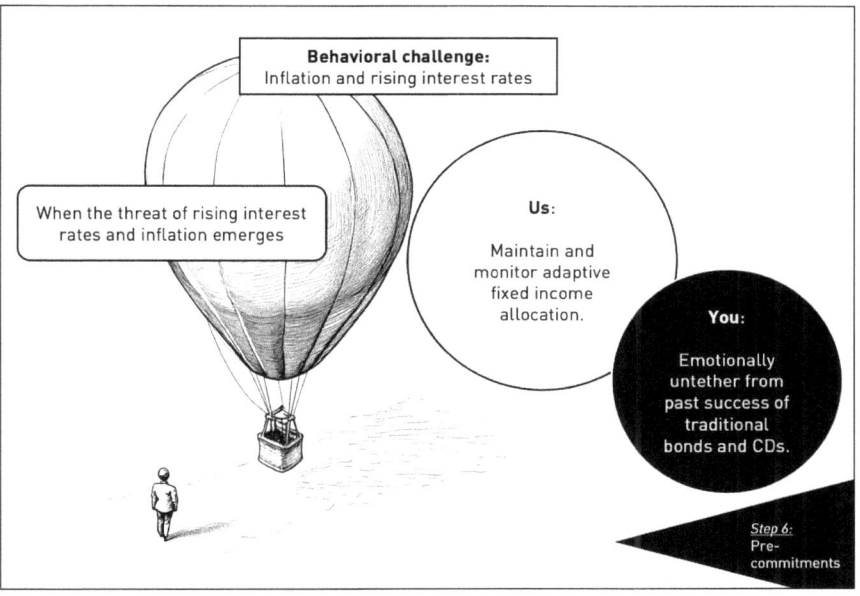

Pre-commitment

The pre-commitment that we will make as advisors is to maintain and monitor adaptive fixed-income allocations. For investors, emotionally untether from past success in bonds and certificates of deposit.

Now that I've outlined the decision-making process for avoiding the six biggest behavioral challenges, in Chapter 11 I'll introduce ways to automate the process by setting "defaults" into your practice.

CHAPTER 11
Automating Good Behavior by Setting "Defaults" in Your Practice

IN 2008, RICHARD THALER AND CASS SUNSTEIN wrote *Nudge: Improving Decisions About Health, Wealth, and Happiness*.[48] They write that a "nudge" is:

> any aspect of the choice architecture that alters people's behavior in a predictable way without forbidding any options or significantly changing their economic incentives. To count as a mere nudge, the intervention must be easy and cheap to avoid. Nudges are not mandates. Putting fruit at eye level counts as a nudge. Banning junk food does not.

In many or even most aspects of life, creating nudges is the best that we can do. You can't make people wash their hands in the loo, but you can place a sign above the sink and ask them to. In our behavioral guidance, however, we want more than a nudge: we want a shared understanding and explicit agreement from clients to take a certain action. But even that can be improved upon by how you configure each client's portfolio.

My preferred approach to managing decision making for investors is expressed by behavioral economists as a "default." Defaults are decisions that are automatically made in the absence of a decision by a person. These decisions require that someone opts out for them not to happen. The most commonly discussed use of defaults concerns 401k plans.

Fifty years ago, defined benefit plans were the preferred way that companies helped provide for employees' retirement incomes. Defined benefit plans are funded directly by companies, without the involvement of employees. When people retire with a defined benefit plan, they collect an income based on their term of employment and income. Investors in these plans don't decide to participate in the plan; it's automatic. They also don't have a say in how the funds in the defined benefit plan are invested; they just get a check. If a company offers a defined benefit plan, it is liable for the benefits to employees according to how the plan is set up, even if the investments of the plan earn less than the actuaries assumed they would.

Over the past 50 years, defined contribution plans have become the dominant way for companies to help employees save for retirement. These plans are optional for employees. They allow them to save a percentage of their earnings pre-tax. In some cases, companies match employee contributions up to 6% of their earnings.

Companies prefer these plans because they have no liability to provide for employees if investments don't perform up to expectations. They also satisfy employee desires to have control of the investments in their retirement plan both before and after retirement.

However, defined contribution plans have a major downside. Employees under defined contribution plans can decide if they want to take all of their income now and buy stuff at Crate and Barrel or save it for retirement. Predictably, many choose to buy waffle makers. According to the Bureau of Labor Statistics, only 75% of employees in civilian companies with access to a defined contribution plan chose to participate in 2022[49]—meaning that nearly 25% of employees have opted to delay saving for retirement. In some cases, this means both paying higher taxes and not receiving company matching dollars that are a direct increase (albeit delayed) of their total pay.

The Pension Protect Act of 2006 was designed to overcome the drawbacks of voluntary enrollment by getting more people to be automatically enrolled in 401k plans. Not all companies have automatic enrollment. However, in those that do, employees have a portion of their pay sent to their 401k plan *by default* unless they opt out of this option. These companies experience much higher participation levels and studies suggest that automatic enrollment plans could reduce the rate of non-participation to less than 15%, significantly increasing retirement savings.

Setting defaults or automating allocation and rebalancing decisions is another opportunity to distinguish yourself from your peers and improve outcomes for your investors. Throughout our Investment Owner's Manual, we have used the term "systematically rebalance" when referring to actions or pre-commitments that we expect investors to make. Ideally, these will all happen without a conscious decision by investors. To the extent possible, advisors should select automatic rebalancing options on investment platforms (understanding that tax management of portfolios may prevent automation of rebalancing). I also recommend that advisors automate payments to insurance policies and monthly or quarterly withdrawals from bank accounts into investment programs. If it's part of their plan and you're able to make it happen automatically, by all means do so!

Changing rebalancing to take advantage of the crowd's poor decision making

Advisors rebalance portfolios quarterly or annually to keep allocations at their target levels, to maintain consistent risk levels, and—frankly—because that's the way it's always been done. But does this type of rebalancing benefit investors?

Surprisingly, in most cases, no. However, it can increase transaction costs and generate taxable gains—two clearly detrimental outcomes. Our research shows that by completely rethinking your rebalancing procedures, you can improve investor returns and lower tax obligations and transaction costs while decreasing your workload. Do I have your attention?

Michael Kitces, in his *Nerd's Eye View* blog, wrote a comprehensive article about rebalancing that discusses many of the issues that should be considered when developing a rebalancing strategy. He first looked at the optimal rebalancing time interval for systematic rebalancing. He highlighted a study from Vanguard that found no material differences in outcomes for rebalancing frequencies varying from monthly to annual. When analyzed using a 60/40 portfolio going back to 1926, the researchers found that rebalancing quarterly or monthly produced no improvement in long-term risk or returns (see Figure 11.1); it simply drove up the turnover rate and the number of rebalancing events (and potential transaction costs!).[50]

Figure 11.1: More frequent rebalancing produced no improvement in long-term risk or returns

	Monthly	Quarterly	Annually
Annual turnover	2.7%	2.2%	1.7%
Number of rebalancing events	1008	335	83
Average annualized return	8.5%	8.6%	8.6%
Volatility	12.1%	12.2%	11.9%

An alternative approach that can help avoid unproductive trading is to wait until any one asset is out of balance by a large enough percentage to trigger a rebalance. This can be accomplished by establishing bands. If an asset class is out of balance by, say, 10% of its target allocation, the behavioral portfolio will be rebalanced to bring that asset class back into line with portfolio targets.

A 2007 study published in the *Journal of Financial Planning* by Gobind Daryanini, titled "Opportunistic Rebalancing," tested banded rebalancing under different scenarios. The study tested data from 1992 to 2004 with portfolios invested in five asset classes (large cap US, small cap US, real estate investment trusts, commodities, and intermediate-term bonds). The study concluded that banded rebalancing often improves returns (see Figure 11.2). It also found that the optimal band that should be met before triggering a rebalance was 20%.

Figure 11.2: Banded rebalancing—or rebalancing at trigger points when an asset is out of balance by a certain percentage—historically improves returns, with the optimal rebalance at 20% and daily analysis to determine when to rebalance

Rebalance bands	Look intervals in market days						
	250	125	60	20	10	5	1
0%	0.26%	0.19%	0.18%	0.07%	-0.05%	-0.29%	-2.32%
5%	0.27%	0.22%	0.19%	0.20%	0.21%	0.20%	0.19%
10%	0.30%	0.25%	0.27%	0.24%	0.27%	0.26%	0.24%
15%	0.29%	0.33%	0.33%	0.35%	0.35%	0.32%	0.31%
20%	0.31%	0.36%	0.38%	0.40%	0.45%	0.43%	**0.50%**
25%	0.17%	0.30%	0.27%	0.32%	0.37%	0.44%	0.43%
100%	0.00%	0.00%	0.00%	0.00%	0.00%	0.00%	0.00%

At the same time that Daryanini studied the optimal bands, he tested different look intervals to find the optimal frequency to test when the bands had been met and rebalancing was required. The results showed that performance is improved when portfolios are constantly looked at and are rebalanced as soon as bands are met.

Of course, this rebalance study looked only at conventional asset classes. Our behavioral portfolio recommendation includes the unconventional asset classes of hedged equities and adaptive fixed income. To guide our advisors toward the best solution when using our behavioral portfolio recommendation, we ran a study that tested a 60/40 portfolio that was invested in conventional assets and the hedged equities and adaptive fixed-income strategies that are included in our recommendation.[51] Our study, like Daryanini's, showed no real benefit from periodic rebalances (monthly, quarterly, or annually). Again, like Daryanini, it revealed the same optimal bands of 20% with a constant look approach.

Automating investor pre-commitments through rebalancing

Our behavioral portfolio rebalance study dictated only six rebalances between 1999 and the end of 2017, or once every three years on average. This means that for advisors who currently rebalance their portfolios quarterly, the workload for their staff could be cut to 1/12th. At the same time, this strategy will likely improve performance, reduce taxable gains, and decrease portfolio transaction costs.

What is genuinely exciting, however, is the way it automates most of the pre-commitments that we discussed in the Investment Owner's Manual. For example, the first rebalance in our study that ran from 1999 to 2017 was in December 2000. This was triggered by losses in conventional stocks during the first year of the internet bubble burst. As a result of this rebalance, money moved from hedged equities back into conventional stocks, fulfilling our pre-commitment that when stocks experience significant losses, investors should rebalance into assets with the steepest declines to take advantage of Black Friday prices.

A second rebalance was triggered in late 2002, after two more years of sizable stock market losses. This rebalance moved assets from hedged equities and adaptive fixed income into conventional stocks at near the lowest levels reached during the internet stock bubble burst. This trade, after nearly three years of stock market losses, would be very difficult for investors to make without:

- training about stock market losses;
- a plan made in advance to take advantage of bargain stock market prices; and
- a researched system that automatically shifts assets at a time which historically is optimal for portfolio performance.

Our study didn't rebalance again until March 2006, after over three years of stock market advances. This rebalance fulfilled another of our pre-commitments: when hedged equity strategies underperform, systematically rebalance portfolios *into* hedged equity strategies to keep portfolio risk in check. The rebalance had the effect of harvesting gains in conventional stocks just prior to the Great Financial Crisis. Again, this "trade" was going in the opposite direction of what I witnessed at the time, which was exits from hedged equities by investors and advisors plagued by recency bias in the fourth quarter of 2007 and the first quarter of 2008. The rebalance positioned the portfolio to have fewer losses than conventional portfolios during one of the worst stock market declines in the past 100 years. Without advance training, a plan and pre-commitment made in advance, and a system to automatically trade into hedged equities, advisors would likely have been unable to persuade their clients to buy into strategies that had trailed markets for the past four years.

This automated strategy continued to make similar trades, triggering purchases of conventional stocks near the stock market bottom in 2008 and purchases of more hedged equity stock during the strong stock market advance following the Great Financial Crisis.

Banded rebalancing strategies promise to address another one of our investor pre-commitments. If a manager or strategy trails enough to be 20% less than its target allocation, more assets will be shifted into that manager to take advantage of a probable return to the mean and outperformance by that strategy or manager.

Even though, during a long period of low or no returns, the behavioral portfolio doesn't show gains, there may be individual assets or managers that do very well or very poorly. Banded rebalancing can potentially harvest gains and allocate into underpriced assets to help improve anemic returns for investors.

Finally, during markets where one asset class is participating in a bubble, banded rebalancing guides advisors to automatically harvest gains and limit exposure to assets that will likely fall once the bubble pops.

Summarizing the effects of managing investor behavior

In Chapter 1, I discussed how investors have historically trailed the funds that they invest in by an average of 1.7% per year. Also, throughout the book I have shown how difficult it is for even educated and well-intentioned advisors to prevent clients from falling victim to investor biases that lower returns and corrupt investor/client relationships.

By deploying behavioral portfolios, a proactive plan for investor challenges, and an automated process for executing those plans, the opportunity to bring real value in the form of improved performance and greater piece of mind is huge. If advisors are simply able to manage clients sufficiently to replicate static portfolios, they stand the chance of performing in line with, rather than 1.7% below, the funds that they invest in.

But our rebalancing study shows that by using a banded rebalancing strategy that supports our behavioral plans, investors stand the chance of taking advantage of the crowd's poor decision making and improving on the performance provided by static portfolios.

In the next chapter, I will show you a step-by-step process to execute all of the ideas that I've shared with you in your practice. But first, let's summarize the potential effects of building an investor behavioral component into your practice. Ideally, it will help you to:

- prevent portfolio underperformance due to investor biases;
- enhance returns by optimizing rebalances that take advantage of the crowd's poor decision-making abilities;
- help safeguard portfolios against severe losses that could devastate clients; and
- provide a smoother return path for investors.

In Chapter 12, I'll outline the final step in transforming your practice, providing a step-by-step plan for executing the ideas discussed in this book.

CHAPTER 12

Implementing an Investor Behavioral Component in Your Practice: A Step-by-Step Plan

IN PART 1 of this book, we laid out the decades-old problem of performance chasing among clients. Through our story about Cornelius and Prudence, we presented the path that advisors will almost inevitably follow. Due to the counterintuitive nature of investment decision making and the deceptive way in which investments fluctuate, you—like Cornelius—will continue to be a victim of investor biases. The old strategy of waiting until investors become frustrated and resentful, and trying to overcome these emotions by telling them to hang in there until things change, doesn't work. And the industry guidance that investors should be disciplined and stick to their plans—without providing a method to instill what is essentially counterintuitive behavior—is a bankrupt idea.

In Part 2, we introduced the behavioral portfolio. Instead of focusing portfolio construction on arbitrary risk measures and returns, we defined specific criteria for building behavioral portfolios and created a quantitative framework for measuring them. Based on these criteria, we constructed a behavioral portfolio recommendation designed to provide portfolio safeguarding against extreme events that could devastate investors. These portfolios are designed to provide a smoother return path and create greater investor peace of mind along the way.

In Part 3, we built a process for training investors about the six biggest behavioral challenges that they are likely to confront and introduced the Investment Owner's Manual, which acts as your clients' map for emergent behavioral challenges. For each behavioral challenge, we discussed how portfolios should be built to address the challenge and laid out a plan, supported by an investor pre-commitment that you and your investors will fulfill when that behavioral challenge emerges. We also introduced a system for automating rebalancing as a way of keeping portfolios near their target allocation and executing pre-commitments for five of the six behavioral challenges.

Virtually all of this content was available through the Behavioral Investing Institute in early 2017. But there remained one problem: once advisors learned this information, they then needed to *do something about it*!

In our experience, some advisors executed nothing; some added a few of the tools to their practices; and a few comprehensively deployed our ideas. We knew that advisors would potentially have greater success if they comprehensively adopted our approach. As a result, near the end of 2017, we built an advisor coaching program into our business. This coaching program is designed to take advisors on the path from knowledge to full implementation of the strategies.

In this chapter, we will focus on the execution of all that you've learned. We will walk you through the processes that you need to follow to transform your practice. We will cover how to:

- position yourself as a behavioral coach who comprehensively addresses market risks;
- build portfolios that attempt to anticipate market dislocations, and that meet both the behavioral and economic needs of your investors;
- discuss with your investors plans of action for market disruptions in advance and ask them to make pre-commitments to take certain actions when market challenges emerge; and
- provide ongoing investor behavioral collateral to guide investors through market stress events.

Positioning yourself as a behavioral coach

Millennials will hold a majority of investable assets in 25 years. They highly value technology; and according to a study by Deloitte, 57% would change their bank relationship for a better technology platform. Robo-advisors, which can be managed via online platforms, are simple to use and provide many investor services traditionally performed by investment advisors for a fraction of the cost.

Training your investors to navigate complex markets will, we believe, dramatically improve both their outcomes and your effectiveness. Positioning yourself as an advisor that has a defined process for making counterintuitive decisions, and that has built portfolios that attempt to navigate a wide variety of markets, potentially gives you a powerful competitive advantage over your peers.

Step 1: Develop a process for determining investors' risk capacity and risk tolerance

"Risk capacity" refers to the economic risk your client is able to take based on their assets, income needs, and time horizon. An investor with $1 million of investable assets who can live on their Social Security and pensions and doesn't need to draw from their portfolio has a high risk capacity, but doesn't need to take on much risk because their needs are met. If the intention of this investor is to pass on a substantial estate to heirs, they might wish to invest aggressively. "Risk tolerance" refers to how much risk an investor is psychologically able to bear. If that same investor is very uncomfortable losing any money, they have a low risk tolerance and might want a conservative portfolio even though they have a high risk capacity.

On the other hand, an investor who has that same $1 million of investments and needs $60,000 of income per year has a low risk capacity, but requires growth in order to avoid depleting their portfolio.

Financial planning software—including the previously mentioned Income Labs, Money Guide Pro, and several dozen other options—help advisors determine their clients' risk capacity. Separately, providers such as Finametrica and Tolerisk allow advisors to gain an understanding of their clients' comfort level with taking on risk. This situation can be complicated as often couples have different risk tolerance levels. Understanding this information for each of your existing and new investors is vital.

By building a process and acquiring the tools for determining the psychological profile of your clients, you are gaining a deep understanding of each client's money personality. In some cases, advisors can also understand the types of communications that investors prefer, with some providers having dashboards that let you know which of your clients are prone to panic or more vulnerable to market stress events.

Step 2: Modify portfolios to incorporate concepts of behavioral portfolio design

Change the makeup of your client portfolios based on the criteria that we outlined. We discussed at length our behavioral portfolio recommendation. Let's refer back to that now.

The portfolio is made up of three broad categories: conventional stocks, hedged equities, and adaptive fixed-income strategies. Start by identifying the managers, funds, or strategies that will comprise each of these categories (see Figure 12.1).

Conventional stocks

Conventional stocks can be made up of passive index funds or ETFs, individual stocks, or any other funds or strategies that remain ... always invested. The most important criterion is: does the manager or strategy have an extremely high likelihood of participating in market rises? As we have stated throughout this book, no other client retention stress is greater than living through a long-term bull market while your clients earn little or nothing. This is the portion of equity portfolios that helps you ensure that your clients participate in market gains. Of course, this means that the strategy, fund, or manager will fully participate in market losses too.

Figure 12.1: In making the transition to a behavioral coach, a critical step is to modify your own investment models to ensure that they address existential risks and behavioral challenges

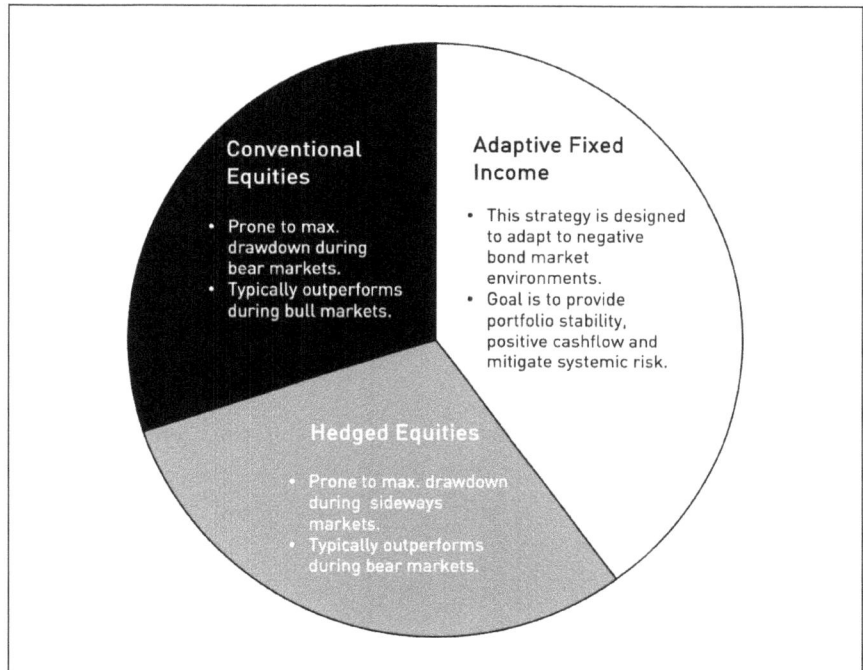

Here are a couple of things to consider when allocating to conventional stocks:

- Fees: Advisors may be able to find solutions with extremely low fees in the form of passive ETFs or direct indexing. If your existing portfolios are comprised of manager fees that don't provide a clear value, use this opportunity to lower costs. When I guide investors, I recommend that the conventional portion of portfolios be comprised of low-cost passive index funds and ETFs.
- Have you chosen an active manager or strategy based on recent past performance? If you have, you may be a victim of recency bias and the odds are that your manager will trail when market trends change—which they inevitably will.

- Is there something inherently compelling about the strategy that you've chosen that justifies any fees charged above passive index strategies? You need to be able to articulate it and justify the reason for the manager's inclusion in the overall strategy.
- Is the management team that was responsible for the long-term performance of a strategy still in place?

Hedged equity strategies

Finding the right hedged equity strategies is one of the most difficult tasks in modifying portfolios because these may be new to advisors and can include complex methodologies. I'll summarize some of the key points of our discussion here:

- Hedged equity strategies should provide robust loss avoidance. This means that they should be designed to attempt to un-correlate from equity markets in order to provide true diversification during market crises.
- Predictive strategies that are designed to guess which direction the market will move should be avoided.
- Look for strategies that have reliable up-capture during bull markets.
- Focus on price-reactive or options hedged strategies that have track records at both loss avoidance and market participation.
- Pay attention to the tax ramifications of these strategies and, where possible, place tax-inefficient strategies within qualified portions of a client's portfolio.

Adaptive fixed-income strategies

When examining adaptive fixed-income strategies or managers, remember the two main objectives that we discussed:

- Attempt to produce above-inflation returns; and
- Help avoid losses due to rising interest rates and/or inflation.

Similar to our recommendations for hedged equities, look for managers with substantial real track records and avoid managers that have only back-tested returns.

Model portfolios using an analysis tool (e.g., Morningstar, Zephyr Style Advisor, or Advisory World)

After the initial round of choosing managers and strategies, we recommend looking at each manager in the context of all the other strategies that you've chosen. When I do an analysis, I first look at returns during each of the major cycles over the past 15 or 20 years, including the internet bubble, the subsequent internet bubble burst years, the 2004–2007 rally, the Great Financial Crisis, the bull market from 2009 to 2020, the pandemic performance, and the bear market and recovery of 2022. We have built a template that shows manager returns during these different periods to help us determine when the drawdowns and positive returns periods were for each strategy. This helps us test the degree to which strategies have achieved their mandates:

- What were the up-capture results for each manager during each period?
- What was the loss avoidance provided by hedged equity strategies and is this consistent with your portfolio objectives?
- With what consistency did the strategies deliver on their mandates?
- Did strategies achieve gains and losses during different cycles, lending support to negative correlation when desired?

Once the comparative analysis of the strategies that you've chosen supports your choices, it is time to begin combining the strategies together in the appropriate percentages for different risk profiles. Using the same basic construct that you likely have been using for more conventional programs, balance allocations among fixed-income and equities strategies to match the different life stages of investors that you work with. I recommend establishing return and maximum drawdown targets for each risk profile.

This report should show the mean return of each behavioral portfolio, the maximum drawdown relative to standard benchmarks, as well as other standard financial metrics like standard deviation, loss deviation, beta, and alpha. It should also include a calendar year return table.

Test each portfolio for the consistency with which it achieves its objectives:

- Do the returns and maximum drawdowns of the portfolios meet investor objectives?
- Are the portfolios delivering loss avoidance at the desired level?
- Are the returns relative to benchmarks acceptable?
- What is the consistency of returns and up-capture during bull markets?

The calendar year return chart will allow you to see in what years (if any) the portfolio trails benchmarks or fails to produce absolute return objectives. Look for any periods of returns when the behavioral portfolio fails to deliver acceptable up-capture. Inevitably, these years will occur. However, if the behavioral portfolio misses entire bull markets or if there are often multi-year periods where the up-capture is too low, this may set you up to have significant investor retention issues. You may have chosen strategies that have insufficient up-capture or don't pair well together.

Try to kill the portfolio now if it is flawed. This is infinitely superior to accepting a questionable portfolio and having 1,000 irate clients.

We tell advisors to "lock down their portfolio choices." By doing the due diligence now, you set yourself up to avoid your own behavioral biases when individual strategies experience their inevitable underperformance periods. If you're vulnerable to performance chasing because you aren't confident in the strategies you've chosen, you won't be able to guide your investors to stay with the out-of-favor investments and execute investor pre-commitments.

Establish a process for firing managers: when to hold 'em and when to fold 'em

As another means of avoiding your own behavioral biases to fire managers when they have underperformed, we recommend creating a process for deciding when they've got to go. *Because of the process you've gone through to select managers, the default position should be that managers stay rather than go.* You should be married to your managers, not just dating them.

We have prepared a "when to hold'em and when to fold'em" worksheet that we provide to advisors to help guide them through the process. Here is some of what we include:

1. Reason the strategist/manager was included:
   a. Market participation____
   b. Risk management____
   c. Portfolio stabilization____
   d. Yield____
2. Is the reason you included the portfolio/strategist still valid?
3. Has the strategist/manager change their stated investment discipline?
4. Did the strategist/manager deviate from their investment discipline?
5. Did any key portfolio managers or investment committee members leave the organization?
6. If the answers to Questions 2 through 5 are YES, does this pose a potential negative material impact on the strategy?

If the reason that you hired a manager is still valid—that is, the manager has not changed or deviated from their investment discipline, and key people in the organization have not changed—this argues for continuing to keep that manager or strategist. Immediate past performance tends to be what people focus on when making decisions about whether to keep a manager in a portfolio. However, a key premise of this book is that markets are mean reverting and managers, asset classes, or strategies that trail in one market are likely to outperform in the following market. Our Investment Owner's Manual asks investors to make a pre-commitment to rebalance into managers or strategies that have trailed. Short-term underperformance is not a valid reason to leave a manager absent another compelling reason.

Step 3: Modify the identity of your firm—highlight your new role as a behavioral coach

You are now poised to bring a well-defined process to help guide your clients through the market's greatest challenges. So, the next step is to let investors know about it, to create sales and marketing materials, and to make behavioral finance a distinctive part of your practice. The steps to doing this are as follows:

- Change the identity of your firm to include behavioral coaching. This means including behavioral coaching on brochures and making it a prominent part of your web presence.
- Create explainer documents and/or videos that discuss your behavioral coaching strategies.
- Modify sales materials and pitch books to include concepts of behavioral portfolios.
- Include behavioral coaching as a key value that you provide in your practice when talking to prospects and onboarding new clients.
- Introduce current clients to the new behavioral coaching services that you'll be providing.

Step 4: Create a new client onboarding process that includes investor behavioral coaching

When I ask advisors to tell me their onboarding process for new clients, most appear sheepish. That's because only about 10% of advisors that I work with have an established onboarding process when we begin collaborating with them. Use the introduction of behavioral portfolios into your practice as an opportunity to create and execute an organized onboarding process. For most advisors, this means taking the educational and analysis tools that you already use and integrating them with your new investor behavioral collateral.

I have created an onboarding template that I use with advisors, shown in Figure 12.2.

Figure 12.2: A possible onboarding template, with specific meetings, is one way to ensure that behavioral and portfolio topics are included in client meetings

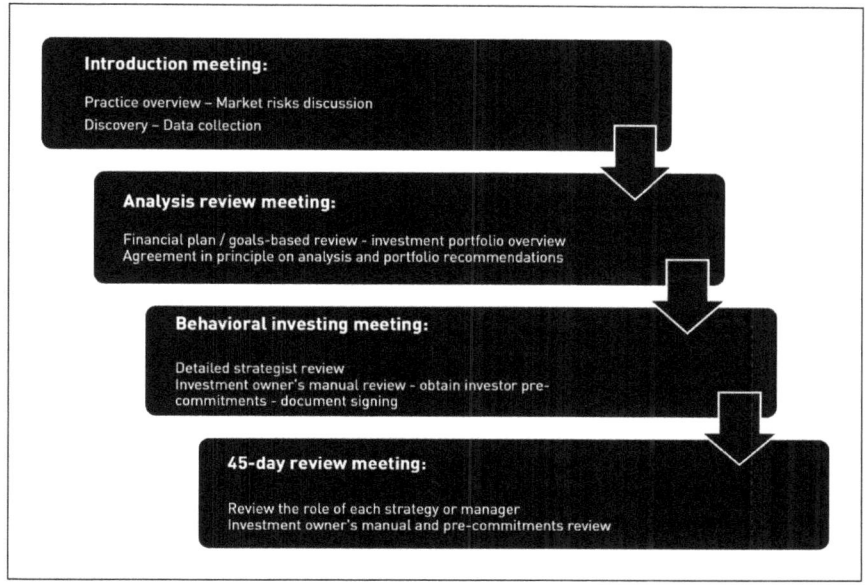

Introductory meeting: illustrating a stark difference between you and your peers

The initial meeting with potential clients should be used to differentiate your practice from other advisors. A great way to begin this process is to highlight market risks instead of diminishing them, as many advisors are inclined to do.

Investors might be under the impression that declines of 30% or more occur very infrequently. Show them the chart that we discussed in Chapter 6, which illustrates that there were on average two bear markets per decade between 1900 and the present, with an average loss of 37% (see Figure 12.3).

Figure 12.3: The statistics in this figure, discussed earlier, assist in communicating to investors the frequency and severity of past market declines

	Years	Number of bear markets	DJIA percentage decline				
	1900s	3	-49%	-46%	-32%		
	1910s	2	-47%	-40%			
	1920s	1	-47%				
	1930s	5	-89%	-52%	-37%	-23%	-22%
Significant	1940s	1	-24%				
declines are	1950s	1	-19%				
part of the	1960s	2	-37%	-27%			
fluctuations of	1970s	2	-45%	-27%			
the markets	1980s	2	-36%	-24%			
	1990s	2	-21%	-19%			
	2000s	2	-54%	-38%			
	2010s	1	-19%				
	2020s	2	-37%	-22%			
	Average number of bear markets		**Average loss**				
	2		**-36%**				

Give potential clients the S&P chart presented in Figure 2.7, showing the maximum drawdown of 84% during the Great Depression, which did not recover to its original principal value for 15 years; and the bond bull/bear chart shown in Figure 2.11, which illustrates the bear market between 1945 and 1981.

Many investors will be surprised at the severity and frequency of market declines, especially if they currently hold conventional portfolios that are exposed to these losses.

Explain to investors that you expect that markets will continue to experience periods of extreme declines, and that you build portfolios that attempt not just to avoid losses, but to capitalize on negative moves.

Make behavioral coaching a second focus of the introductory meeting. The best way to illustrate this is through stories of client struggles that you have witnessed during your career. Explain that the portfolio that you recommend for them can be counterintuitive and at times take the opposite position that the herd is following. Therefore, it's essential that investors understand why they are invested in each strategy that they hold. Finally, explain that you will put in place a specific plan for the actions that you will take (and will ask investors to take) for each market challenge that they are likely to experience during their investing life. To illustrate this, I have prepared a simple behavioral cheat sheet, shown in Figure 12.4, that highlights the biggest behavioral challenges and the pre-commitments that you'll be asking them to make.

Figure 12.4: This cheat sheet summarizes much of the content in the Investment Owner's Manual

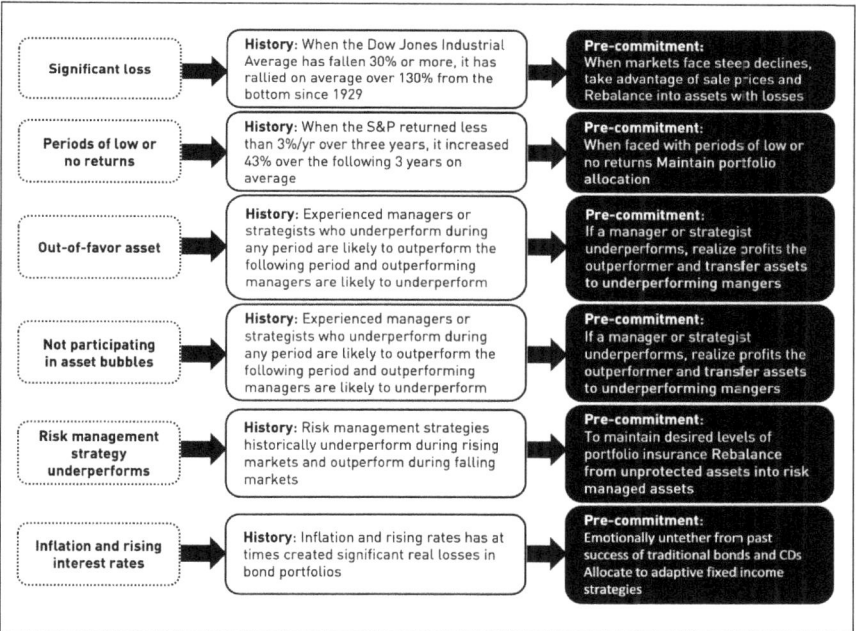

Assuming investors are prepared to proceed, collect all of the information that you'll need to prepare financial plans, goals-based analyses, and investment portfolio recommendations. This is also the time to ask them to complete or send them an investor behavioral questionnaire, to gain an understanding of their risk profile and communications preferences.

Analysis review meeting

The second meeting should be used to show potential clients the results of your analysis and discuss an overview of your portfolio recommendations. The analysis should show the rate of return they need to achieve to be able to meet their goals and their risk capacity, communicated as the maximum drawdown they are economically able to endure in order to meet their goals. You should discuss the results of their investor behavioral profile and how that correlates to their risk capacity analysis.

If a client's goals are too optimistic and aren't likely to be achieved, this is the time to help them set more realistic goals and adjust their savings, retirement age, or retirement living expectations.

Although we recommend completing a comprehensive portfolio proposal for this meeting, it might be best to focus the conversation on an overview of the portfolio and how it meshes with their goals and risk capacity, and the broad ways that it addresses the risks that you talked about in the introductory meeting.

The objective of this meeting should be to help them understand their situation and generally how your approach will help them reach their goals. While not getting a commitment to move forward, ask if they agree in principle with what you've discussed and tell them that you will go over this in more detail at the next meeting.

Behavioral investing meeting

At the third meeting, you will want to spend time talking about each strategy in the portfolio and the role it plays in matching your risk capacity and risk tolerance. However, the context for this will be discussing the six behavioral challenges. This is best done with the Investment Owner's Manual.

Although one of your objectives is discussing strategies in detail, each is introduced in the context of how it meets a specific market or behavioral challenge. This is a good time to introduce specific aspects of each strategy and help them gain understanding. Once you have reviewed the Investment Owner's Manual, ask them to sign it to agree to the pre-commitments it discusses.

Investment strategies can be complicated. What is important for investors to understand, however, is how each strategy is likely to play out in different market environments. We have created a document called "Who, What, Why, When ..." (see Figure 12.5). Before moving on to signing forms, fill out this document as a reference. It helps investors understand that each strategy will perform well at times, but poorly at others. Juxtaposing strategies against each other illustrates the various ways in which they may perform during different markets.

Figure 12.5: Asking clients to complete this form helps them to internalize the role that each investment strategy plays in the portfolio

```
Who, What, Why, When...
_____s objective is to_____
In a significantly rising equity market, they will likely _____
In a significantly declining equity market, they will likely _____
In a choppy equity market, they will likely _____
In a rising interest rate environment, they will likely _____
In an inflationary environment, they will likely _____

_____s objective is to_____
In a significantly rising equity market, they will likely _____
In a significantly declining equity market, they will likely _____
In a choppy equity market, they will likely _____
In a rising interest rate environment, they will likely _____
In an inflationary environment, they will likely _____
```

If investors agree to your proposal, ask them to complete the documentation, open accounts, and complete investment transfers. Issue them copies of signed documents, as well as the Investment Owner's Manual and the "Who, What, Why, When ..." document.

45-day review meeting

As all experienced advisors know, setting up and transferring accounts takes time. Around 45 days after clients initiate transfers, schedule a review meeting. At this meeting:

- review their goals, along with target returns and maximum drawdowns. Explain that when you review your portfolio, you will be referring to these goals rather than comparing their portfolio to benchmarks;
- review market risks and the overarching objectives of their portfolio;
- briefly review the most relevant section of the Investment Owner's Manual (based on what investor challenge currently predominates) and the role of each strategy in the portfolio. Explain that this is their primary reference document to refer to if they feel uneasy about their portfolio; and
- tell them that before each meeting, you would like them to guess which market/behavioral challenge is emerging and what action you will be asking them to take in their portfolio.

Step 5: Introduce behavioral coaching to your current clients

Advisors may be tempted to focus more on communicating their new identity in order to gain new clients, but they would be better served to focus first on training their existing clients. And the best way to begin this process is at your quarterly or annual review meetings.

For current clients, explain that you have decided to add an investor behavior coaching component to your practice. Here is an example of how advisors can introduce this concept to their clients:

> For years now, I've watched my clients struggle with volatile markets and a sense of uncertainty about their future. In some cases, clients suffer from anxiety. In more extreme cases, they feel compelled to chase performance or depart from their plans. As a result, I have decided to broaden the services that I provide to include behavioral coaching.
>
> First, I'd like to build in additional risk management strategies that increase the loss-avoidance capacity of your portfolio. These strategies will be designed both to attempt to lessen losses and potentially to capitalize on the major market dislocations that I expect that we'll experience over the coming decades.
>
> I'll discuss what I believe are the six biggest investor behavioral

challenges facing investors and how the portfolio has been designed to address these challenges.

Next, I'll make plans for the specific steps that we'll take when these six market challenges present themselves. These plans are all based on over a century of market data that supports the best course of action.

Finally, I'll ask you to make some pre-commitments to take specific actions when market disruptions occur.

Through this process, my hope is that we will be prepared for anything that the markets throw at us and as a result, we'll all have greater peace of mind and be more likely to follow through on our plans.

After the introduction, we recommend that advisors spend the time walking investors through their new Investment Owner's Manual. As a guide, refer to Chapter 10, where we discuss each part of the manual. Issue a copy of the manual to each client and tell them that when they feel uneasy about the way the markets are behaving, they should refer to the manual. A number of advisors even tell clients that when they prepare for meetings in the future, they will ask their client if they believe a market behavioral challenge is emerging and if so, what it is.

Step 6: Execute portfolio changes to current investor portfolios

As a natural follow-up to conversations with investors about behavioral portfolios, advisors should execute a well-thought-out plan to modify portfolios across their practice. This is a multifaceted process that includes taking into consideration each investor's goals, target returns, and risk capacity or ability to tolerate market drawdowns. It also includes an evaluation of any tax consequences of portfolio changes.

If you decide—as many advisors do—to make major changes to the makeup of portfolios, we recommend building a system to see through the execution of portfolio modification across your practice to ensure that no clients are missed. This is important. If you have embraced portfolio changes that attempt to meaningfully reduce portfolio risk, you don't want any investors left behind with significant losses when markets turn lower.

As part of this process, explicitly discuss the target return and target maximum drawdown of the new portfolio with each investor. These are important anchors for client reviews and help keep investors focused on their own goals and away from arbitrary market benchmark returns.

Use your customer relationship management system or spreadsheets to track all of your target investors and each step in the execution process. A sample tracking spreadsheet is presented in Figure 12.6.

Figure 12.6: Track progress at bringing your existing clients into conformity with your new behavioral portfolios and behavioral guidance

Client / Household name	Review owner's manual and receive signed copy	Issue investor copy in progressive 3-ring binder	Set and explain portfolio return objective for investor	Set and explain portfolio maximum drawdown target for investor	Discuss modified behavioral portfolio with investor	Reallocate to modified portfolio

Step 7: Provide ongoing investor behavioral guidance to your clients

In 2011, an advisor attending one of our first behavioral workshops in Denver told a story about his experience during the Great Financial Crisis. He said that in the years before the crisis, he discussed at every meeting how a big market decline was inevitable at some point in the future and reminded investors that if that happened, it would be a huge opportunity to rebalance their portfolios to buy stocks at perhaps once-in-a-lifetime prices. In the teeth of the crisis, when most investors were calling their advisors to get out of the stock market, his investors were calling to see if it was time to rebalance and buy more stocks.

This is the type of behavior that you should attempt to encourage for all of the big market challenges confronting your investors. Successfully onboarding investors and introducing them to your behavioral guidance is just the start. But as we all know, investors can forget what we say and get caught up in the momentum of the markets.

Ongoing behavioral guidance involves two key steps. First, review all of the challenges and pre-commitments at each meeting and point out to investors how the portfolio not only may lessen the risks of those challenges, but could actually benefit from them. Second, watch carefully for emerging challenges and send clients newsletters or other communications reminding them of your plans and explaining how this is the opportunity that you have discussed with them from the start.

The hero's narrative

A winning strategy for creating a high-grossing film is to base it on what is called the "hero's narrative." Innumerable blockbuster films have deployed this storyline, including *Star Wars*, *The Lion King*, the Harry Potter films, and many more (see Figure 12.7). In the hero's narrative, a protagonist (Luke Skywalker) has a call to adventure (save Princess Leia!), meets a guide (Obi-Wan Kenobi), travels to a new world, faces significant challenges (Darth Vader), and returns triumphant.

Figure 12.7: The hero's narrative, used in many top-grossing films, can be applied to an advisor's progression over the course of growing their businesses

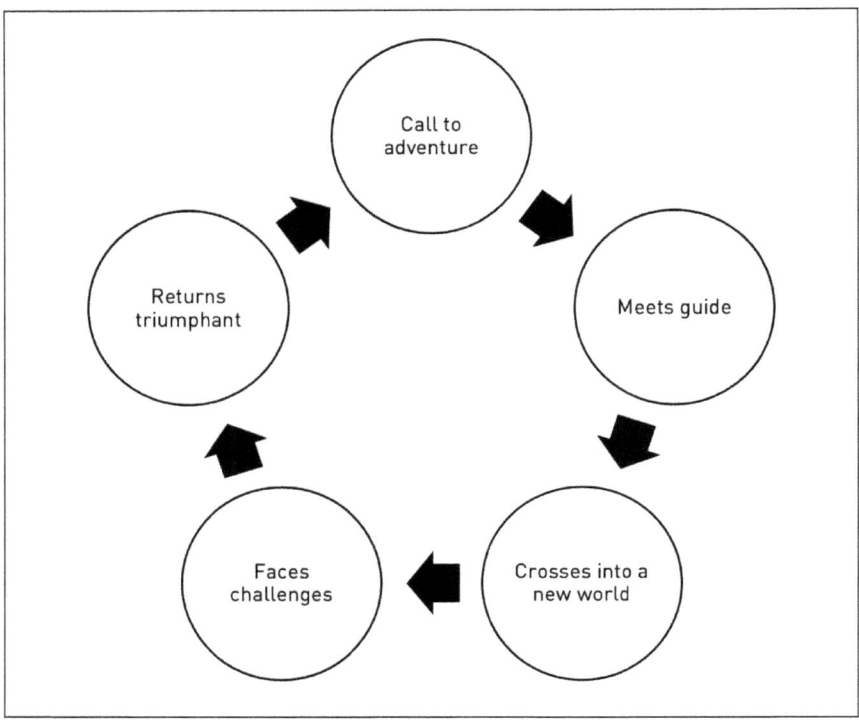

Brilliant behavioral finance author Brian Portnoy framed the trajectory of an advisor's path as fitting this narrative. Most who start a career in financial advice fail. Most require a mentor. All face significant challenges, as both businesspersons and investment counselors. And few succeed. In a 2023 study, Cerulli Associates revealed that 72% of trainee advisors failed in their first year alone.[52] So the fact that you are in business and dedicated enough to read this all the way to the end means that you have been triumphant in building your career!

However, this movie isn't over. Our clients are constantly faced with challenges as markets vacillate in a world fraught with risk. At the firm outside of Philadelphia where I worked in the early 1990s, we had roughly 300 retired clients. We imagined a scenario where stocks entered a multi-year bear market and our clients became destitute. Under this bleak imaginary scenario, we, as their advisors, would have led them to their demise. Luke crashes into the Death Star and the rebel force is crushed.

Our most important role as financial advisers is to address the possibility of crisis markets and help our clients navigate them when they occur. In a way, this is everything. But crisis preparedness cannot be achieved with a conventional stock/bond portfolio. The era of benchmark centricity for investors needs to end.

We also need to acknowledge that our clients are maladapted to make counterintuitive investment choices. Our traditional habit of preaching to clients that they should "stay the course" when regrets and fear surface is ineffective. Providing a framework for guiding investors to make wise choices is also a vitally important role we can play for them.

The behavioral portfolio improves investment outcomes and points to a brighter future for investors. Our strategies for managing investor behavior involve working for advisors, helping them differentiate their practices, streamline decision making, improve outcomes, and enhance peace of mind for their investors.

The most important step for you now is to implement these ideas.

ACKNOWLEDGMENTS

THE NEBULOUS VERSION of this book has been in my head since near birth. Thanks to Janna Morishima for helping to bring it to the world as my writing coach and friend. This book would not exist without your inspiration.

Toews' Behavioral Investing Institute and its many ideas were built organically as we tried and failed and tried again. Instrumental to this process were Eben Burr and Dan Kullman, who have acted as coaches and advisor mentors over the years. Also, thanks to Blake Jordan, our behavioral guru and the author of the introduction to Part 3 of this book, for his unique perspective on and contributions to investor communications.

Greg Brunck provided vital analytics to help construct the behavioral portfolios in this book, as he does every day in advisor consultations. A big thanks to Jason Graffius, Charles Collins, and Randy Schroeder for their indefatigable efforts on building behavioral portfolios, with a special shout out to Landon Gould who **owns** and delivered virtually every point of data shared here, as well as Yu-Jin Kim for his careful review and curating this book.

Thanks also to Kelly Bradley for helping to form clear communications digestible to investors and to the thousands of advisors who over the years have helped to form this work.

ENDNOTES

1   Hackethal, A., Haliassos, M., and Japelli, T. (2009). "Financial Advisors: A Case of Babysitters?". CFS Working Paper No. 2009/04. This study of 32,751 randomly selected individual investors concluded that "Involvement of Independent Financial Advisors tends on average to reduce both the total portfolio return and the excess return, once the characteristics of the owner are taken into account. This reverses the impression from descriptive statistics that IFAs improve performance …"

2   Mullainathan, S., Noeth, M., and Schoar, A. (2012). "The Market for Financial Advice: An Audit Study". NBER Working Paper No. 17929

3   Hackethal, A., Haliassos, M., and Japelli, T. (2011). "Financial Advisors: A Case of Babysitters?". Available at SSRN: ssrn.com/abstract=1360440 or dx.doi.org/10.2139/ssrn.1360440.

4   Goyal, A. and Wahal, S. (2008). "The Selection and Termination of Investment Management Firms by Plan Sponsors". *The Journal of Finance*. Vol. LXIII, No. 4; Agapova, A., Ferguson, R., Leistikow, D., and Rentzler, J. (2018). "Chasing Performance and Identifying Talented Investment Managers". *The Journal of Investing*. Vol. 27, Issue 1, pp. 52–64.

5   Source: Bloomberg

6   Holton, L. and Bates, J. (2009). *Business Valuation for Dummies*. Wiley Publishing, Inc.

7   January 1871 to December 12/23 Source Shiller Data.

8   Period January 1, 1962 to December 29, 2023.

9   Paulson, Jr., Henry M. (2013). On the Brink: *Inside the race to stop the collapse of the global financial system* (Business Plus).

10   www.bis.org/publ/bisbull69.pdf.

11   Returns from the Dow Jones Corporate Bond Total Return Index from 1915–2023 and the S&P 500 Index. Source: Global Financial Data and Bloomberg. Note that the date range of bond data differs from the stock analysis data due to the limited availability of reliable bond data. The Dow Jones Corporate Bond Index provides data that goes back further than most other bond indices, which is why it was chosen.

12   2022 returns of the Dow Jones Corporate Bond Total Return Index.

13   Source: Schwab Center for Financial Research with data from Standard & Poor's 2022 U.S. Corporate Default Study, as of 6/13/2023.

14   Giesecke, K., Longstaff, F. A., Schaefer, S., and Strebulaev, I. (2010). "Corporate Bond Default Risk: A 150-Year Perspective", NBER Working Paper 15848, www.nber.org/papers/w15848.pdf.

15   Hanke, S. H. and Krus, N. (2012). "World Hyperinflations", Cato Working Paper 8, August 15.

16   In 1945 the interest rate on a 10-year Treasury Yield was 2.5%. In 1981, the 10-year Treasury yielded 13.9%. Source US Treasury.

17   Figure 2.14 represents the hypothetical growth of $1,000 if it were possible to invest directly in the DJ Corporate Bond Index Real Return (bond declines) and the S&P 500 Index Real Return (equity declines). It also looks at data within a narrow timeframe which may not accurately reflect overall equity and/or bond trends given multiple market cycles.

18   www.federalreservehistory.org/essays/banking-panics-1930-31.

19   www.vanguard.com.

20   According to the Social Security Calculator, the joint life expectancy of a 65-year-old couple would be closer to 89, or 24 years. However, more affluent clients that seek investment advice would likely have longer life expectancies; and as life expectancy has historically increased over time, we find it reasonable to assume a 30-year time horizon.

21   Based on a portfolio invested 60% in the S&P 500 Index and 40% in the Dow Jones Bond Total Return Index from 1916 through 2023. Returns shown are the arithmetic mean.

22   www.morningstar.com/lp/mind-the-gap.

23   This example assumes that a portfolio trails by the behavioral gap and is net of average advisor all-in fees. Results improve if the investor is able to achieve market returns less fees. The assumed starting portfolio value is $1 million.

24   www.risk.net/definition/modern-portfolio-theory.

25   www.phys.sinica.edu.tw/.

26   www.ineteconomics.org/.

27   IMF Global Debt Database, 2023.

28   Statman, M. (2010), *What Investors Really Want* (McGraw-Hill), p. 3.

29   A skewed distribution chart was first suggested by Brian M. Rom and Kathleen W. Ferguson, in the Winter, 1993 and Fall, 1994 editions of *The Journal of Investing*.

30   Campbell, J. Y. and Shiller, R. (1998). "Valuation Ratios and the Long-Run Stock Market Outlook". *The Journal of Portfolio Management*. Vol. 24, Issue 2.

31   Malkiel, B. G. (2003). "The Efficient Market Hypothesis and Its Critics", Princeton University, CEPS Working Paper No. 91.

32   Hedged equities returns include all strategies, funds, and ETFs on Morningstar that had an inception date of January 1, 2008 or earlier. Chosen strategies were correlated with stocks (MSCI World Index) during rising markets with an up-market correlation of .5 or greater, and generally had a low correlation with stocks during falling markets (with a down-market correlation of lower than .5), excluding any strategies that did not invest in stocks.

33   The study was built by Toews Asset Management and the Investments and Wealth Institute, and was conducted by Absolute Engagement. Input was gathered from 751 investors in the US between March 10 and March 24.

34 www.empirical.net/wp-content/uploads/2014/12/Andrew-Lo-Reconciling-Efficient-Markets-with-Behavioral-Finance.pdf.

35 Montier, J. (2010). *The Little Book of Behavioral Investing: How not to be your own worst enemy* (Little Books, Big Profits (UK)) (pp. 42–43). John Wiley and Sons. Kindle Edition.

36 Montier, J. (2010). *The Little Book of Behavioral Investing: How not to be your own worst enemy* (Little Books, Big Profits (UK)) (pp. 156–157). John Wiley and Sons. Kindle Edition.

37 Source: S&P data obtained from Global Financial Data and Bloomberg from 1916 through 2023. Calculations by author.

38 Source Data: The Callan Periodic Table of Investment Returns (2004–2023).

39 www.psyfitec.com/p/the-big-list-of-behavioral-biases.html.

40 Emerging Markets Stocks calculated using the MSCI Emerging Markets Index. US stocks represented by the S&P 500.

41 www.spglobal.com/spdji/en/documents/spiva/persistence-scorecard-europe-year-end-2022.pdf.

42 S&P Persistence Scorecard December 2017.

43 Shiller, R. J. (2016). *Irrational Exuberance: Revised and Expanded Third Edition* (p. 90). Princeton University Press. Kindle Edition.

44 Shiller, R. J. (2016). *Irrational Exuberance: Revised and Expanded Third Edition* (p. 91). Princeton University Press. Kindle Edition.

45 www.forbes.com/sites/greatspeculations/2010/12/13/the-biggest-ipo-flops/#a1ca6d46391f.

46 Teeter, P. and Sandberg, J. (2017). "Cracking the Enigma of Asset Bubbles with Narratives". *Strategic Organization*. Vol. 15, No. 1, pp. 91–99.

47 www.federalreserve.gov/newsevents/speech/bernanke20120413a.htm.

48 Thaler, R. H. and Sunstein, C. R. (2008). *Nudge: Improving decisions about health, wealth, and happiness*. Yale University Press.

49 www.bls.gov/opub/ted/2023/retirement-plans-for-workers-in-private-industry-and-state-and-local-government-in-2022.htm#:~:text=Sixty%2Dnine%20percent%20of%20private,up%20rate%20of%2075%20percent.

50 www.kitces.com/blog/best-opportunistic-rebalancing-frequency-time-horizons-vs-tolerance-band-thresholds/.

51 Our study was limited to a maximum frequency of one-month periods due to limited strategy data for hedged equities and tactical fixed-income models.

52 2023 Cerulli Edge—U.S. Asset and Wealth Management Edition.

www.ingramcontent.com/pod-product-compliance
Ingram Content Group UK Ltd.
Pitfield, Milton Keynes, MK11 3LW, UK
UKHW020008020225
454465UK00005B/133